SYMPTOM REDUCTION THROUGH CLINICAL BIOFEEDBACK

Ivan Wentworth-Rohr, Ph.D.

St. Vincent's Hospital and Medical Center
Professor Emeritus in Residence at Pace University,
New York City

HUMAN SCIENCES PRESS, INC.
72 FIFTH AVENUE
NEW YORK, N.Y. 10011-8004

Paperback edition copyright © 1988 by Human Sciences Press, Inc.
Original hardcover edition copyright © 1984 by Human Sciences Press, Inc.
72 Fifth Avenue, New York, New York 10011

Printed in the United States of America
987654321

Library of Congress Cataloging in Publication Data

Wentworth-Rohr, Ivan, 1918–
    Symptom reduction through clinical biofeedback.
    Bibliography: p.
    Includes index.
    1. Medicine, Psychosomatic. 2. Biofeedback training. I. Title.
[DNLM: 1. Psychophysiologic disorders—Therapy. 2. Biofeedback (Psychology)
WL 103 W479s]
RC49.W43 1983   616.08   82–21199
ISBN 0-89885-135-1 (hard)
     0-89885-366-4 (paper)

CONTENTS

PREFACE

The preface to the original edition indicated that the volume focussed on methods and techniques used in clinical biofeedback to reduce a wide variety of symptoms. The application of the biofeedback machines are supplemented by psychotherapy techniques from cognitive therapy, relaxation methods, hypnotism, behavior therapy and psychodynamic procedures. In this fashion, a "psychophysiological therapy," to use Dr. Charles Stroebel's phrase, had been created in the 1960's which provides a non-invasive, short-term, symptom-oriented treatment procedure.

Clinical biofeedback continues to prove its usefulness, as well as its low cost, in treating psychophysiological disorders such as migraine, gastrointestinal spasms, Raynaud's, both smooth and striate muscle spasms, hypertension, stress disorders, TMJ syndrome and tension headaches. Many psychiatric patients suffering from anxiety-related symptoms, both psychotic and neurotic, also find help. Among the symptoms that are amenable to psychophysiological therapy are fears and phobias, obsessions, sexual dysfunctions, motor restlessness, over-repression of emotionality, unbound anxiety, insomnia, some respiratory and circulatory dysfunctions and learned depressions.

The use of the biofeedback instruments allows for the precise focussing on the residence of the anxiety-related symptom in whatever physiological system it might be located. The physiological information is then fed back through the patient's sensory system, thereby providing a psychophysiological modality of treatment instead of the therapy being confined by the constraints of verbal psychotherapy. The psychological aspects of the symptom can be dealt with in conjunction with the modification of the biological aspects.

The volume has summarized the major research and clinical applications and has been found suitable for a text or reference in clinical biofeedback in particular or for studies in short-term, symptom reduction techniques.

PREFACE TO THE ORIGINAL EDITION

This volume was planned as a concise and informative account of symptom reduction techniques utilizing clinical biofeedback as a central procedure. Ancillary techniques from behavior therapy, relaxation methods, cognitive approaches and hypnosis are combined with biofeedback procedures to provide efficacious treatment approaches. Biofeedback focuses on the psychophysiology implicated in symptoms and provides a concrete, observable experience for the patient during the application of the various psychotherapeutic methods. The patient is directly involved in monitoring his own mental and bodily components of the complaint and the therapist is provided with an objective, ongoing measurement of change in symptom formation. Clinical interventions and introspection are thereby improved. The collaboration in treatment is also enhanced as both patient and therapist observe and participate in the process of treatment.

The wide range of biofeedback applications in clinical and research areas has been sampled to present a balanced review of such applications. Reports emanate from several sciences and disciplines, each contributing technical knowledge and clinical methods that are often adaptable to useful treatment applications. Many of these were poorly conducted and the reports are often overstated and of little assistance in pragmatic clinical work. An attempt has been made to present those whose usefulness has been reasonably verified through clinical trials and laboratory research. Needless to say, the efficacy

9

and the validity of treatment procedures are always open to question, verification and improvement. This principle holds for the procedures presented here as much as for any other kinds of procedures.

The presentations in this volume are designed for the practitioner in psychiatry, clinical psychology, rehabilitation medicine, physiotherapy, nursing, pediatrics, psychotherapy and in the allied services of the helping professions. The advanced student in these areas will find the introductory material on learning theory, bioinstrumentation, neuromuscular physiology and clinical applications a substantial basis for specialized study in the sciences and the treatment procedures that constitute the developing fields of clinical biofeedback and behavioral medicine.

No attempt has been made to present a detailed and extensive account of each of the fields that comprise clinical biofeedback. The audience that may read this text could be comprised of professionals who are novices in some of the material and expert in the remainder. They may wish to scan the chapters that are familiar to them and to concentrate on the unfamiliar. Experience in teaching seminars and workshops in symptom reduction through clinical biofeedback and ancillary therapy techniques has revealed the gaps in knowledge within the different helping professions. Those from medicine usually have a limited background in the active techniques of symptom reduction, and those from the nonmedical fields are limited in their knowledge of anatomy and psychophysiology. Often many from psychiatry, psychology, and nursing have been trained in verbal psychotherapy and find it difficult to conceptualize and carry out symptom reduction techniques that are devised in open collaboration with the patient and necessarily applied in a consistent and circumscribed series of planned procedures. Ordinarily, symptom reduction techniques do not use free-association and introspection as the *primary* modalities of treatment. However, these are used by any sensitive therapist when clinically appropriate during the course of any treatment procedure, including clinical biofeedback.

It is hoped that the technical data and the clinical procedures will serve to fill whatever gaps in background one may bring to the study of symptom reduction, and that the singular nature of the clinical approach is adequately demonstrated.

Many students, patients, and colleagues have contributed to this work. The Faculty Committee for Scholarly Research of Pace University funded and encouraged the endeavor. Drs. Carmine Casella and David Marsh were particularly helpful in reviewing and correcting the manuscript. Any errors remaining are mine. Several colleagues have been helpful in providing consultations and support—Drs. Thomas McShane, Andrew Cannistraci, Benjamin Fialkoff, Stefan de Schill, C. Harold Taylor, Edward Rabinowitz, Ralph A. O'Connell, and Frank Catalano. Nancy Nicomini and Teresa Paduano patiently read my handwriting and typed the manuscript. Most important, my wife, Ruth, was forever helpful and encouraging during the many months of work.

FOREWORD

Several ingenious premises qualify this book as a third generation exploration of biofeedback applications. The author passes beyond the development arrest of the awe and speculation of the first generation and the tentative clinical procedures of the second generation to integrate biofeedback methods as core procedures within a variety of psychotherapeutic modalities. Potential pitfalls of such an undertaking are avoided by restricting the scope of outcome goals to symptom reduction rather than the nebulous tangles of psychodynamic resolution.

What emerges is the first balanced and clearly written guide for psychotherapists lacking familiarity with biofeedback methodology; and, conversely, one also for those health professionals who should be using biofeedback but lack familiarity with the crucial larger framework of psychotherapy and its variants.

Biofeedback applied to human subjects usually lacks effectiveness in the sterile setting of a double-blind laboratory without sensitivity to psychotherapeutic issues. Dr. Wentworth-Rohr sets the stage for this premise early in the book through insightful analysis of operations, targets, and goals of various application strategies to distinguish between the experimental laboratory paradigm (which he calls BFT or biofeedback training) and the broader, clinical biofeedback paradigm.

Failure to make this very distinction is a source of considerable confusion to the uninitiated in these fields. For example, numerous anecdotal single case and uncontrolled small sample studies claim to demonstrate the efficacy of biofeedback for the treatment of a variety of psychophysiological conditions. However, little convincing experimental evidence supports the application of biofeedback as a specific treatment for any psychologic condition. Further, except in animal experiments claiming to demonstrate instrumental conditioning of normally involuntary physiological functions, there is no single unilateral application of biofeedback "hardware" per se to achieve any convincing result. Positive outcomes have been reported only when the hardware is combined in a passive, nonthreatening therapeutic alliance situation with such adjunctive "soft-ware" procedures as psychotherapy, behavior therapy, progressive relaxation, autogenic therapy, physical therapy, relaxation response, quieting response, imagery, hypnotic variants, and coping procedures.

Given a paucity of definitive data but a growing consensus among psychiatrists and psychologists using biofeedback as a treatment tool that it does "something" to facilitate treatment of many patients. I would like to propose the following rationale for biofeedback's applicability as a psychotherapeutic tool, which is in agreement with Dr. Wentworth-Rohr.

Psychotherapy, per se , is probably too narrow a term to describe the process whereby a therapist deals not only with cognitive material, but with associated emotional-physiological manifestations as well. The term "psychophysiological therapy" more appropriately describes the actual process and is in keeping with the belief structure of many patients that their physical symptoms are in their body and cannot be resolved through talking therapies alone.

While the therapist may be acutely attuned to sensing latent covert structures and dynamics in linguistic or cognitive communications from patient, his or her sensitivity, as well as the patients, to associated covert physiological variations is relatively meager. Biofeedback, often termed a "real time physiological mirror," may serve to extend significantly both therapists' and patients' sensitivity to the subtle emotional-physiological components of the basic therapeutic process. Thus, within the context of this rationale, biofeedback may be viewed as an adjunctive tool for refinement of more traditional therapeutic approaches and not as a new entity of itself.

This is the very essence of Dr. Wentworth-Rohr's book and he is to be congratulated on his penetrating clarification and systematic presentation of the foregoing issues with extensive case study material as examples. This book will provide a meaningful core text for introductory and graduate courses integrating biofeedback and psychotherapy. It will provide consolidation as well for the more seasoned practitioner who may have had nagging concerns about the experimental vs. clinical paradigm controversy.

Charles F. Stroebel
M.D., Ph.D.
Director of Research
Institute of Living

Professor of Psychiatry
University of Connecticut Health
Center and Medical School

Lecturer in Psychiatry
Yale School of Medicine

Part I

HISTORY AND PRINCIPLES OF BIOFEEDBACK

Chapter 1

INTRODUCTION

Singularity of Biofeedback

Clinical biofeedback has become a widely used procedure in symptom reduction over the last decade (11, 17, 19, 72, 74, 219). The investigation of psychophysiologic activities in both normal and abnormal subjects has contributed substantial evidence that feeding back to the subjects current information about their physiologic activity can enable significant degrees of self-regulation (7, 76).

Indeed, this procedure is the special asset of biofeedback methodology. The feedback machines are sensitive monitoring aids in their capacity to record physiologic functioning, to process the information, and to inform the subjects of much of their functioning that is otherwise below their ordinary awareness. Considerable assistance can be given to persons who suffer a wide range of symptomatic dysfunctions in physiological systems. Psychogenic muscle spasms in tension headaches and bruxism (39) are among the responsive symptoms to biofeedback procedures. Vasoconstrictive disorders that are caused or exacerbated by anxiety or stress also remit well to biofeedback retraining (185). Gastrointestinal dysfunctions are frequently alleviated insofar as the intensity of the symptoms of constipation or diarrhea is concerned (217). Brudney et al. (29, 30) have had success treating spasmodic torticollis. In targeting neuromotor disabilities, Basmajian (11) and Marinacci and Horande (127) have increased neuromotor competence. These are some examples of the successful use of biofeedback as an adjunctive procedure which adds to the efficacy of standard practices in treating many symptoms that are expressed in physiologic dysfunctions which arise from anatomic change or from stress and anxiety (see Part III).

The biofeedback procedure itself is a straightforward method of training persons to use the instruments as self-teaching devices to the end of self-regulation of their physiological functioning. Specifically, the procedure consists of the *operations*, or electronic machine applications, that *target* psychophysiological processes, with the *goal* of revising selected parameters of physiological and psychological functioning (Figure 3).

The physiological systems targeted by the biofeedback procedure are determined by the diagnostic study of each patient. The systems that are most commonly monitored are the striate and smooth musculature, brain wave activity, the cardiovascular, and the eccrine sweat glands (Table 1). The systems innervated by the autonomic nervous system (ANS) are used as mediators to increase or decrease arousal level of the ANS. Decrease in level of activation of the sympathetic nervous system is crucial in most clinical applications of biofeedback. The interaction of the ANS and the hypothalamic-pituitary-adrenal axis in the release of epinephrine, norepinephrine, steroids, and other hormones can be influenced by biofeedback and other stress reduction methods. Selye's (186, 187) general adaptation syndrome, other classes of stress disorders (156), and anxiety states (130) are therefore appropriate referrals for clinical biofeedback.

The confluence of several sciences and theories in physiology and psychology have led to the development of biofeedback. The investigations of physiologic activity in human and animal biology laid the biological foundations for psychophysiology, which is the focus of biofeedback applications (91). Concurrently, studies in the behavior of humans and animals gave rise to behaviorism and its multiplicity of learning paradigms. Among them, Skinner's (193) and Pavlov's (155) theories of learning have been adopted as the chief sources of the techniques and explanations of biofeedback procedures, but are often supplemented by principles and methods from psychodynamic theory (219). Developments in electronic bioinstruments simplified the hardware technology of biofeedback for the researcher and clinician, and an almost endless variety of psychotherapy techniques comprise the "software" of treatment procedures.

The physiological machine method of limiting biofeedback procedure to feeding back physiological information, which the subject uses to revise a physiological parameter, may be properly designated as biofeedback training (BFT). That is, a given bioinstrument such as an electromyograph (EMG) or an electroencephalograph (EEG) is applied to the targeted physiology and the subject uses the feedback information to revise the frequency, intensity, or direction of the physiological function. In this model of biofeedback, Brudny et al. (29) have had success in treating torticollis, and Blanchard and Epstein (19) have targeted cardiovascular dysfunction with promising results. Psychogenic subvocalization has been reduced by Hardyck (89), masseter spasticity by Budzynski and Stoyva (33), and tension headaches by Budzynski et al. (34). Closer normalization of EEG activity through BFT can also be achieved in some cases of epilepsy that have not responded to usual procedures (112). When BFT is used as the sole treatment technique in complex disorders, the results are minimal at best.

Conversely, when BFT is one part of a multimodal treatment procedure for varieties of anxiety-related symptoms in neurotic and psychophysiologic disorders, the clinical outcomes are reasonably rewarding (7, 22, 28, 38, 46, 63, 219). This approach is often referred to, in contrast to BFT, as clinical biofeedback in that it includes in the treatment procedure many kinds of psychotherapy techniques. With the addition of such techniques as BFT, considerable assistance can be provided patients who present a wide diversity of symptoms, directly or indirectly related to a wide range of diagnoses. In most instances, the primary disease or condition is *not* being treated in clinical biofeedback. Rather, some of the symptoms resulting from primary diagnostic complaints are treated through both physiological and psychological modalities. For example, peripheral vasospasms in Raynaud's syndrome, migraine headaches, tachycardia, and essential hypertension are symptomatically responsive to clinical biofeedback, especially when the symptoms are exacerbated by stress or anxiety. When psychic factors are components of the dysfunctions, the reduction of the maladaptive learned responses or resolutions of the internal conflicts are often necessary changes in order to alleviate the symptoms.

These successes have by no means established biofeedback as the treatment of choice for all symptoms based on physiopathology. Nor can the procedure claim more than reasonable usefulness to justify its inclusion in treatment plans (28, 219, 232). Many limitations are present in clinical biofeedback. The self-regulation of physiological functions through biofeedback is limited by biology itself, as well as by the motivation of the subjects, their personalities and life styles. The causes and severity of the malfunctioning, placebo effects, the skill of the practitioner, and the extant body of scientific and clinical knowledge also influence the degree of success in assessing the value of biofeedback as a clinical technique. The assets of the approach are that it is a non-invasive, low-risk method of returning homeostatic dysfunctions to within normal boundaries; it can also be used as a powerful tool in psychotherapy procedures to treat psychogenic symptoms such as phobias, impotence and frigidity, reactive spasms in both smooth and striate musculature, insomnia, and other disturbing neurotic symptoms (Part III).

The historical argument in physiology concerning the voluntary control of the ANS, which is implicated in many psychogenic symptoms, is still a matter of debate (76). Miller and Dworkin (140) reported on the problem in determining the degree of direct control of the visceral organs regulated by autonomic functions. A significant degree of deconditioning is possible, whether or not the learning is mediated by the somatic nervous system and the skeletal muscles. There appears to be ample evidence that the autonomic system can indeed be highly controlled, whatever the mechanism.

There is no disagreement about accomplishing direct self-regulation of the voluntary musculature. We learn to write, skip, speak, etc., through learning to control the striate muscles, and equally fine motor control can be achieved through feedback instrumentation. Whatever the sequence of internal mechanisms may be, the major systems of the body are accessible in varying degrees to direct or indirect influence through physiological feedback procedures.

The part the "mind" plays in biofeedback applications is another area of the field filled with disagreement, opinion, and theory. There are even disputes as to its existence, let alone its nature (14). A good deal of the problem is one of definition and theoretical structures. If one assumes that observable behavior is the sole basis for understanding and interpreting human behavior, then the observer need not concern himself with a subject's introspective reports. The observer, in biofeedback applications, can depend on the readouts of the instruments for determining change in behavior. On the other hand, if one assumes that a significant amount of human experience that is vital is not observable, then the covert, subjective experiences of the patient are used by the biofeedback therapist as clinical data in the treatment procedure.

We have found few cases, if any, in which mental activity of simple to complex forms has not been connected with the symptom under treatment. As a matter of fact, we approach each patient as though there is a mind at work throughout the procedure. Our view does recognize mental activities as a major system in human behavior, and the bulk of the instruction and case histories in this volume reflects that view. The mind is accepted as an integral dimension of physiology, and the *interaction* of mind and body is the key dependent variable in clinical applications. That is, biofeedback procedures are not applied to the body *or* to the mind, but to the processes of their interactions. A treatment plan usually begins with relaxation and a direct feedback of bodily events and then shifts to the patient's mental manipulation of such events, as in reducing premature ventricular contractions (PVC), spasms, or vasoconstriction. Or, the conscious, verbal documentation of a phobia through constructing a hierarchy can precede the induction of autonomic hypoarousal through biofeedback instruments. But, in both cases, the interactions between the patient's mental and bodily dimension of the PVC, the vasoconstriction, or the phobia, appear to be the principal, internal processes that are revised, rather than merely one of the dimensions.

Specifying which dimension takes precedence does not imply predominance of mind over body or body over mind. The advantage of specifying which dimension is to be selected as the initial pathway for clinical intervention merely provides the clinician with a stated position that serves to clarify his treatment plans and his clinical hypotheses. We have found this kind of clarification necessary, as a rule, in order to use biofeedback-behavioral therapy models for treating anxiety-related symptoms in schizophrenics, and in unusual cases of long-standing duration where etiology is unclear.

Different presenting symptoms appear to be derivatives of the biological, psychological, or the social parameters of the patient's history. Many symptoms demonstrably originate in the first, due to disease or injury, or even to a possible genetic malfunctioning of homeostasis. Others are more clearly learned responses that have become habitual or are reactive to particular situations or objects. Whatever the basic etiology, the patient usually has incorporated elements of all three parameters in the symptomatology by the time he arrives for treatment. The initial interviews and the treatment phases are therefore developed within a biopsychosocial model. The biological substrate, which the bioinstruments target, is the physiological dimension of the mind-body interaction. The psychological is the mental-emotional dimension that is treated with the psychotherapy techniques. And the social is the environmental domain, past, present, and future, in which the symptomatic behavior originates or persists.

Severe or long-standing symptoms require clinical attention to all three domains. The healthier patient, whose disorder and symptom have not contaminated his life, may be treated effectively in only one or two of the domains.

Varieties of Applications

The reader who wishes a quick, condensed overview of the varieties of diagnoses and symptoms reported in the literature, and the bioinstruments used in their treatment, may refer to Table 1. The reports cited are both research and clinical studies. Many of the applications are not yet established clinical procedures, but are reported to illustrate the wide range of symptoms and diagnostic groups that have been treated or investigated.

Most of the disease entities reported, such as hypertension, Raynaud's, and epilepsy, are not the treatment targets. Rather, some of the symptoms such as high blood pressure, vasospasms, or

Table 1.   Overview of operations, targets and goals of biofeedback instruments for symptomatic treatment.

I.   Overview—Biofeedback

    A.   Operations: application of electronic or mechanical machine systems that feedback information of physiological functioning.

    B.   Targets: musculature; circulatory system; eccrine sweat glands; brain waves; cardiac activity, autonomic nervous system; respiratory system; gastrointestinal system.

    C.   Goals: to enhance the subject's awareness of ongoing information about his/her physiological functioning and to provide training in self-regulation.

    D.   Clinical applications: most clinical applications involve use of a combination of instruments, relaxation techniques and methods from the realm of psychotherapy to reduce presenting symptoms. Only instrumentation is presented here.

    E.   Symptom: as indicated.

II.   Treatment procedures—EMG, GSR, Thermistor, EEG, EKG, EGG, Sphygmomanometer, Plethysmogram, stethoscope.

    A.   Instrument: electromyogram (EMG).

    B.   Targets: voluntary musculature.

    C.   Machine operations: body surface (or needle) placement of electrodes which pick up electrical output signal of muscles being monitored; amplifies, rectifies, integrates, and displays the signal in auditory-visual forms to the subject.

    D.   Goals: to provide subject with ongoing information of muscle activity in order to increase voluntary control of rate of firing, degree and sequence

of contractions, control of internal/external
stimulation of motorneurons, or through inducing
a bodily state of relaxation to enhance the
application of psychotherapeutic techniques.

E. Symptoms:

1. Chronic spasms in voluntary muscles (4, 11, 22, 28, 78, 89, 225).

2. Tension headaches (2, 11, 13, 28, 31, 32).

3. Bruxism (TMJ spasms) (6, 38, 39, 74, 233).

4. Voluntary control of involuntary motor activity (choreiform movements) (9, 28, 187).

5. Writer's cramp (11, 72).

6. Throat constriction (dysphagia spastica) (221, 93).

7. Menstrual pain (28, 232).

8. Sleep disorders (3, 13, 65, 72, 74, 225).

9. Torticollis; tics (7, 9, 11, 28, 29, 30, 43).

10. Restoration of impaired neuromotor function after injury or surgery (6, 7, 9, 11, 111, 127, 139, 179).

11. Cerebral palsy (increase-decrease of motor activity) (64).

12. Irritable colon (11, 217).

13. Recto-sphincteric reflex dysfunction (83).

14. Bronchial asthma (respiratory spasms) (1, 47).

15. Stress reduction (17, 22, 23, 28, 32, 46, 72, 76, 200).

16. Chronic pain spasms (26, 40, 192, 219, 221).

17. Ruminative vomiting (118).

18. Chronic drug abuse, tension element (28).

19. Hypertension (46, 153, 154, 165).

20. Bell's palsy (104).

2. A. Instrument: body surface thermometer (thermistor).

B. Targets: vascular and sympathetic systems.

C. Machine operations: body surface placement of

temperature sensors to monitor distribution of blood flow to major areas of body, particularly the hands, feet, head, and genitalia.

D. Goals: to provide the subject with ongoing information of changes in temperature level of skin in selected areas of the body in order to relax the sympathetic system and redistribute blood volume to extremities; relaxation preparatory to desensitization, recall, internal searches.

E. Symptom:
1. Vasoconstrictive disorders; Raynaud's (7, 11, 27, 28, 185, 232).
2. Migraine (7, 11, 27, 53, 161, 175, 176).
3. Essential hypertension (28, 46, 60, 219).
4. Autonomic overactivation (11, 46, 202, 203, 209).
5. Alcoholism, autonomic hyperarousal element (27).
6. Asthma (1, 47).
7. Irritable colon (11, 217, 227).
8. Sexual dysfunctions (95, 158).

3. A. Instrument: dermogram (GSR)
B. Targets: eccrine sweat glands; sympathetic system.
C. Machine Operations: placement of electrodes on fingertips or palmar surface to monitor skin conductance (or resistance) level and electrodermal potential, thereby monitoring autonomic arousal levels and emotionality.
D. Goals: to provide subject with information of fight-flight response of the autonomic system in order to acquire increased control of autonomic activity, achieve reduction of anxiety, induce relaxed state and to monitor emotional responses to internal/external stimuli.
E. Symptom:
1. Autonomic overactivation (27, 28, 200, 209, 223).
2. Stress reduction (11, 28, 49, 72, 209, 223).

3. Essential hypertension (7, 11, 19, 153, 154, 156).
4. Hyperventilation (47).
5. Neurodermatitis, stress-related (178).
6. Phobias (28, 72, 115, 209, 203).

4. A. Instrument: electroencephalogram (EEG)
   B. Targets: cerebral cortical action potentials.
   C. Machine Operations: scalp surface placement of surface electrodes to monitor brain wave activity; EEG filters permit visual or auditory output signal of desired wave forms and amplitudes.
   D. Goals: to provide subject with information about brain electrical activity in order to achieve self-regulation; to learn to intervene in irregular brain waves; to learn to sustain control over given wave patterns in order to induce given psychologic states.
   E. Symptom
      1. Epileptic seizures (28, 72, 112, 197, 198).
      2. Obsessions; ruminations (27).
      3. Sleep-onset insomnia (3, 7, 27).
      4. Concentration dysfunction (7, 144, 145, 191).
      5. Reduce diffuse anxiety (88).
      6. Increase hypnogogic revery (3, 156).
      7. Adjunctive to treatment in psychiatric disorders (7, 11, 28, 63, 74, 76, 79, 100, 121, 177, 219).
      8. Drug abuse (3, 28).
      9. Chronic pain (26, 28).
      10. Relaxation (79, 88, 107, 162).
      11. Stress reduction (11, 27, 28, 88).
      12. Hyperkinesis (28).

5. A. Instrument: electrocardiogram (EKG).
   B. Targets: cardiac activity; autonomic nervous system.
   C. Machine Operations: surface electrode placement to feedback normal activity or arrhythmias.

D. Goals: to provide subject with moment to moment information about targeted cardiac activity for appropriate intervention; to teach decrease in heart rate to achieve relaxation, or to correlate with cognitive or emotional activity and their changes.

E. Symptom
   1. Atrial arrhythmias (60, 117, 180).
   2. Premature ventricular contractions (19, 117).
   4. Phobias (7, 11, 17, 27, 28, 72, 76, 219, 232).
   5. Acute anxiety (76).

6. A. Instrument: sphygmomanometer.

B. Targets: cardiovascular system; autonomic nervous system.

C. Machine Operations: standard placement of cuff to feedback information of blood level pressure.

D. Goals: to provide subject with information about blood level pressure in order to monitor changes in autonomic system as reflected in vascular changes.

E. Symptom:
   1. High blood pressure (7, 60, 153, 154).

7. A. Instrument: plethysmogram.

B. Targets: cardiovascular and sympathetic system; voluntary muscles of vaginal tract.

C. Machine Operations: placement of strain gauge around limb or organ, or within an organ to feedback information on blood flow; to teach voluntary control of vaginal muscles.

D. Goals: to provide subjects with information of increase in blood flow to limb or organ in order to decrease vasoconstriction; to provide feedback of muscle activity of vagina to decrease spasms, or increase voluntary control.

E. Symptom
   1. Psychogenic impotence (95, 158, 232).

2. Vaginismus (158).

8. A. Instrument: electronic stethoscope.
    B. Targets: respiratory system; GI tract.
    C. Machine Operations: surface placement of head of stethoscope on chest to monitor bronchial spasms, or in abdominal area to monitor borborygmi of GI tract, and to feedback signals of muscular dysfunction.
    D. Goal: to provide subjects with information of muscle spasms and peristalsis to reduce dysfunctions.
    E. Symptom:
       1. Asthma (1, 72).
       2. Irritable colon (27, 72, 227).
       3. Colitis (28, 217).

---

abnormal brain waves are the treatment targets. In addition, patients are usually taught stress-reduction techniques which serve to alleviate a source of exacerbation of many of the diseases (3, 79, 219).

Appropriate applications of biofeedback are obviously dependent on accurate diagnosis of the presenting problems, as well as the quality of the treatment procedures. As indicated, most clinical applications are symptom oriented and do not presume to treat the underlying causes. Patients whose primary complaints require medical or intensive psychological treatment should not assume that symptom alleviation has removed the cause of the symptom. Migraine, asthma, hypertension, and other psychophysiologic disorders, among other diagnoses, can be treated for symptomatic relief but many cases appear to need other or additional treatment modalities in order to maintain any gains achieved through biofeedback, or to reduce the conditions themselves.

Limitations and assets

Biofeedback is evidently a clinical procedure that is not self-sufficient in most applications. Clinicians invariably apply a multi-modality treatment procedure consisting of biofeedback instruments, relaxation techniques, and methods adopted from hypnotism, behavior therapy, and traditional psychotherapies (17, 28, 72, 219). These approaches appear to enhance each other when used simultaneously, or in sequence. There are few verifiable, high-return treatment plans that one is able to apply with minimal variations. Most clinicians begin with relaxation techniques, augmented through biofeedback instruments, and then apply individualized treatment programs in terms of the patient's age, level of cooperation, the kind and severity of the complaints, the diagnosis, the particular physiological systems involved in the complaint, and the ongoing response to a program. Clinical applications are essentially quite pragmatic and eclectic in the conduct of a given treatment plan.

Behavior therapy (80) has contributed most of the specific therapy techniques that are ancillary to the biofeedback operations. Table 2 presents an outline of the principles, applications, and techniques of behavior therapy and relaxation methods that are most commonly used in treatment plans. Biofeedback's limited usefulness in clinical applications has compelled practitioners to use ancillary techniques in order to meet the clinical criteria of significant reduction in symptomatology that lasts a significant length of time.

The usefulness of clinical biofeedback, as indicated above, requires motivation on the part of the patient and clinical acumen on the part of the therapist. Their joint efforts are also necessary for any degree of success, even though the patient is engaged in the treatment procedure in a pre-eminent role. The patient cannot perform accurately within the patient-instrument-therapist feedback loop without adequate knowledge of the technology of the instruments, the physiology, and the therapy techniques.

The patient is not required to be a physiologist or an electronics engineer, but he or she must learn something about the implicated physiological systems and be trained in "driving" the instruments. Most patients find the latter to be a simple task when trained on the EMG. A brief description of the relevant physiological process that allows them to visualize the gross features of the anatomic structures involved in the symptom and self-demonstrations on the machine usually suffice.

The most difficult task the patient faces is to learn consciously the *passive concentration* required in relaxation training in order to allow any psychological overactivation to diminish. Once the "letting go" attitude is grasped and established, the treatment can proceed.

Table 2.   Overview of principles, applications, and treatment procedures in behavior therapy used in
conjunction with biofeedback instruments.

I.   Overview—Behavior Therapy
   A.   Principles: Neurotic symptoms are learned
      behaviors or responses which are maladaptive and
      are susceptible to being modified or unlearned.
   B.   Methodology: Maladaptive responses are described
      in detail (behavior analysis), particular behaviors
      to be changed are identified (target symptoms),
      appropriate techniques are applied to modify the
      target symptoms (applications), and outcomes are
      assessed (validation).

II.   Applications
   A.   Counterconditioning of anxiety through reciprocal
      inhibition techniques.
   B.   Reconditioning through the acquisition and rein-
      forcement of new, desirable motor habits or
      cognitions.
   C.   Extinction of undesired responses through
      withdrawal of reinforcing stimuli or use of
      aversive techniques. (N.B. Clinical applications
      are used in various combinations or sequences
      and often in conjunction with drugs, biofeedback,
      recordkeeping by the patient, group procedures,
      or environmental manipulations. Many behavior
      therapy techniques are useful in symptom reduc-
      tion in changing behavior in the context of inten-
      sive psychotherapy.

III.   Treatment procedures
   A.   Relaxation: progressive, focus of attention, or
      hypnosis including relaxation of autonomic and
      voluntary muscle systems.

    a. Target symptoms
1. Autonomic hyperarousal.
2. Muscle tensions.
3. Preliminary to desensitization of fears and phobias.
4. Sleep disturbances.
5. Constipation.
6. Menstrual disorders.
7. Pre- and Post-operative tension.
8. Stress reduction.
9. Hyperkinesis.
10. Vasoconstrictive disorders.
11. Asthma; respiratory spasms.
12. Tics.
13. Dysphagias.
14. Hypertension.
15. Pain.
16. Smoking.

B. Systematic desensitization in vivo or imaginal re-experiencing of feared or phobic objects or situations simultaneous with counterconditioning through relaxation.

    a. Target symptoms
1. Phobias (animal, object, social).
2. Test anxiety; school phobias.
3. Sexual fears.
4. Functional impotence and frigidity.
5. Acrophobia, agoraphobia, claustrophobia.

C. Assertive training, behavioral rehearsal, modeling.

    a. Target symptoms
1. Social anxiety.
2. Authority problems.
3. Emotional withdrawal.
4. Deficient socialization.
5. Inappropriate social behavior.
6. Alcoholism and other drug abuse.
7. Marital discord.

D. Positive reinforcement: to increase the frequency or strength of desired responses.

    a. Target symptoms

    Not applicable inasmuch as the undesired responses (symptoms) are ignored during this form of contingency management. Positive reinforcers increase the rate of response through reward of desired responses; therefore, this technique is utilized essentially in the training of new or normal behaviors and is applicable in a wide variety of cases.

E. Aversive conditioning: punishment applied to decrease the frequency or strength of undesired responses.

    a. Target symptoms
        1. Smoking
        2. Dysphagia.
        3. Fetishes.
        4. Sexual deviations.
        5. Self-injuries.
        6. Drug abuse.

F. Thought stoppage: sudden intrusion on patient's ruminations.

    a. Target symptoms
        1. Obsessions and ruminations.

G. Implosive or flooding therapy: extinction of anxiety response to eliciting stimuli through in vivo or imaginal saturation of consciousness of the eliciting stimuli in their most extreme forms.

    a. Target symptoms
        1. Phobias and fears.
        2. Generalized anxiety with obsessive ideation as eliciting stimulus.

H. Autogenic technique: verbal method of inducing relaxation, and change in blood flow through autosuggestion.

    a. Target symptoms (see Luthe (125) for extensive list)

1. Migraine.
2. Vasoconstrictive disorders.
3. Hyperarousal.
4. Insomnia.

During the training and treatment phases, the therapist functions as a guide assisting the patient in continuing successful use of the feedback signals. The therapist also provides the specific therapy techniques that target psychological processes, such as phobias or other anxiety-related symptoms.

Although many of the research and clinical papers in the field do not report patient activity emerging during the sessions beyond the responses of the targeted physiology or symptom, it is a rare patient who does not report complex mental and emotional events occurring throughout treatment sessions. Even the monosymptomatic patient will report varieties of reactions, if permitted by the therapist. Indeed, the need many patients have to talk out their internal reactions to the experience of biofeedback is a commonplace. The clinical decision of concentrating on the self or the symptom, or both, and by the feedback therapist or some other professional, is of considerable importance. Discussions about the possible choices ordinarily resolve the problems of appropriate treatment plans. Clear information in these matters is essential to informed consent and for the required participation of the patient.

In summary, clinical biofeedback can serve as a low-risk procedure to reduce homeostatic imbalances that are not limited to anatomical change due to injury or disease. As an adjunctive technique in rehabilitation medicine, the instruments provide a highly discriminative signal of viable neuromotor action potentials, and the retraining of impaired muscle groups can be sharply enhanced. Maladaptive motor habits respond well to BFT. It is especially useful in reducing psychogenic stress. In psychotherapy, the physiologically generated signals provide an additional pathway to psychological processes. Moreover, one of the major accomplishments of clinical biofeedback is the involvement of the patient in the responsibility for the treatment of his or her disorder and in the maintenance of personal health, thereby reducing the passivity and dependency so common in psychosomatic disorders in both adults and children.

Various medical, psychiatric, and psychological disorders, for which the treatment of choice is not biofeedback, nevertheless may present symptomatology that exists apart from the illness or disability. Sometimes these symptoms pre-date the illness, and some may be psychogenic reactions to the shock and stress of a serious injury which then complicate treatment or convalescence.

The field of biofeedback is still in its infancy. "Old literature" is dated from 1970; and quite recently clinical procedures have been refined through research and practice that modify clinical views of a few years ago. At present, one might say that the technique shows strong promise in both clinical and research areas, but the future will establish the nature and degree of that promise.

Chapter 2

HISTORY AND DEFINITION
OF BIOFEEDBACK

Origins

The technique of feeding back to a subject some attribute of his or her physiological functions was reported as early as 1935 by Lindsley (123). His research was devoted to determining the degree of voluntary control that could be gained over a single motor unit (SMU), the smallest self-contained structure of the neuromotor system. The motor action potential of a SMU was fed back to the subjects who were able to discriminate its activity from the many hundreds of neighboring motor units with excellent precision. The task also requires inhibiting the firing of hundreds of the other SMUs. No other method of physiological training had achieved that fine a degree of self-regulation. Basmajian (10) confirmed that remarkable feat in mind-body control in a series of replications in the 1960s.

Marinacci and Horande (127) also used the EMG in 1960 to pick up motor action potentials, in cases of neuromotor impairment, to feed back signals of viable motor fibers to the patients who then attempted to increase the strength of the signals. As the patients acquired increasing degrees of voluntary control over the signals— and the neuromotor functioning—improvement in function and control increased in the impaired regions. The authors did not conceptualize their procedure as biofeedback, although they obviously used that methodology. Whatmore and Kohli (225, 226) had applied EMG feedback in the 1950s to teach muscle relaxation to patients suffering from psychogenic disorders; and Jacobson (101) had included EMG monitoring of muscle tone since his early research in the 1930s in order to assess the depth of muscular relaxation achieved by tense patients. Jacobson did not feedback the ongoing EMG output signals; however, he told his patients how they were performing. Jacobson was practicing an indirect, somewhat time-delayed, biofeedback procedure. If he had allowed the patients to hear directly and immediately the output signal, and instructed them to revise the signal in a desired direction, he would have been applying biofeedback as it is now practiced.

Joe Kamiya is noteworthy in the history of biofeedback as the scientist who discovered that subjects could learn to intervene in the ebb and flow of various of their brain waves. He was studying the electrical activity of the brain through use of the EEG and concluded that his subjects could increase the rate of alpha rhythm after having learned through feedback when alpha was occurring. Kamiya (106, 107) was demonstrating through objective, quantifiable research that people could read and revise bodily processes that were out of awareness. One cannot ordinarily sense one's own brain waves, or blood pressure, or minute changes in muscle tone; but with appropriate information about these bodily processes, one can learn to read them. Hassett put it succinctly: "Feedback makes learning possible" (91).

Kamiya's subjects' reports of their subjective, psychological states while in "alpha-on" may well be the catalyst that set the clinical community in pursuit of therapeutic applications of the new physiological feedback technique. The subjects had reported feeling calm, peaceful, tranquil, refreshed, during and after alpha enhancement. The direct production of "alpha-calm" through EEG feedback was and is questionable to many scientists and practitioners, but that finding suggested the possibility of using physiological feedback technique to reduce distressing symptoms or disruptions in mental, emotional or physiologic parameters. The search was undertaken by numerous experimentors and clinicians (27, 28). Practitioners and scientists in psychology, psychophysiology, rehabilitation medicine, and psychiatry also turned to the use of other standard research and diagnostic instruments in the conduct of their research and practice in biofeedback.

Many of these instruments had been in use for decades as devices to measure varieties of physiologic processes, some directly, some indirectly (Table 1). The dermogram or galvanic skin response (GSR) machine utilizes sweat gland production as a measure of sympathetic nervous system activation and the electrocardiograph (EKG) monitors the electrical activity of heart muscle contraction. Surface body temperature is measured by the thermistor which reflects changes in blood flow in arterioles to and from the skin; the sphygmomanometer measures blood pressure; the plethysmograph (a strain gauge) measures changes in volume through blood flow of a limb of organ, such as a finger or penis; and the stethoscope monitors heart activity and sounds of the respiratory system and the gastrointestinal tract. It is surprising that no one until the recent decades had thought to instruct patients in reading their own physiologic functions and to encourage them to gain useful control over one or more of the parameters of such functions.

Early advocates of teaching self-regulation of disrupted homeostatic processes were gratified by significant successes in their beginning attempts to investigate a wide variety of disorders. Budzynski and Stovya (32) were among the first to treat the psychogenic muscle spasms of tension headache. They also used EMG biofeedback to reduce temperomandibular myofacial pain and bruxism by relaxation of spastic masseter muscles of the jaw (33). Cannistraci (39) was also using the EMG applications in dental practice for treating temperomandibular joint syndromes. Barbara Brown (27, 28) conducted experimental biofeedback applications with several feedback instruments and contributed enormously to the research and clinical literature of feedback. Pelletier (156) and Sargent et al. (174, 175) reported many successful endeavors in stress reduction and in treating psychophysiological disorders. Basmajian (9) extended his research in muscle activity to rehabilitation of neuromotor impairments; and Andrews (6) and Brudny et al. (29, 30) also contributed to the clinical methodology of reducing spasticity or increasing the level of control over impaired muscle groups. Gleuck and Stroebel (79) and Wentworth-Rohr (221) adopted biofeedback technique in treating anxiety and other symptoms in psychotic conditions.

The EMG has become the principal instrument among clinician in the treatment of tension, regardless of etiology. Its particular value is in its ease of operation, the clarity of the output signal which simplifies biofeedback learning for the patient, and its clinical flexibility in the treatment of many complaints. The EMG is an invaluable bioinstrument in the reduction of tension in skeletal muscles, in teaching general somatic relaxation, and in neuromotor rehabilitation.

Whatmore and Kohli (225, 226) developed an original paradigm in biofeedback theory regarding functional disorders of physiology. They conceptualized physiopathologies as errors in the neuromotor-endocrine signaling systems resulting in "dysponesis," or errors in effort. Dysponetic signaling and subsequent activation of misdirected motoric efforts are seen in "headache, backache, various other somatic pains, fatigue and exhaustion, insomnia, anxiety states, depression, gastrointestinal disturbances, and a number of other conditions" (225, p. 1). In pathophysiologies there are underlying alterations in structure; there are none in physiopathology. The alterations in dysponesis are in the functions of the physiology, although structural changes can sometimes eventually occur.

Reducing homeostatic overactivation in both striate and smooth muscles was recommended in the early years of biofeedback to be therapeutic in and of itself (32, 200). Other relaxation procedures used by Pascal (150, 151) and Schultz and Luthe (184) had already established that finding in their treatment of phobias and an extensive variety of psychosomatic disorders. Their relaxation methods included specific use of imagery, indicating that the relaxation training was combined with mental or cognitive training. The predominance of disorders of the viscera and other organ systems regulated by the autonomic nervous system (ANS) led clinicians and experimentalists to concentrate on autonomic functions and their relationship with stress and anxiety.

The importance of hyperarousal of the sympathetic nervous system (SNS) division of the ANS in various psychiatric disorders and in anxiety itself had been discussed by many investigators (1, 82, 201). One of the earliest and most popular physiologic systems to be studied was the ANS, especially the SNS division (8, 82, 130, 159) in the search for the physical correlates of psychologic states. The GSR has been a chief monitoring device of sweat gland activity since the late nineteenth century, when it was determined that increase in body sweat occurred when persons were upset, frightened, embarrassed, anxious, or similarly stressed (97).

However, the ANS was not considered to be responsive to instrumental conditioning. Historically, the ANS was viewed as directly accessible only to classical conditioning (See Chapter 5), and biofeedback theory and practice fall within the model of instrumental learning. Nevertheless, research was undertaken to determine whether the dichotomy in physiological learning of classical-autonomic and instrumental-somatic was in fact a biological given. In the 1960s Kimmel and Hill (109) found that the number of spontaneous changes in skin resistance responses, a sympathetic function, could be varied through instrumental conditioning. Miller's work (138, 140) with curarized rats in the late 1960s investigated the instrumental conditioning of the ANS through biofeedback techniques and the initial success he reported encouraged others to follow his lead.

The psychophysiological model and the GSR were quickly adopted by biofeedback practitioners as the treatment modality and the instrumentation to be used in cases of anxiety states, hyperventilation, phobias, vasoconstrictive disorders (adding the use of the thermistor), gastrointestinal disorders, insomnia, and other psychosomatic conditions involving homeostatic imbalances in the ANS and smooth musculature. Reducing sympathetic hyperarousal was found to be fundamental to stress reduction in general and in the multimodality treatment of many conditions (1, 150, 203, 205, 209).

Other experimental applications of biofeedback that were conducted in the late 1960s have provided possibilities for low-risk, therapeutic interventions. The EKG has been applied in biofeedback training in premature ventricular contractions (PVCs), among other cardiac arrhythmias (19, 117), by feeding back to the patient information about heart activity with acceptable levels of success. Heart rate has also been used as a measure of anxiety, or sympathetic hyperarousal, as well as being targeted by the EKG as a means of reducing arousal level and accompanying fears and phobias (28, 74). However, most of the reports are confounded by the addition of other techniques. The clinical methodology included significant use of relaxation and cognitive techniques which may be the effective agents, rather than the biofeedback itself, particularly in the treatment of stress, fears, and phobias (20, 76).

Other attributes of the cardiovascular system have been targeted in treating homeostatic imbalances in the ANS. The thermistor is commonly used in vasoconstrictive disorders. Sargent, Green, and Walters (174, 175) at the Menninger Clinic combined relaxation, the autogenic techniques of Schultz and Luthe (184), and thermistor biofeedback in treating migraine headaches. The rationale is that migraine is a vascular disorder in which excessive blood flow to the head causes the migrainous pain. They began the procedure with relaxation technique, fed back desired temperature increases in the periphery (hands) and decreases at the forehead, instructing the patients to think simultaneously various autogenic phrases such as "My hands are warm."

Increasing peripheral temperature is surprisingly easy for most persons when relaxed. The Menninger Clinic group's success led Sedlacek (185) and others to use a similar approach with Raynaud's disease. But, again, it is not clear which of the techniques is the effective agent—the relaxation or the biofeedback.

High blood pressure is a major, life-threatening disorder (156). Essential hypertension is high blood pressure without known etiology and is one of the most commonly presented cardiovascular complaints in biofeedback practice. Any method that would be effective, noninvasive and self-sustaining would make a useful contribution to the control of hypertension.

Schwartz (181) conducted several elegant projects in the self-regulation of cardiac functions. Among the findings was the ability of normotensive subjects to raise and lower systolic and diastolic blood pressure, or to decrease heart rate. Specially designed sphygmomano-meters provided the biofeedback information. Application to hypertension became the obvious next step.

Patel (153, 154) employed GSR biofeedback, a cognitive-physical method of achieving relaxation, focusing on breathing, and autogenic phrases in reducing BP successfully. Combining relaxation techniques and biofeedback that targets the ANS simultaneously in order to lower sympathetic tone has been a standard procedure among clinicians for several years (219, 228). If the patients practice relaxation, change stressful life situations, and otherwise maintain good health habits, the lowered levels are usually maintained. There is also considerable clinical experience that suggests that sympathetic hypoarousal is a necessary though not sufficient agent, regardless of treatment modality and complaint presented (11, 16, 220) in cases of visceral problems.

The plethysmogram has long been in use in research laboratories to measure blood volume change in an organ. The modern device of a simple coil that fits around the penis, measuring degree of penile erection as a function of blood flow to the genitals, has been applied as a feedback technique for treating psychogenic impotence or psycho-sexual disorders. Herman and Prewitt (95) report a case study which is typical in procedure. The coil is placed around the flaccid penis and the subject is stimulated by erotic pictures. It is a questionable use of biofeedback training as a technique in the treatment of psychogenic impotence, let alone psychosexual disorders in general. Sexual arousal is highly dependent on the ANS, but even more dependent on attitude. Attempting to increase blood flow to the penis or vagina to reduce psychogenic sexual dysfunction is a naive approach in treating sexual disorders. Human sexuality consists of more than genital ade-quacy.

Sexuality in humans is a mind-body process and not simply a matter of physiological sexual drive or changes in blood volume. In the cases of learned fears of sexual activity where the patient has out-grown or resolved the early learning that resulted in attitudes of fear, shame, or mild inhibition, and the physiological sexual systems were conditioned not to respond to normal stimulation, retraining of the physiological processes via clinical biofeedback is indicated and may be sufficient. These cases are autonomous habits of response that persists after their causes are no longer present. They respond well to retraining of the homeostatic loops involving the ANS and the circulatory system. With few exceptions, the patients also require desensitization of their anxiety responses to sexual acts, some resolution to their immature attitudes to human sexuality, and often the reduction of social anxiety.

Cases of deep-seated conflicts, anxiety, and defenses that are inherent dynamics of the sexual dysfunction require intensive psychotherapy. Biofeedback applications are then useful, eventually, in the reduction of symptoms that are expressed in physiological dysfunctions.

The stethoscope has been applied to the feedback of sounds from the respiratory system and the gastrointestinal (GI) tract. The former was attempted by Abdullah (1) with asthmatics. He taped the chest piece of the stethoscope to a patient's chest and while being taught a "simple breathing exercise combined with a meditation-relaxation procedure" the patient learned varying degrees of voluntary control over bronchial spasms. Abdullah did not report the numbers of patients treated but stated that the method was generally useful. Currently, practitioners use the stethoscope to monitor or to feed back the sounds of airway resistance, as well as adding other instruments to achieve relaxation states, in various kinds of respiratory disorders.

The electronic stethoscope amplifies the physiological output signal permitting a more sensitive reading of low amplitude signals of a mechanical nature. This has permitted an effective use of the stethoscope in picking up the peristaltic rumbles, or borborygmi, of the intestinal tract in the treatment of disorders of the GI tract. Fuller (72) suggests that the feedback of borborygmi is the most straightforward biofeedback application for spastic colon. The patients are individually instructed in reducing the rumbles, or smoothing out the extremes of peristaltic activity while relaxed.

An EMG of low frequency (2Hz) filter or a standard electrogastrogram (EGG) have been used with promising reliability as monitors or feedback instruments of GI activity (72) but little has appeared in the literature regarding their use.

Many other scientists and practitioners have contributed to the field of biofeedback. Miller (140) has continued his seminal research in the instrumental conditioning of the ANS, Mulholland (144) has refined his research of cortical action potentials and Blanchard and his colleagues (19) continue to report on the treatment of cardiovascular disorders.

The pressing need for clinical biofeedback is basic research in problems of crossover in systems treated, the role of mentation or cognition in the various complaints treated and in different diagnostic groups regardless of presenting complaint, the role of relaxation itself in biofeedback, and factors such as advanced age, placebo effects, masochism, secondary gain, selection of instruments, and the development of testable treatment plans.

Training vs. treatment

From the earliest days of the clinical application of biofeedback technique there has also been a confusion in the literature between BFT and clinical biofeedback (3, 11, 72, 156, 219). However, the more recent evaluations of the research and clinical literature appears to be recognizing the limitations of BFT and the confounding in its applications by personality variables (76). Undoubtedly, the multi-modal clinical biofeedback approach is confounded by the use of a multiplicity of machine, relaxation, and therapy operations. But BFT, too, is confounded by the patients' motivations, expectancies, reactions to the machines and to the therapist, and by the virtual impossibility of removing from the BFT procedure the patients' historical and newly gained perceptions of biofeedback. Evidently, BFT is merely a much less complicated procedure than clinical biofeedback. Determining which model should be followed in treating pathologies is as much a clinical judgment as it is an issue for experimental resolution. In reality, the choice often appears to be a matter of one's clinical view.

Many of the practitioners of clinical biofeedback seem to accept the existence and power of covert, mental-emotional components in the formation of symptoms, and even some accept the unconscious element of personality as a factor in human behavior (74, 78, 79, 177, 220).

Generally, research and clinical reports indicate that bioinstruments are not necessary in reducing some symptoms. Among these are peripheral vasoconstriction, general somatic tension, insomnia, high blood pressure, sexual dysfunctions, headaches, ruminations, phobias, and impaired neuromotor units. These, and other symptoms, respond to traditional therapies or to various kinds of relaxation training, hypnotic suggestion, behavior modification techniques, change in life style, growth, desensitization, and even a pleasant vacation.

What, then, is the unique value of using bioinstruments in these complaints? One is that the patient is doing his own treatment, which is a valuable contribution to developing self-care. Many conditions are chronic and incurable, requiring constant attention and medication. When the patient learns a self-applied, noninvasive method to reduce the severity and frequency of a symptom, such as recurrent headaches, high blood pressure, or vasoconstriction, he is less likely to increase medication to dangerous levels, his life is less disordered by the symptom, and the cost in time and money are reduced. A second value is that the feedback instrument can focus on a specific organ and provide highly discriminative training, quickly, in changing the direction of the function in a desired fashion. This precision may not be reached at all through other methods, or may require inordinate amounts of time. Progressive relaxation (101) and TM suffer these limitations.

A third possible value is that the direct reading through the output signal of the physiological circuits from the cortex to the periphery through the use of a bioinstrument may produce a more profound neurophysiological change in the pathways than accomplished by other less sensitive and less direct training procedures. Whatmore and Kohli hypothesize such a consequence of biofeedback training in treating physiopathologies.

Other values may hold for particular persons. One is that the person alienated from somatic experience may find that biofeedback can reintegrate mind-body-feeling experiences simultaneously in a manageable procedure.

These foregoing values indicate that bioinstrumentation is relatively necessary in clinical biofeedback. The instruments alone, though, are probably not sufficient to achieve long-lasting remissions of many symptoms. Since most psychosomatic and neurotic symptoms are intertwined with thought and feeling, additional psychotherapy techniques appear to be essential for meaningful change in mindbody interactions, which lead to symptom reduction.

Definition of Biofeedback

Biofeedback can be defined by its *operations, targets,* and *goals.* The operations consist of the application of the instruments, the targets are the physiological systems, and the goals are desired changes in one or more attributes of those systems. In BFT the operations do not add other treatment techniques to the machine applications; and the targets do not extend much beyond the directly expressed activities of the physiology, such as signs of muscle contractions or variations in percentage of particular brain waves. The complexities of the mental domain are not explicitly included. The model excludes free association, guided imagery, introspection, the use of an observing ego, and the interaction and integration of affect and intellect in relation to bodily functioning on different levels of consciousness. Admittedly, some kind or degree of mental process is at work in BFT. Asking a subject to focus his attention on a muscle group being targeted obviously includes mental activity.

However, there are significant clinical and psychological differences between BFT and clinical biofeedback as to operations and goals. Clinical biofeedback adds to the operations of BFT elaborate instructions and guidance in using varieties of psychotherapy techniques (28, 74, 228). It also targets the mental domains of psychophysiological systems through adding the goal of revising the biophychosocial matrix of personality.

Clinical biofeedback applications purport to deal with more aspects of the person than BFT. The latter is devoted predominately to symptom reduction; the former to achieving a change in the more complex psychological processes of the person that may underlie the symptom. Briefly, the goal of BFT is change in the symptom; the goal of clinical biofeedback is change in the self. These treatment models are obviously not mutually exclusive; but their differentiation can be described through the different operations conducted by the therapists and by the stated goals of the treatment plans.

In BFT the operations are identified as the application of the feedback instrument, and the goals are stated as the revision of physiological functions. The sensors of a feedback instrument are applied at selected sites of the body in order to monitor and feed back the activity or attribute of given physiological functioning. Although the procedure may seem to be uncomplicated, there are indirect and complex psychological activities inherent in the procedure. The intervention in BFT is direct on the level of the operations and less direct on the level of the targets. Evidently, more than one physiological system is involved in the simplest of biofeedback technique. Which physiological systems are in fact the functional targets of the operations, let alone what methods the subject uses (219) to achieve the goal of self-control, remain major questions in the field of biofeedback.

Blanchard and Epstein's definition (19, p. 5) is an example of defining BFT in terms which minimize psychological variables. "Biofeedback is a process in which a person learns to reliably influence physiological responses of two kinds: either responses that are not ordinarily under voluntary control or responses which ordinarily are easily regulated but for which regulation has broken down due to trauma or disease." Presumably, when a "person learns" in this model, the learning process is in the behavioristic model of stimulus-response, and excludes reference to internal, nonobservable variables. It is a classical laboratory research model that minimizes, if not excludes, mental activities of a subjective nature. The advantage of the model is precision in control of the independent variable (the operations), and their relationship with the dependent variables (the targets).

Fuller's definition of biofeedback (72), and his descriptions of the individualized, multimodality approach to treatment illustrates a concept of biofeedback that recognizes more complexities of the person and the clinical data. Indeed, in actuality, few biofeedback applications in the clinical and research literature fail to include attention to thinking, mental content, concentration, emotionality, and individual differences among patients even though many reports omit any such references.

Perhaps the differences between research and clinical attitudes structure the definitions of biofeedback and consequently the nature of the procedures. The classical psychodynamic therapist as opposed to the classical behaviorist would approach the clinical application of biofeedback with different perspectives, would develop different treatment plans, and would probably set different criteria for assessing outcomes.

If change in physiological functioning is the treatment goal, and the treatment techiques are limited to BFT, it follows that the criterion is the revision of physiological functioning that demonstrably covaries with machine operations. One is then testing the validity of biofeedback in terms of retraining physiology through machine applications. Blanchard and Young's review (20) of several research and clinical reports used this model and found that biofeedback was efficacious in reducing some muscle spasms with the EMG, and that *when BFT is combined with relaxation techniques* and home practice good results were also obtained in treating phobias.

Hume (100) noted that several disorders have responded to clinical applications: tension headaches, migraine, hypertension, and neuromuscular dysfunctions. Others, epilepsy, cardiac arrhythmias, and phobias, "may be modified," but the few controlled studies available had not demonstrated biofeedback's superiority to existing methods.

Blanchard and Epstein's and Hume's reviews reflect the confusion between BFT and clinical biofeedback. Very few symptoms treated with biofeedback technique, and reported in their reviews, respond to only machine operations; and most of the projects reviewed used various psychotherapy and relaxation techniques as treatment agents in conjunction with the machine operation. Virtually all used relaxation methods as the clinical base for the applications of other techniques. The exceptions might be some cases of neuromotor re-education (127). However, relaxation to reduce anxiety and general tension is usually a necessary pre-treatment step.

Strictly speaking, it is unlikely that biofeedback procedures do not tap mental activities during research or in clinical applications.

In clinical biofeedback, the elaborate treatment procedures confound the operations to a great degree. Adding to the machine operations relaxation techniques that affect emotions, attention, physiology, and deliberately revising mental content, increases the number of operations and their interactions. The targets are multiplied by the addition of the instructions to relax and the application of other therapy methods, such as self-statements, guided imagery, free association, desensitization hierarchies, etc. It is then impossible to determine which of all these operations influence which targets and which goals. The justification for using such complex clinical procedures is pragmatic. When the simpler approaches, such as BFT, are insufficient in achieving the clinical goals, as they usually are, the clinical routinely adds varieties of techniques to the machine operations until a desired change occurs. This kind of complexity appears in the use of biofeedback for treating even mild, monosymptomatic complaints, as well as psychosomatic disorders, other complex, non-psychotic conditions, and in the treatment of some anxiety-related symptoms in chronic schizophrenia or long-standing hysteria (219).

Individual differences in use of and degrees of responsiveness to biofeedback suggest that more than a stimulus-response model is necessary to explain the actualities of biofeedback. For example, the idiosyncratic interpretation of the feedback information by subjects becomes self-evident through the wide differences subjects display in their use of the information. All subjects are not equally capable of perceiving feedback information usefully; and some persons can not revise the physiological processes that are malfunctioning, regardless of their endeavors, or of the therapists' assistance.

Some definitions that exclude the mental activity of the subject or patient may be defining a particular kind of theoretical orientation in therapy, rather than biofeedback itself.

The lack of certainty in the nature and activity of the targets at work in biofeedback, coupled with the dynamic quality of the subject's use of feedback ,suggest that the principle referent in the procedure is one that is universal in biofeedback: *interaction between physical and mental systems.*

In that context, the following definition appears relevant. *Biofeedback is the process of acquiring through feedback instruments comprehensible information about the interactions of psychophysiological systems to develop skills in their regulation.* The definition departs from current ones in that it explicitly includes mental systems, in the manifestation of consciously perceived and self-applied feedback information, as a major parameter of the procedure. And it requires self-regulation of mind-body interactions as the principle goal. The definition emphasizes the interactions of mind-body as the central dependent variable in conducting the procedure.

What is treated

By specifying the principle referent as the interactions of the mind and body the therapist and patient would monitor and attend to the activities of the physiology and the psychology of the patient before, during, and after the biofeedback procedure, and set criteria for change in all relevant parameters, not only in the physiological parameter. Treatment procedures appear to be conducted in this model, by clinicians, even though some of them define their operations, targets, and goals as though the mental target is insignificant. Biofeedback operations are useful and sometimes necessary, though rarely sufficient, in clinical applications. The addition of other operations that target mental activities often comprise a sufficient combination for treatment purposes.

It is also well worth emphasizing the obvious: physiological and psychological functioning cannot be fragmented and isolated within a *person*, and treated or studied as though each physical or mental process or event functions independently within the person. If one could in fact do so, the human subject would no longer be human, or even alive. The interactions of the biopsychosocial matrix is the essence of clinical biofeedback inasmuch as the person is a product of the matrix and exists within it. Any human activity is shared among the domains of the matrix and influenced to some degree by those domains. Assuredly, clinical biofeedback procedures must attend to each domain as it exerts its particular influence on any disorder and every behavior of the patient.

Chapter 3

PHYSIOLOGY AND BIOFEEDBACK

Physiologic feedback

Physiology, as the study of the functioning of anatomy, is of particular interest to the biofeedback specialist. What each physiologic system does, and its interactions with behavior, provides the modality in machine applications for intervention in the mind-body feedback loop. The potential activities form the biological bases of biofeedback procedures.

Through biofeedback procedures, the potential activities of some organs can be revised in ways not previously accomplished. For example, overriding the chronic constriction of small blood vessels in Raynaud's disease through clinical biofeedback procedures increases the potential for dilation of the vessels and the flow of blood to the periphery (185). That is, in biofeedback-assisted dilation of blood vessels the potentialities of the circulatory and central nervous systems are influenced to a significant degree. Generally speaking, a purpose of biofeedback is to *re-establish or to increase the biological potential of psychophysiological activity*. There is no evidence, incidentally, to suggest that new potentialities can be created. What may seem new is probably a variation of the natural, physiological potential.

Physiologic feedback within and among the various systems is a general law of biologic functioning. A feedback system consists of the interactions among the parts of a system so that as one part changes, other parts change in adjustment. The common room-temperature thermostat is a simple example of a feedback system.

The feedback principle is also the basis of electronic servomechanisms, such as a radar tracking unit. The radar sends a beam to a moving plane or missile; the beam is reflected back to the tracking mechanism which automatically revises the direction of the outgoing beam as the incoming beam registers changes in the movement of the object. In human movement, the neuromotor system is a servomechanism. Weiner (215) termed such a system *cybernetics* when a machine and an organism were interacting in a feedback loop—as the actions of one changes, the actions of the other changes. He specified the system as a closed-loop method of controlling a dynamic system by reinserting into the system the results of its past performance. Biologically-given systems interact among themselves and with the external environment on both a learned and unlearned basis. Their purpose is to maintain relatively automatic patterns of behavior which regulate moment-to-moment living. It is through these systems that normal growth proceeds in an orderly sequence of internal changes, and in adaptive relations with the external environment.

The constancy and purpose in physiological functioning were conceptualized by Cannon as *homeostasis* in *Wisdom of the Body:*

> Repeatedly in foregoing chapters I have called attention to the fact that insofar as our internal environment is kept constant [homeostasis] we are freed from the limitations imposed by both internal and external agencies that could be disturbing. The pertinent question...is freedom for what? It is chiefly freedom for the activity of the higher levels of the nervous system and the muscles they govern. By means of the cerebral cortex we have all our intelligent relations to the world about us.

> They are made possible by such autonomic regulations of the routine necessities that the functions of the brain which subserve intelligence and imagination, insight and manual skill, are set free for the use of these higher services (36, pp. 302-303).

By complex, interactive feedback loops, within and among the physiological systems, the person maintains his normal, adaptive patterns of living, moment to moment, situation to situation. Most of the functioning is out of awareness, and will alert the person only when a significant departure from within the ordinary ranges occurs. Most departures are normal events, such as urinary pressure in the bladder, alerting one to the need to urinate. An unusual event, such as an injury, an infection, nausea, or a muscle spasm, will fill the mind with information that the body part involved is not in its usual anatomical or physiological state. One then takes actions to reduce the distress.

Figure 1 illustrates homeostatic mechanisms in biological feedback loops in the context of the environment. The central area represents the central nervous system (CNS), consisting of the brain and the spinal cord. The area surrounding the CNS represents the internal environment of the body; and the outer regions constitute the external environment. Stimuli in the external environment in the form of sounds, light, pressure, heat and cold, smells, movement, etc., impinge on the sensory receptors (the exteroceptors) of the five main senses at the surface of the body. The receptors convert the energy of the stimuli into electrical impulses which are sent along the sensory nervous system (afference) to the spinal cord and on to the brain. The brain then processes the impulses giving many a conscious or preconscious significance (cognition) in order to make a judgment about responding to the stimuli. Whatever judgments and decisions are made, and whether in or out of awareness, the brain then sends electrical impulses along the efferent nervous system to the effectors— glands and muscles— to make appropriate internal, environmental adjustments. The adjustments can be, and often are, expressed in overt interactions with the external environment.

Many of the internal adjustments are automatic, as Cannon describes, and without any cognitive events occurring. Changes then take place in various organs and biochemical processes in different

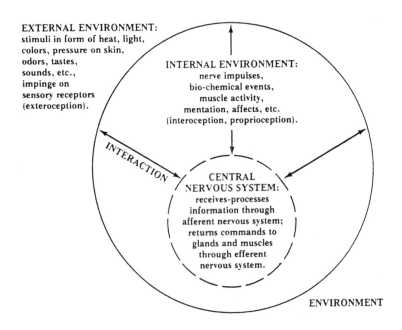

FIGURE 1. SCHEMATIC OF BIOLOGICAL FEEDBACK LOOP.

physiological systems. Among them could be increase or decrease in heart rate, respiration, muscle tension, body movements, body temperature at the surface or at the core, elimination, sweating, etc.

A similar process takes place when the brain is stimulated by internal activity. The interoceptors, located within the body, of pressure, pain, heat and cold, sexual excitement, alimentary canal peristalsis, etc., send afferent messages of their activities to various brain regions which respond with appropriate efferent signals, resulting in further internal adjustments in homeostasis. Proprioception deals with body position and movement through receptor sites at muscle fibers and at the joints of the body (55).

Interoception and proprioception interact in many body movements, if not all, and since one's body is always in an external environment, exteroception is normally involved as well.

Electronic biofeedback monitoring

Sensory reception is enhanced through use of physiological feedback instruments. The feedback signals generated by the internal activity of the body, register on the sensors of the biofeedback instruments and are displayed to the subject whose exteroceptors receive and forward the signal to the CNS.

Figure 2 shows a schematic outline of the sequences of events and the path of the signal in the electronic biofeedback loop. If, for example, muscle contractions are being monitored by an EMG the electrical activity of the muscle's output signal is the input signal for

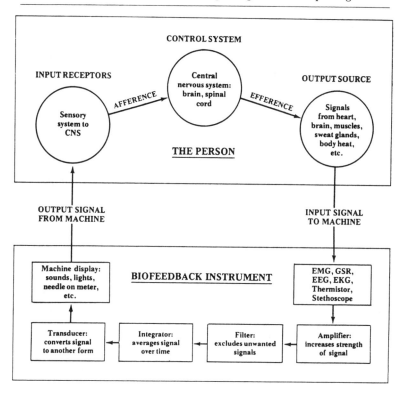

FIGURE 2. SCHEMATIC OF ELECTRONIC BIOFEEDBACK LOOP.

the machine. The electronics of the EMG amplifies the muscle's minute current whose intensity is in thousandths of a volt (millivolt: mV), or millionths of a volt (microvolt: uV).

The EMG bandpasses filter out signals from other physiological systems such as the heart beat, brain waves, and sweat glands. The muscle contractions are summations of numerous SMUs arising from both surface and deeper muscles and their raw signals are not in a form of information useful to the subject. The integrator accumulates the raw signals over a predetermined period of time and averages their microvoltage. Various time periods can be set by most machines, in epochs of seconds or minutes. The averaged signal is then converted by the transducer into a selected display form, of sounds, flashing lights, or on an oscilloscope. These output signals are returned to the subject who can then track the functioning of the muscle, moment to moment. As the muscle contracts or relaxes, the signal reflects the increase or decrease immediately and directly.

Voluntary Musculature

Muscles provide the basis for all movement within the body and between the person and the environment (9). Whatever action one takes, it is taken via muscle movement. Overt and covert muscle movements are the physical mechanisms one uses in responding to the environment. The fact that all relationships with the environment are conducted through the musculature gives these organs special importance in biofeedback procedures and involve the neuromotor systems, directly and indirectly.

The striate, or voluntary, muscles, illustrated in Figures 3 and 4, make up most of the muscle tissue of the body and are innervated by the somatic, or cerebrospinal nervous system. The striate muscles are the movers of the body through space. They are responsible for posture, locomotion, antigravity functioning, for exploring the environment, etc. They can also interact with smooth muscles in respiration, urination, defecation, swallowing, speech, and in many spinal reflexes (75).

All muscles contract, or shorten their fibers when innervated. Contraction occurs when the muscle fibers are stimulated by efferent impulses terminating in the motor end-plate (myoneural junction).

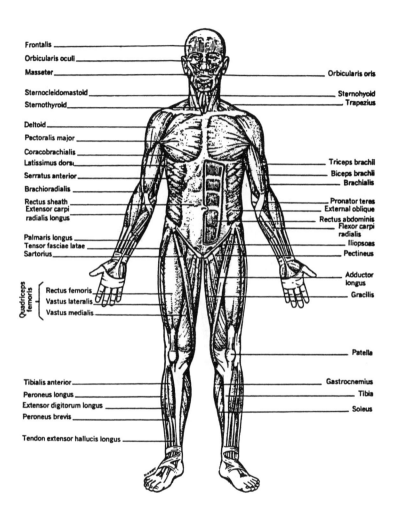

Figure 3

Muscles of the body, anterior view. Source: Chaffee, E. E., & Greisheimer, E. M. *Basic Physiology and Anatomy*, Philadelphia: J. P. Lippincott Co., 1974. Reprinted with permission.

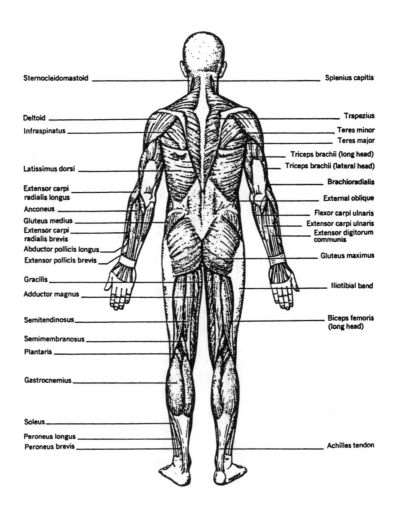

Figure 4

Muscles of the body, posterior view. Source: Chafee, E. E., & Greisheimer, E. M. *Basic Physiology and Anatomy,* Philadelphia: J. P. Lippincott Co., 1974. Reprinted with permission.

When not stimulated by the motor cortex or spinal reflex centers, muscles are relaxed. Continual firing results in sustained contractions.

Two forms of muscle contraction are monitored and worked with in biofeedback. The isotonic is a muscle contraction that is accompanied by a shortening or reduction in length of around 50 percent in the muscle, resulting in body movement through space. An arm is lifted, or a finger is wiggled. The second is isometric, a contraction in which the length of the muscle does not vary from its resting length. Isometric contraction inhibits body movement, as in the case of synergistic muscles firing simultaneously and flexing the arm to only part of its total possible movement (6, 9). A general rule regarding muscle firing is that a muscle should be relaxed unless it is involved in work. Muscle spasms resulting from chronic stress, anxiety, maladaptive habits, damage, or other causes of neuromotor dysfunctions, are not considered to be work. Noteworthy psychogenic spasms are contractions arising from psychological activity which is firing the motor cortex. Much of clinical biofeedback concentrates on psychogenic spasms that cause headaches, back pain, bruxism, or are directly implicated in anxiety and stress.

Although voluntary muscle movement is learned (the potential for self-regulation in shaped by the learner during use), the final complex movements learned are usually conducted as though they were involuntary reflexes. Walking, talking, posture, sitting down, etc., are voluntary acts initiated mainly in the motor cortex of the brain, but they become so thoroughly learned and automatically carried out that when they are signaled to activate they can appear to be involuntary.

Involuntary Musculature

The involuntary or smooth muscles compose the walls of the circulatory system and the great bulk of the visceral organs. Their contractile rates are slow and they are not susceptible to fatigue. These muscles automatically propel substances through the body: blood, food, waste matter, bile. They also regulate the circumference of body passages and openings of the blood vessels, alimentary and urinary systems, the bronchioles, etc. Smooth muscles are innervated by the autonomic nervous system and in normal states these homeo-static neuromotor loops maintain the life functions of the body, leaving the mind free for its own work. Significant disorders in these life functions, such as constipation, diarrhea, heart palpitations, urinary or fecal incontinence, or intestinal hypermotility, result in constant mental attention and disrupt the sufferer's life.

The autonomic nervous system (ANS), with its two subdivisions of the sympathetic nervous system (SNS) and the parasympathetic nervous system (PNS) regulate visceral functioning and is of central interest to the biofeedback specialist. Figure 5 illustrates the ANS and its pathways to visceral organs which are listed in Table 3. The SNS functions as an involuntary, reflexive, stimulator of visceral organs. The SNS has the purpose of mobilizing the organism to flee or to fight, when threatened, by bringing about widespread changes in res-piration rate, heart rate, blood distribution, increase of sugar supply in the blood stream, etc. The SNS normally readies and maintains the organism in a state of heightened preparedness against possible injury. The PNS functions predominantly in tandem to the SNS and inhibits or slows down the accelerated SNS responses, thereby conserving body resources.

For most persons in a state of abnormal excitement, anxiety, or overstress, the SNS is firing at an increased rate, maladaptively, and usually producing a subjective awareness of ''racing tension,'' anxi-ety or fearfulness. Reduction of the SNS overactivation that is out of normal homeostatic boundaries is a basic technique in the biofeed-back treatment of most psychogenic disorders. Lowering sympathetic tone to achieve lower arousal is probably one of the effective agents in relaxation methods (201, 219) that target SNS overactivation. Chronic autonomic overactivation frequently and perhaps always results in tension in the striate muscle, as the hyperaroused person attempts to control the arousal or to take actions that might alleviate the feeling of distress. The action might be gritting the teeth, bracing the shoulders as though ready to fight, clenching the hands, or motor restlessness. Compensatory symptom formation such as these voluntary but maladaptive reactions produce spasticity and increased discomfort. The spasms are targets for EMG biofeedback application, in addition to the targeting of the ANS (226).

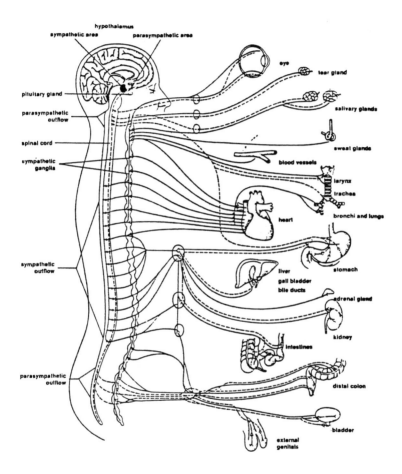

Figure 5

Autonomic nervous system and related visceral organs (broken line, parasympathetic system; solid line, sympathetic system). Source: Krech, D., Crutchfield, R. S., & Livson, N. *Elements of Psychology* (2nd ed.), New York: A. A. Knopf, 1969, p. 578. Reprinted with permission.

Table 3. Functions of the Autonomic Nervous System

Organ	Para-sympathetic	Sympathetic
Digestive System		
peristalsis	Increased	Decreased
sphincters	Relaxed	Contracted
secretions of		
stomach	Increased	
intestines	Increased	No direct effect
salivary glands	Thin, watery	Thick, viscid
Respiratory System		
rate	Decreased	Increased
bronchioles	Constricted	Dilated
Circulatory System		

rate of heartbeat	Increased	Decreased
force of heartbeat	Increased	Decreased
blood vessels		
in skeletal muscles	Dilated	No direct effect
in abdominal viscera	Constricted	No direct effect
in skin	Constricted	No direct effect
in heart muscles	Dilated	Constricted
blood pressure	Increased	Decreased
Genitalia (male and female)	Vasoconstriction	Vasodilation
ejaculation	Increased	No direct effect
Sweat glands	Increased	No direct effect
Adrenal glands		
adrenaline	Increased	No direct effect
noradrenaline	Increased	No direct effect

Electrodermal system

The skin's ability to conduct an electrical current is one of the two main bases for dermographic biofeedback. Changes in the skin conductance (SC) of a current reflects complex, not fully understood, biochemical processes taking place in the sweat glands and their surrounding tissues. This physiological process is regulated by the SNS, which, in turn, is responsive to stimuli that vary sympathetic arousal. Internal stimuli, such as one's thoughts and emotions, as well as external stimuli influence SNS arousal level. The paradigm of stimulation of the SNS, increase in sweat production, allowing a corresponding increase in SC, is the psychophysiological process monitored in dermographic biofeedback. Lowered SC, or increase in its reciprocal, resistance to the passage of the current, co-varies directly with lowered SNS arousal level. Anxiety, stress, and other stimuli accelerate SNS firing and the biofeedback practitioner utilizes the end product of SC in treatment procedures for anxiety, guilt, stress, etc.

The presence of neural pathways from the cortex and lower brain structures suggest that both cortical-cognitive events and reticular arousal mechanisms are involved in variations of SC. SC cannot be considered to be an indicator of specific thoughts or emotions, or of the kind of stimuli at work. Only some rather broad relationships exist that can serve as clinical hypotheses for biofeedback applications.

The major relationship between increase in skin conductance for most people is, of course, the fight-flight response of the SNS. Among the various bodily changes the response contains an increase in sweat gland production, hence increase in SC, as the current finds easier passage. The sweat glands of the palms of the hands and soles of the feet are particularly sensitive to SNS stimulation due to external stimuli and stress (91).

Generally, increase over baseline in the level of tonic activity of skin conductance level (SCL) and an increase in the number of spontaneous skin conductance responses (SSCR), or the phasic activity, are used as signs of SNS activation that are related to clinical events such as guilt, stress reactions, and anxiety. A SSCR is a momentary increase in conductance and is typically about 1 micromho per CM^2. Most SCLs fall in the range of 5 to 20 micromhos per CM^2, according to Grings and Dawson (86), with few SSCRs. Patients who are below these norms may be affectual under-responders; while those above may be over-responders. This dimension of reactivity, particularly while stressed or stimulated normally, is a clue to the degree of repression or hypersensitivity to arousal among patients. As Toomin has reported (209), some patients are under-responders, others are over-responders and they both have clinical significance (See Part II).

Cardiovascular system

The heart and the blood vessels are the most commonly moni-tored organs of the cardiovascular system in clinical biofeedback. Both are responsive to stress and anxiety and the anatomic divisions of the system can interact with other physiological systems under normal and abnormal conditions (114). The most frequent complaints encountered are high and low blood pressure (11, 28, 156), tachycardia and bradycardia (74, 114), peripheral vasoconstriction or dilation (85, 185, 219), premature ventricular contractions (19), migraine headaches (7, 11, 53, 174, 219), and sexual dysfunctions related to lack of blood flow to the genitals (51, 158).

The ANS itself can be monitored indirectly through monitoring cardiovascular functions such as blood pressure, heart rate, and peripheral vasoconstriction. The anxiety or stress that is causing the ANS dysfunction can then be treated with biofeedback techniques through these physiological parameters (209, 219).

The thermistor is a direct measure of the heat of the blood flow to the periphery of the body through placement of the sensors on the hands or feet. These are the standard applications in vasoconstrictive disorders such as Raynaud's disease. Increasing blood flow to the periphery through thermistor feedback is also an efficient method of lowering sympathetic tone. Normal hand temperature is about 90^0 to 95^{0}F; the lower the temperature below 90^{0}F, the more serious the vasospasm. Temperatures of below 80^{0}F are common in Raynaud's and require appropriate treatment, whether or not Raynaud's is diagnosed. Any patient reporting cold hands, chronic or reactive, should receive thermistor feedback and training in hand-warming.

The plethysomograph can be used to feed back heart rate to treat diffuse anxiety. The strain gauge is placed around a finger to pick up the pulse and the patient is instructed to relax and to allow the pulse to slow down.

The EKG gives a direct print-out, or oscilloscopic readout, of cardiac activity and can be used to treat arrhythmias such as premature ventricular contractions.

The sphygmomanometer's application as a feedback instrument to treat high blood pressure (HBP) is limited by the complications of the device and the discomfort of prolonged use. Ordinarily, other bioinstruments and techniques are used to modify blood pressure.

Central nervous system

Brain wave activity monitoried through the EEG focuses on the psychological correlates (106) of the predominant wave forms (Table 4) and their amplitudes. A great deal of debate continues as to the reliability of the psychophysiologic correlates and the clinical or biofeedback methods used to induce given neurophysiologic states in the central nervous system. The reader is referred to Brown (27, 28), Gazzaniga (77), Ornstein (149), and Gatchel and Price (76) for extensive discussion of the EEG technique in research and clinical biofeedback.

The brain waves monitored by EEG are summations of the incredibly complex patterns of very low voltage electrical activity of billions of neurons within the brain. Surface electrodes sense the final output signal at particular areas of the scalp, the signals varying from area to area as well as from moment to moment. "The EEG pattern is thus a constantly changing pattern and at best a faint mirror of brain events occurring at some distance from the recording" (27). The pattern being recorded is a voltage, or cortical evoked potential (CEP), that is constantly changing in many of its attributes, such as amplitude, phase, and frequency. Brown (27, p. 234) lists "at least eleven quite different elements of alpha that have been demonstrated to be of individual and significant specific importance to specific and significant subjective or behavioral characteristics."

Very likely other predominant waves are equally complex. At best, then, in clinical applications, one is severely constrained when presuming to identify a specific cortical potential as a reflection of a specific or nonspecific response. And most clinical work appears to concentrate at the present time on feeding back frequency ranges of alpha and theta, along with increase or decrease in amplitude in order to intervene and revise general psychological states. Some current refined applications are feasible, such as increasing the abundance of given waves for concentration enhancement, the normalization of brain waves for seizure control, and inducing states of relaxation for sleep problems and obsessiveness, as an aid to meditation and pain control and in drug abuse (11, 28, 74, 88, 145, 233). Results are inconsistent and most of these applications have also been conducted with satisfactory results with EMG, GSR, and thermistor biofeedback coupled with various therapy techniques.

In summary, the physiological systems are the biological targets of the biofeedback procedure. Retraining of psychogenic imbalance in homeostasis is an efficient and low-risk treatment procedure. Retraining in cases of severe changes regardless of etiology can also be efficacious for selected patients.

The principal systems targeted are the smooth and striate musculature, the CNS and the ANS, the circulatory, respiratory and sweat gland systems, and the GI tract. Relaxation and psychotherapy techniques applied in conjunction with BFT are essential in the reduction of stress and other conditions involving physiological overactivation, anxiety, and symptom formation.

The particular physiological system that is targeted in treating physiological overactivation is idiosyncratic among anxious patients. Some manifest anxiety through sweating or through increased respiration, rather than through a cardiovascular function. Other patients may present symptomatology in one or more systems, in addition to the cardiovascular.

The various organ systems regulated by the somatic or the autonomic system do not act and react in a tandem, one-to-one change. An increase in parasympathetic dominance does not automatically lead to a decrease in skin conductance, for example. Desired changes in one physiological function through biofeedback training does not necessarily generalize to produce changes in other physiological functions. In clinical pratice one cannot expect one physiological target to "stand in" as the treatment target for all the physiological systems.

Table 4 Frequency ranges and some psychological correlates of EEG waveforms.

0.0	flat line: death.
0.5– 3	delta: deep sleep.
4.0– 7	theta: drowsiness; creativity; relaxation.
8.0–13	alpha: relaxed wakefulness; receptivity.
12.0–14	sensorimotor rhythm: seizure control.

Table (continued)

14.0–28 beta: alert; problem solving; stress;
            anxiety; attention.

40.0   beta: short-term memory consolidation;
            problem solving; concentration.

N.B.   Frequency ranges are somewhat arbitrary and
        psychological correlates not identical from
        person to person.

Generally speaking, in physiological biofeedback the subject intervenes in the psychophysiological feedback loop in order to modify one or more attributes of the physiological processes. For example, *intensity* (of body surface temperature, blood pressure, autonomic arousal level, muscle tone), *rate* (of heartbeat or muscle contractions), *percentage time increase or decrease* (of brain waves), *direction* (of blood flow), *or interactions* (synergism in muscle groups, mental activity, and body response) are among the attributes modified (219).

Mind-body feedback

The interactions of physiological and mental activities are manifested in the biofeedback output signals. As the bodily information is perceived by the mind, the mind regulates change, even though we have no knowledge as to how the brain, reflected through mental activity, achieves awareness of itself and tells itself what to do. The information the brain receives may be about the external or internal environment. The mind or mental activity cannot be located in all its complexities in the physical and chemical realms. But, however complex such activities are, we do read the mental through the physical expressions of the body. Mental activity is communicated to others through muscular activity. We know, too, that when information is delivered to the mind through biofeedback signals, or from any source, the mind reads itself and the body and can intervene in mental and physical processes appropriately and deliberately. It is difficult to conduct biofeedback training or clinical procedures without acceptance of mental activity existing as a significant variable

The mental activity is, of course, not separate from the neuromuscular activity. Jacobson's (103) position in the question of cause-effect sequence in brain-muscle (or mind-muscle) interaction is that for every mental activity there is a corresponding muscular activity, and vice versa; but that it is not a simple matter of the motor cortex action potential discharging along efferent neurons to muscles which then react. He states that his studies of muscular and brain impulses "indicate that with negligible lag, the muscular and corresponding brain functions proceed simultaneously" (103, p. 33).

In reality, when a biofeedback therapist is intervening in the mind-body loop, he is entering an established, ongoing, afferent-efferent process which has no specific and sole point of initiation or termination. There appears not to be any brain firing that does not include body activity, particularly muscular activity. The brain-body, or mind-body, is a complex, interactional process, not a sequence of discrete events. The mind is sometimes looked upon as an emergent property of these brain-body interactions.

The brain is the focus of and the instrument for the mental activity in biofeedback procedures, but not the sole locality; similarly is the body. By some elegant but obscure means, after the brain receives information, processes it, integrates memory and foresight, and regulates motivations and goals, the mind then directs bodily changes, as the bodily changes directed the brain to respond.

In order to use feedback instruments with a reasonable degree of reliability in the clinical monitoring of psychophysiological responsiveness, one must add the subjective monitoring by the patient of his own physical and mental private events. The physiological signals are made public by the instrument but many of the unexpected deviations in the signal can reflect either normal or abnormal mind-body interactions. Since mind reading is not possible by the therapist, the patient is called upon to provide his report of any private events that rise to consciousness and may be related to the physiological activity. In this way the mind-body feedback loop is tapped as a source of useful information for therapeutic interventions.

Chapter 4

INSTRUMENTATION AND BIOFEEDBACK

A profusion of biofeedback instruments has flooded the market over the last few years (169, 170, 171). They vary widely in reliability, flexibility, and cost. Some are overloaded with gadgetry and varieties of output signals; others presume to give feedback information that is useless in ordinary clinical practice. The most expensive models are not necessarily the best workhorses, and the cheapest machines may lack adequate sensitivity, resolution, or flexibility in machine-person interface. On the whole, the established medical instrumentation and biofeedback manufacturers have produced many excellent instruments, at low cost.

Assistance in selecting machines can be obtained from distributors of biofeedback equipment, and from consultations with experienced biofeedback clinicians and electronics experts. These sources can provide information about the technical reliability and clinical usefulness of equipment.

However, the beginning practitioner must decide what kinds of complaints he wishes to treat. Clinical decisions will determine selection of the kinds of machines needed, their complexity, and their cost. Experience dictates that the EMG is the central clinical instrument of any practice, and that the dermogram and thermistor complete the basic matrix. Specialization in treating conditions that call for highly specialized instrumentation will influence the selection of other instruments and accessories. For most practices, the problem of buying equipment consists of deciding which firm to buy from and which grade machine in a given line of instruments should be selected. As a rule of thumb, the middle grade machine is usually sufficiently elaborate to meet most clinical demands. Firms that offer three or four machines in a line of EMGs, thermistors, dermograms, and EEGs often classify the top of the line as the "research level" machine. If one should wish to do research that requires highly precise monitoring of physiological systems with quantification and statistical treatment of output signals in preselected time intervals, with print-out facility, then one is not thinking about inexpensive, clinical instrumentation. Fortunately, the more complex machines in a line are suitable for most research projects in clinical or laboratory methodology. These have outputs for interfacing with computers, counters, and printers.

Recent designs offered by several manufacturers include lines of clinical machines that can be used separately, or in groups, and integrated with a minicomputer, or a counter, and print-out recorder. These modular designs permit purchasing desired instruments, one by one, for individual use, as well as combining several into a matrix with appropriate accessories that can simultaneously monitor, feed back, store, and print-out physiological data. The advantages for research are obvious, but in clinical use the issue in the selection of machines is that of their efficacious, clinical value, not merely data acquisition.

The specifications for any instrument are obtained from the manufacturer and provide the necessary information about the number of electrodes, the kinds of signals that are processed, the output modalities, filters, etc., in terms of which biofeedback applications are conducted. The technical explanations of these specifications which are beyond this introduction can be found in references on biophysics and electronics. Particularly useful are Brown (27, 28), Basmajian (9, 11), Gaarder and Montgomery (74), Venables and Martin (211), Dickinson (55), Grings and Dawson

(86), the *Handbook of Physiological Feedback* (7), and in Rugh and Schwitzgebel's evaluations of several commercial EMGs (169) and EEGs (171).

The original biological signals processed by machines are electrical (EEG, EMG, GSR), mechanical (sphygmomanometer, stethoscope, plethysmogram), and thermal (thermistor), and they indicate the nature of the physiological activity. The signals are detected by sensors which receive the end product, the signal, of the physiological activity, and transmit the signal to the instrument which processes it for useful output information for the patient.

Instrumentation requires accuracy in receiving the signal, and accuracy begins with the sensors. The sensors should be among the best available, and should be given meticulous maintenance. Sensors that accompany machines are not always interchangeable with other machines, any more than instruments from different manufacturers can be considered comparable in design and can be integrated into a matrix. One should consider purchasing one line of different instruments from the same manufacturer with the sensors manufactured for use with those machines.

There are a number of design specifications that are basic to the efficiency and use of biofeedback equipment. These specifications state the limits and flexibility of the machine in reference to the properties of physiological functioning, and the biofeedback applications. Some of the design specifications will be presented briefly. Extensive details can be found in the technical references.

Sensitivity is the capacity of the machine's amplifiers to produce an electrical output signal that is in correspondence with those properties of the physiology. The machine is of little use if it is not sensitive enough to detect, amplify, and reproduce the physiological signal proportionally. However, the sensitivity must not permit the undesired signals form other sources, either environmental or biological, to be picked up or to be processed for output as part of the desired signal. This machine function is expressed as the common mode rejection ratio (CMRR). The ratio should be at least 100,000 to 1, or 100db, at 60 Hz, for both EMG and EEG. High input impedance of sensors of more than 1 megohm is essential to rejection at the biological source of artifacts that can occur at the site of the sensors. Input impedance must be of the order of 10 times greater than source impedance in order to minimize errors found in variations in electrode impedance and to provide accurate amplitude data.

The *range* of an instrument refers to the span of the frequencies (or Herz: Hz) that the machine will process. These frequency ranges are functions of the filters, or bandpasses, of the machine. Some machines will provide several that can be set by dial; less expensive machines may have only one filter. EMG frequencies on complex machines may range form 20 to 30 to 1000 Hz, with several bandpasses that can be set by a bandpass switch, such as 100 to 200 Hz, 20 to 1000 Hz. Smaller machines usually have a standard 100 to 200 Hz filter, which is the range recommended for routine EMG biofeedback. Filters on the EEG also vary with the complexity of the machines. The common alpha-theta EEG has filters for 8 to 14Hz and 4 to 7 Hz respectively. More complex instruments that can cover ranges up to 100 Hz are not used in clinical biofeedback. Clinical machines can incorporate special filters for use at 40 Hz for training in concentration, and in various ranges for the normalization of brain wave forms in the treatment of epileptic seizures.

Amplitude is the measure of the strength, or voltage, of a signal and is expressed in microvolts for the EMG and EEG, and in a ratio, micromhos, for the GSR. There are various measures of EMG voltage: peak-to-peak, integral average, and root mean square. Disputes exist as to which is the most useful method for measuring the electrophysiology. The instruments should have the capability of registering the desired minimum amplititudes of the output signals of the targeted physiology, and in reference to the specific biofeedback applications conducted. The EMG requires a sensitivity dial that can be set to pick up as low an amplitude as 0.1uV, in order to conduct relaxation techniques and to reduce spasms; the maximum cut-off should not be lower than 1000uV for use in neuromotor retraining. A logarithmic meter display read-out, which registers the rise and fall of the amplitude of muscle contractions, provides an analog of the changes in tension level. The gain can be set so that the ranges in microvolts reflected on the display dial, through sweeps of the needle, are multiples of the gain, or sensitivity setting. When the gain is set at a given level, 1uV for example, any output below 1uV of physiological functioning would not be read out by the machine. The needle would hang at the left end of the dial and no other output modality would release a signal. The gain would then have to be set at a lower level, say 0.5uV or 0.1uV, to read out such lower amplitudes. The gain is essential in shaping the physiological parameter of the strength of the process being monitored by allowing the patient to increase, or decrease, the parameter by small and easily controllable amounts.

Average time setting, the time during which all the action potentials are averaged before readout, is also a matter of machine complexity. Most have a dial which sets the time average from zero, or instantaneous response time, or in epochs such as 1, 3, 5, 10 seconds, etc.

Threshold is the level of amplitude below (or above) which the output modalities are automatically nulled. It is used as a clinical goal in turning on or off the output signal as a sign of and a reward for controlling amplitude. The threshold and time average settings are often co-varied in their dial settings by the therapist to reduce the monotony that can occur in prolonged biofeedback training.

Resolution is the characteristic of the machine in discriminating fine differences along the range of a signal. Resolution varies with different designs, but the thermistor should discriminate to 0.1°F, and the EMG and EEG to 0.1uV. These fine degrees of resolution are rarely essential in adjusting the feedback information for the patients' use, especially in the early stages of training, but they can be necessary at later stages of training, or under special clinical circumstances.

Feedback modalities are visual or auditory, and appear in different kinds of displays. Changes in light emitting diodes (LED) of different colors can signal increase or decrease in amplitudes. The meter displays read out degree of microvoltage, temperature, micromhos or frequency range, on the EMG, thermistor, GSR, or EEG. Auditory feedback is integrated with the LED and meter output signals, and can be in "trills, clicks," or other kinds of sounds. The auditory and the meter display are minimum required feedback modalities for efficient use by patient and therapist. The complex machines usually have several feedback systems beyond the minimum. Digital displays are useful in record keeping over and across sessions but lack the advantage of the information contained in the sweep of the meter readout. Auditory feedback appears to be the modality most desired by patients and is a feature on all machines.

Safety features are established by the fact that clinical machines being battery operated pose very little risk, if any. Those that derive their power from electrical wall plugs must be isolated to prevent danger to the patient.

Smaller EMG instruments usually have only one input receptacle for one electrode assembly; larger machines have two or three inputs. Clinical need is, again, the best basis for decision. In dealing with muscles at a joint, two electrode assemblies are necessary to feedback desired increase on one side of the joint, and decrease on the other side, or to reduce spasticity in both temperomandibular joints in concert. A multiple input selector that is plugged into the EMG and receives three or four electrodes assemblies provides the necessary number of electrodes for multiple placements. These selectors can therefore be used with machines having only one input receptacle and provide greater machine flexibility.

Similarly, a thermistor may have only one sensor, or may have a multiple sensor input from which the thermistor would average the surface temperature at the placements of the several sensors. This permits a larger area to be monitored. The limitation is that skin temperature can vary by several degrees at different spots within a small area. One equally flexible and precise system is that of two channels, each having two or more sensors. Each sensor can be used to read out the temperature at its placement and if there is a significant difference in absolute degrees, the lower area can be concentrated on clinically until it is raised close to the higher one. At that point, the sensors can be averaged by manipulating the appropriate switch. Two channels also allow for feedback from right and left hands individually or averaged, and the second channel used for the right and left feet, individually or averaged. This kind of flexibility is valuable in severe cases of vasoconstriction, such as Raynaud's disease. One sensor is adequate for targeting the sympathetic nervous system via peripheral vascular flow.

A liquid crystal wrist thermometer that reads out surface temperature over a wide range is quite accurate and acceptably sensitive to blood flow to the hands. The patient can wear the wrist thermometer with no discomfort or detraction from personal appearance throughout the day. Recordkeeping draws the wearer's attention to place, context, and stress level for each recording, thereby increasing awareness of any environmental stressors. Hand-warming exercises and relaxation can be immediately practiced. Finger-tip readings are taken by merely inserting the finger tips between the undersurface of the plate and the wrist.

Skin conductance (SC) measures the ease of penetration of a minute electrical current, in microamperes, through the skin when applied by a dermogram. Increase in eccrine sweat gland activity increases conductance of the current. SC is the generally preferred measurement of sympathetic nervous system activity, as reflected in increase, or decrease, in sweating (91). The SC unit of measurement is expressed in micromhos for those instruments that feature meter displays for output signals. All machines have audio output signals, such as rate of clicks or changes in pitch of a constant tone, that both patient and therapist can monitor. The complex and expensive dermograms provide various refinements of meter displays that allow for quite precise discrimination in resolution of the visual signal. The audio output is also an analog of the meter display. A useful feature on some dermograms that can be used in psychotherapy is an automatic reset function which frees the therapist of having to make frequent dial adjustments as the conductance level increases or decreases over a session.

There are a number of small, very inexpensive dermograms that feedback audio signals only, but are useful for a general measure of sympathetic tone. They are rarely applicable in cases of under-respon-sers in the autonomic nervous system because of the instruments' limited range and resolution.

There has not yet been established universal specifications for machine design. Various organizations have appointed committees to begin the task of standardizing design specifications that relate to "good" design. The variations of output tones, size of electrodes, filter band width, portability, etc., which have more to do with differences of opinion rather than with electronic reliability and validity, exist among almost all manufacturers. The "best" clinical machine is probably a reflection of the clinician's taste and clinical practice rather than a matter of electronic design and biophysics. There are few machine specifications among manufacturers that are identical. Consequently, output data in research and clinical practice is, at best, grossly comparable.

Rugh and Schwitzgebel (171) summarize the situation regarding instrumentation in biofeedback:

> What general conclusions can we draw...? Inexpensive physiological monitoring devices if standardized are potentially very useful and valuable to the health care professional. Many of these devices (are) of good quality, excellent design, and would provide reliable data. The major problem...is that no standards exist in the design, in functional characteristics, in calibration, or in test procedures used to specify instrument characteristics. Before these devices can be of widespread use, standards must be developed. We must be able to compare readings made by different devices in different laboratories or clinics. (p. 240).

Technical considerations suggest the impossibility of designing machines for research or clinical use that are perfect and complete, even if cost were not a factor. The selection of clinical instruments is probably best based on the clinical needs the therapist predicts he will encounter in his practice, after he has established the general areas of pathology that he can treat within his competencies.

Chapter 5

LEARNING PARADIGMS

Learning—a change in behavior due to experience—is the basis of biofeedback. The subject receives feedback information and develops an internal method of comprehending and using the information in order to change his behavior. In attempting to establish biofeedback procedures on a scientific basis, learning theory was recognized as a ready-made and useful choice. It is a reasonably straightforward, parsimonious, and testable theory of human behavior that contains an adequate number of manageable hypotheses, principles, and findings that are applicable to the procedure. Learning theory is also based on known facts of physiology, and biofeedback procedures find a reliable correspondence between the physiological output data of feedback instruments and the use of these data as treatment variables.

Most biofeedback specialists use learning theories as the source of explanation, research models, and treatment plans (7, 11, 28, 74). Pavlov's *classical conditioning* (155) is one of the principle sources of theory and technique in biofeedback. Classical theory draws on the physiological functioning of the autonomic system as the basis of emotional learning. Skinner's *instrumental conditioning* (193) utilizes the voluntary nervous system and musculature as the physiological basis for treating maladaptive patterns of behavior. A third theory, also of direct application in biofeedback, is *avoidance learning,* which has been described by Mowrer (143) as a combination of classical and instrumental learning. Finally, the learning principles of psychodynamic theory have also been related to the interpretation and treatment of clinical events occurring in biofeedback practice.

Classical conditioning

Pavlov established classical conditioning theory when he found that a dog's inborn, reflexive, salivary response (an unconditioned response: UR), to the smell of food (an unconditioned stimulus: US), could be modified in that the UR could be elicited by a previously neutral stimulus, such as the sound of a bell. When the sound and the food are presented contiguously for a number of trials the sound itself acquires the property of eliciting a similar salivary response. At that point in the process the sound is then identified as a conditioned response (CR). One should note that the response is not new. Rather, the sound had acquired a new property in its ability to evoke the response. The UR is now a CR because the CS can elicit the CR.

Classical conditioning is based on the capacity of the autonomic system to acquire responsiveness to previously neutral stimuli. The learned responses are still involuntary reactions of the autonomic system and its related visceral organs. One then may learn to respond with an accelerated heart rate, intestinal hypermotility, rapid and shallow respiration, etc., to situations or objects that one learns to fear. Various psychosomatic disorders are thus established, according to this theory of learning.

Psychosomatic disorders involving dysfunction of homeostasis in the ANS and related functions include colitis, hypertension, peptic ulcer, hyperthyroidism, asthma, irritable colon, chronic diarrhea, and rheumatoid arthritis (125). Although these and other psychosomatic disorders very likely have more than a simple psychogenic etiology (216), the onset of intense stress evidently can precipitate or aggravate the conditions.

It has been postulated that such disorders may originate in early childhood learning experiences, and that individual differences in temperament, tissue, or organs may be predispositions to the particular organ implicated in a given disorder (200). All persons do not manifest anxiety in the same organ, and it is unknown as to how or why individual selections are made.

The principle of *generalization* of a response to similar stimuli is behaviorism's explanation of how a person may develop a fear of a particular object or situation that he has never confronted before. Fears of varieties of objects, experiences, situations, and persons are thus acquired throughout life.

The ANS has been traditionally considered accessible only to Pavlovian conditioning (54, 137). This principle is now highly debated in the experimental literature. Although there has been success in conditioning visceral responses through instrumental learning techniques (138, 140), the possibility has remained that the conditioning that occurred was mediated by the skeletal muscles. DiCara (54), however, indicates that he and other physiologists have been successful in visceral and glandular conditioning through instrumental procedures. In clinical practice, the question is probably moot, if for no other reason than the clinician's inability to control or remove the autonomic or the skeletal system from the clinical situation. The clinician is well aware that they are interacting in the complaints under treatment. He or she may select one or both as the treatment modalities in biofeedback applications, knowing full well the probability of intervening in both during the course of treatment, although the clinician will target the particular system implicated in the complaint.

In deconditioning autonomically based symptoms, reduction of SNS tone itself, or "cultivating low arousal" as Stoyva (202) puts it, is a standard, initial step. If one of the organs innervated by the SNS should predominate in showing homeostatic imbalance, the appropriate feedback instrument would be used to target that organ as the modality for cultivating low arousal, as well as to apply biofeedback retraining. Anxiety reactions specifically require lowering sympathetic tone, even though there may be no well-defined symptoms in evidence, such as excessive sweating, vasoconstriction, or heart palpitations. Most patients who complain of "fearfulness" will describe ANS overactivation during a phobic episode, or as a chronic condition which exacerbates episodically. The diagnostic issue is of course important in terms of the etiology of bound versus free-floating anxiety and the differences in treatment planning (201, 219, 228).

Patients may have also sustained a "spreading" of the anxiety to other systems, and skeletal muscle spasms will have developed. However, in the biofeedback treatment of classically conditioned symptoms the physiological targets are those related to autonomic functioning and are first order targets. Any skeletal spasms can be treated in conjunction or in sequence.

Instrumental conditioning

Skinner's theory of learning is of direct application in biofeedback. Instrumental conditioning utilizes the physiological model of the voluntary (somatic) nervous system and the striate musculature as the basis for the development of complex learning.

Skinner's paradigm begins with an overtly active animal, in vivo, emitting numerous responses to internal and external environments. The stimuli innervating any given movement are both complex and difficult to distinguish from any other of the multiple stimuli in the environment. In all this complexity of behavior, the animal is acting on its environment in emitting its repertoire of responses, not merely passively, reflexively, responding to a given stimulus, as in the case of Pavlov's dog. As the responsiveness to stimuli continues, the animal will begin to increase the rate of its responses to the particular stimulus in the environment that is *rewarding* to the animal. In other words, any behavior pattern or response that is rewarded (positively reinforced) will increase in the probability of its recurrence.

The procedure of conditioning an organism is through *shaping* behavior in successive approximations of the goal—the desired behavior. When the learner emits a response or behaves in the direction of, or close to, the desired goal, he or she is rewarded for each such response. The final, complex learning that is the goal is acquired piece by piece, until all the elements have been established as a learned pattern of behavior.

In the biofeedback context, shaping is the standard procedure the patient uses, aided by the feedback instrument. For example, the desired goal may be to regain voluntary control over impaired motor use of a limb. The EMG is used to locate viable motor units in the impaired region. Such signals are the emitted, instrumental responses to be shaped. The EMG feeds back signals of the viable motor units in analog form which tells the patient whether he or she is increasing the rate of firing those units. The increase of firing (and often the recruitment of other motor fibers) is heard by the patient via the feedback signal and constitutes the reward. The signal is also providing correct, immediate, and useful perceptual information, moment to moment, of the patient's own functioning. This is the same method he or she used in learning how to handle a knife and fork skillfully.

One should notice that whatever idosyncratic method the patient uses, it is trial-and-error learning. He or she tries one image, or movement until coming upon some kind of internal event that results in an approximation of the desired goal; and then, step by step, shapes his or her responses (up), in successive approximations.

In the event the opposite goal, reduction in the rate of involuntary contractions, is desired, the patient's goal is to *decrease* the rate of the analog signal. In the search for the method of relaxing the muscle a decrease is used in the rate of the signal (shaping down), or negative feedback, to inform and reward him or herself on the desired progress. The difference in the demands to be met by the learner requires different learning sets. In the first example, the demand requires *conscious effort*; in the second, the demand requires *conscious relaxation*.

Avoidance learning

Avoidance learning (164) is a literal term: one learns to avoid a frightening or aversive aspect of life. The aversion (CR) is acquired by the classical conditioning of emotionality (UR) and the learner reacted by escape or an avoidance (instrumental) response which removed him or her from the aversive stimuli (CS). Such avoidance is an instrumental response in that the learner acts on the environment by escaping from the aversive stimulus. The escape also rewarded the patient with the cessation of the distress that had been experienced (a negative reinforcement). If one has at least a vague identification, even if it is incorrect in reality, of the stimulus that evoked distress, one then engages in anticipatory avoidance which keeps him or her away from the aversive stimulus.

Commonly experienced, distressing affects such as guilt, shame, rejection, embarrassment, and anxiety are the kinds of punishments or aversive stimuli to which humans are peculiarly susceptible.

It is a simple step to the use of aversive conditioning as the explanation for the acquisition of social phobias, fears of personal intimacy and social relationships, test anxiety, interview anxiety, authority problems, and sexual anxieties and dysfunctions. Other phobias can be included under this rubric: claustrophobia, acrophobia, agoraphobia, fear of airplanes, escalators, or elevators. It is equally simple to use avoidance responses as the explanation for the sufferers' minimal participation in living in the areas affected.

The principle of generalization holds in the aversive conditioning paradigm. Learning to fear others or to fear a given manner of relating to them, emotionally, or in groups for instance, could have originated early in life through significant adults instilling fear or shame or anxiety in the child during the child's socialization and interaction with those around him. The discordant emotional response could then generalize to similar experiences in living at later ages, with other people, in different forms.

Aversive conditioning is also characterized by its durability. The burnt child reaction illustrates the quick acquisition and durable nature of learning through aversive conditioning. Extinguishing the fear or anxiety underlying the avoidance behavior is not of sufficient assistance to lead to healthy activity if the patient lacks the skills to participate successfully. The treatment plan should include acquisition of coping skills that would help the patient deal with the previously aversive situations.

Psychodynamic learning theory

Changes in behavior due to experience, in Freud's psychodynamic theory (70), is manifested in the development of the ego and superego, the defenses against anxiety and the formation of symptoms. By specifying that the ego and superego develop through maturation and interactions with external reality, and contain both conscious and unconscious memories, affects, and fantasies, Freud outlined the learning aspects of his theory. Individual differences in genetic endowment and in experiences account for the variations in personality among people, but the major aspects of personality structure are species specific. Other complex patterns of behavior, either normal or abnormal, are also involved in these principles of personality development.

The ego functions deal with the realities of the external world in order to satisfy the demands of the instinctual drives, particularly sexuality, and to reduce drive tension. The ego regulates behavior, unless it is overcome by drive energy, and the behavior reflects the learning of the individual. Much that is learned is unconscious or preconscious and the learning, at whatever level it exists, has changed the person's behavior. The ego and superego are formed from birth on, in the process of learning methods of reducing tensions arising from the interaction of the instinctual needs and the restrictions of culture.

In this model of learning the unconscious is considered to be a major, explanatory construct of the presenting symptoms and of the anxiety. In the neurotic person, the unconscious contains the internal conflict between the id impulses of aggression and sexuality and the rest of the personality (ego-superego) which had not found the impulses to be acceptable. Attempts at repression are not wholly successful and the impulses continue to rise to consciousness and continue to disturb normal functioning. Waelder (212, p. 37) summarizes the process: ''. . . the formation of the psychoneuroses follows the pattern: inner conflict—unsuccessful repression—return of the repressed.''

The inner conflict includes the (signal) anxiety that was engendered during the development of the conflict. The anxiety is the ego dystonic affect against which the ego defenses defend the stability or integrity of the ego. Symptom formation, or compromise-formation, is a substitution in act or thought that reflects the repressed conflict. That is, psychogenic symptoms are the consequences of the repressed conflict and the need to sustain some degree of relief from the tension that is in the conflict (25). The conflict arises in the family, and the anxiety and other disturbing affects and memories that are part of the conflict are liable to emerge during the course of living, usually in disguised forms.

The application of clinical biofeedback in the psychodynamic model presumes that the applications would take place in the context of intensive psychotherapy. The purpose of the biofeedback would be to target the anxiety in diffuse and bound forms in order to lessen the threat of the anxiety to ego functions. The ego defenses (66), including repression, are also diminished in their defensive strength and the anxiety and the unconscious materials are freer to enter consciousnes. The therapist would then analyze the memories and affects of the unconscious conflict as they enter consciousness. The reduction of the anxiety would permit consciousness to maintain its capacity to tolerate abreactions, or recall of the anxiety-laden memories, and to be able to resolve the conflict on the level of consciousness.

A recent use of clinical biofeedback is as an adjunctive procedure with patients in intensive psychotherapy (167, 209, 219). In cases of severe obsessives, the applications target the intellectualization and the isolation of affect from consciousness. The patients undergo relaxation training and biofeedback-behavioral techniques that reduce the tension level and allow more direct interactions among body sensation, emotionality and consciousness. The relaxation aids in diminishing the strength of the defenses and the interactions are enhanced. Persons who are prone to dissociative phenomena during analytic regressive episodes that interfere with communication with the analyst can also be treated through similar approaches (219). Reducing the anxiety bound in particular physiological systems allows these patients increased body-mind integration through biofeedback experiences. Other analytic patients report symptoms such as muscle spasms, phobias, or maladaptive habit patterns that do not appear to be related to any current, underlying psychopathology. The symptoms do not always respond to the intensive psychotherapy as expected and can be treated through the biofeedback-behavioral model, adjunctive to the psychotherapy.

The personality theory the therapist selects through which explanations and treatment plans are devised in clinical biofeedback may be less important to successful treatment than clinical eclecticism. Personality theories can provide guidelines for practice, but the limited verification of any theory suggests that no one theory is adequate for all patients or all symptoms. The realities of the patient and the clinical data presented requires some flexibility in devising treatment plans, regardless of theoretical orientation. The final arbiter of clinical technique is reality—the efficacy of the technique—not a particular theory.

Chapter 6

STRESS, ANXIETY, AND RELAXATION

Stress

The concept of stress has undergone considerable revision and development within the last five decades. Selye (186, 187), Jacobson (101), and Cannon (36) have contributed basic research related to human reactions following stressful experiences. Selye focused on the actions of hormones in his studies of the biochemistry of stress and eventually examined the psychological correlates of stress reactions. Jacobson investigated relationships among muscle tension, relaxation, and symptom formation; and Cannon formulated the fight-flight response, or the emergency reaction of the ANS, as well as the concept of physiological homeostasis. These and many other contributions to the problem of stress have been drawn on by investigators and practitioners in biofeedback applications, particularly in the areas of stress-related (psychosomatic) disorders.

Cannon's emergency or fight-flight reaction is an organismic state produced by the interaction of the sympathetic nervous system acting in time with the hormones secreted by the adrenal medulla, adrenaline, and noradrenaline (Figure 5 and Table 3). The reaction's purpose is to mobilize the resources of the body for immediate action, fight or flight, as such actions are needed. There is then an increase in respiration to take in more oxygen, an increase in heart rate and strength of each beat, and the spleen releases red blood cells to transport the oxygen throughout the body. Sugar stored in the liver is released for use by the muscles as energy, the blood is withdrawn from the periphery and the viscera to provide extra flow to the brain and muscles, dilation of the pupils increases visual acuity, and an increase in supply of lymphocytes improves the body's repair mechanisms in case of injury.

Ordinarily, the counteraction of the parasympathetic nervous system slows down these responses and the bodily systems return to within normal boundaries of homeostasis once the "emergency" has passed. In psychogenic fight-flight reactions the overactivation can be caused by learned fears, such as phobias, and can persist beyond the duration of the apparent emergency. That is, the sufferer of chronic anxiety, or of heightened stress levels caused by the work or family situation, or by one's own fearful thoughts, can remain in a state of emergency reaction with its attendant increase in physiological activity. One may then suffer acute or chronic symptoms of hyperventilation, cold hands or feet, excessive sweating, a racing feeling in the trunk of the body, etc. The emergency reaction may then cause one to tighten voluntary muscles in the scalp, neck, hands, jaws, or elsewhere, resulting in painful muscle tension.

Selye was a prime mover in medicine and psychology in drawing attention to the fact that increasing levels of stress in an organism can result in anatomical changes as the organism exhausts its capacity to adapt to, or cope with, stressors of increasing intensity or prolonged impingement. His general adaptation syndrome (G.A.S.) identifies the stages of stress reactions as ranging from normal to lethal conditions. Selye (186, p. 55) defines stress as "a nonspecific response of the body to any demand placed upon it."

The stages of the G.A.S. are, first, the *alarm reaction* in which the body calls on a generalized (nonspecific) defense to deal with the stressor. No specific organ system is involved in the defense, although pituitary-adrenal flow is increased and other adaptive responses occur. The hormonal flow diminishes when the body defenses are successfully coping with the stress. However, if the stressor continues to stimulate the minimal defenses, the stage of *resistance* is activated during which the organism mobilizes more specific organ systems to counteract the stress and to confine it to as local a body region as possible. Adaptation is then taking place in this stage of resistance.

"Wear and tear" on tissues can result from extended demands that the body resist and adapt to the stress.

The third stage develops when prolonged resistance and failures in adaptive mechanisms occur and the organism collapses into *exhaustion*. Selye is emphasizing the importance of the capacities of the persons in responding effectively to any demands made in order to cope successfully (healthily) with the resultant stress. "Derailments of this G.A.S. mechanism produce *diseases of adaptation,* that is, stress disorders" (187, p. 56).

Some consequences in behavior of the G.A.S. is that continued stress inhibits thyroid and anterior pituitary activity possibly leading to inhibition of body growth. During the stage of resistance there can be a suppression of production of spermatazoa and testosterone in the male, and, in the female, interference in the menstrual cycle, failure to ovulate, or even a difficulty in the implantation of the fertilized ovum on the lining of the uterus, and a decrease in lactation. Prolonged stress can therefore result in significant malfunctioning of bodily processes that involve resistance to diseases, growth, and reproduction.

The concept of demands-resistance and adaptation-exhaustion is inherent in the more elaborate of the psychological theories of human behavior—Freud (67), Sullivan (204), Jung (105), Horney (199)—and in the treatment techniques of Jacobson (103) and Wolpe (229) that target stress reactions. The concept has also become a basic principle in the clinical application of biofeedback procedures.

In the psychological as well as the biological arena, what constitutes a stressor is often an individualized or idiosyncratic matter. Differences in genetic endowment, temperament, learning, health, etc., are influential in determining effective resistance to stressors. A promotion, in school or work, is frequently stressful, but to some the new demands are overwhelming. Other normal activities, such as marriage, the birth of a child, or a change in residence are ordinarily stressful but can lead to pathological consequences when one is unable to cope with and to adapt to the change. Similar consequences can occur in response to the undesired changes of death of a spouse or child, serious losses or failures, or divorce (58).

Lazarus (121) recently suggested that the cognitive aspects of stress management are crucial in determining the consequences on the person stressed. He points out that unless a victim is aware of an injury or threat, the pituitary-adrenal-cortical response is not initiated. Therefore, the G.A.S. is not initiated. That is, patients dying from injury or disease because they remained unconscious revealed normal adrenal cortical conditions on autopsy. Conversely, autopsies of persons who knew they were under lethal threat did show adrenal changes. In applying these findings to biofeedback procedures, Lazarus points out that disturbances treated in biofeedback cannot be isolated from the psychosocial matrix in which these biological phenomena occur. What one knows and thinks about what is happening to one has a direct influence on physiological consequences.

Humans can react with mental as well as physical alarm and resistance to significant events in their lives, good or bad, that demand a reordering of their social status, style of life, etc. When able to cope and to adapt to the change, provided they are not restressed by additional stressors, they can achieve a healthy adjustment to the change.

Frequently people develop a stereotyped—automatic—response to any stressor even when the response is of no adaptive value. It is possible that the response was originally adaptive, or perhaps a particular system was vulnerable to the development of such a response. Whatever the reason might be for such a selection, the response can become a potential and maladaptive reaction to any stressor.

This kind of response is referred to as "response stereotypy" (113, 201), in which physiological overactivation in a given system, or a given parameter of a system, becomes the stereotypical location of responsiveness under stress, regardless of the stressor. For example, if one is prone to cardiovascular homeostatic imbalance manifested in vasoconstriction, or striate muscle spasms as in tension headaches, one is most likely to respond through that system and with that symptom first and foremost when one is stressed.

A related phenomenon was pointed out by Cameron in 1944 (35) in his classification of the bodily residences of anxiety in the musculature, the cardiovascular, or the gastrointestinal system, or in the last two simultaneously. The taxonomy obviously suggests that anxiety-ridden people somatize in the skeletal muscles or in the autonomic systems, where symptoms then develop.

The repeated response of a given system to any kind of stressor in stress-prone people aggravates the normal wear and tear on that system. Moreover, since we ordinarily adapt to increasing levels of pain, distress, or discomfort, response stereotypy can lead to increasing levels of intensity in the symptom formation before the intensity reaches the terminal (pain) threshold. At that point, if not before, the symptom is interfering with living.

Most patients who undertake biofeedback treatment (and other therapies) present response stereotypy as a chief complaint. Indeed, some have developed two or three, and of varying degrees of disruption to their living. In some cases, the symptoms of lesser intensity can be masked by the chief complaint and reduction of the chief complaint will allow the lesser symptoms to enter awareness.

The mechanisms or reasons for which given people select given systems for the residence of symptoms are unknown. Stoyva, for example (200) proposes a learning model to explain the development of stress disorders. He considers several variables as being implicated: (1) the failure (instability) of homeostatic processes that lead to their vulnerability to stress, (2) the presence of response stereotypy, (3) the triggering (through CNS involvement) of the (maladaptive) response, and (4) the social reinforcement of any phase of the pathological process. Figure 6 outlines the sequence of events over time in the development of a stress disorder. The "preferred response" is functionally equivalent to the concepts of residence of anxiety and response stereotypy.

Note Stoyva's comments in Figure 6: "Prompt return to baseline levels" and "Slow return to baseline levels (homeostatic failure)." He is pointing out a prime difference between normal and abnormal functioning in the duration of physiological responses. The abnormal course is one of *prolonged* overactivation of a physiological response, continuing long after the stressor has disappeared. That is, in the stress-related disorders, not only has the sufferer learned to react with inappropriate levels of intensity to ordinarily mild stressors, but the reaction to mild or severe stressors tends to persist at inordinate levels, thereby perpetuating the distress, discomfort, pain or, even disability. The sufferer would then be persistently disturbed mentally by the response, and his or her mind would not be free to engage in thinking, planning, judging, or enjoyment.

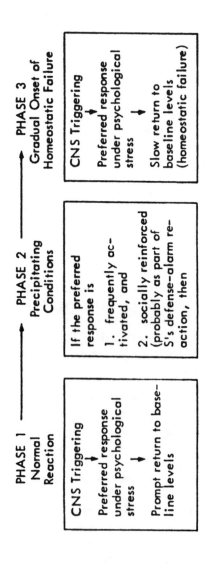

Stoyva's model, as he states, is insufficient as an etiological system in that many unknown variables exist, any of which might account for the susceptibility to homeostatic overactivation (genetic defect or variability, trauma, early learning, nutrition?). However, the model is clinically useful as a frame of reference for applying and assessing some aspects of clinical biofeedback. For example, most clinicians target physiological overactivation routinely in most presenting problems; and most establish their criteria for symptom remission as decreased frequency and shorter periods of activation of response stereotypy.

Anxiety

Anxiety and stress disorders have in common a significant increase in physiological activation accompanied by a subjective awareness of mental or physical discomfort. There are also endless variations among both anxiety-ridden and stressed people regarding the frequency, causes, intensity, duration, symptomatology, insight, coping mechanisms, defenses, etc., of their responses to anxiety and stress. These variables are among the major issues in clinical biofeedback. Patients' complaints will contain references to physical or mental symptoms of anxiety, in diffuse or specific forms. Bodily discomfort is reflected in homeostatic imbalances: pain, restlessness, tension, and mental symptoms are often expressed in terms of feeling apprehensive, guilty, ashamed, inadequate, shy, and so on.

The sufferers of anxiety are in mutual agreement that anxiety is an affect that they do not seek out. They will report the need for experiences that evoke fright, awe, sexual arousal, sadness, joy, horror; but anxiety is avoided to any possible degree in real life or in imagination. In contrast to anxiety, stress in work or play can be experienced as desirable, provided the stressors are manageable or do not cause anxiety. Planned occurrence of fear is also engaged in with pleasure so long as the circumstances are under one's control and do not elicit anxiety. The peculiar characteristic of anxiety is its unpleasant character (25, 204).

Anxiety feels like fear, but fear is likely to mobilize one's skills to act to avoid or to manage the source of the fear since the source is usually recognizable and definable in realistic terms. Anxiety episodes can occur in contexts that may be realistically nondangerous, such as riding an elevator. The unknown or unmanageable dimension or source in anxiety may well constitute its threatening character. Anxiety reactions are bound in specific objects or situations, such as enclosed spaces, that are not realistic sources of fear; other reactions are diffuse and vaguely related to aspects of the real world. Anxiety disables human functioning by its severity or because the source of the anxiety is a mystery and the sufferer has great difficulty in coping with the apparent source.

Behaviorism's assumption that anxiety is a learned fear is at odds with the psychodynamic assumption of the causes of anxiety. Both assume that fear is an innate drive having survival value. Behaviorism offers several paradigms to explain the acquisition of irrational fears, or anxiety, each of the models utilizing stimulus-response learning in some variation.

The general thesis Freud proposed is that anxiety is a necessary component of ego control over impulsive acting out, but that excessive or inappropriate anxiety drains one of energy and is part of symptom formation. Anxiety in this theory incorporates the concept of a mental attitude laden with irrational fear as being a cause of anxiety. The psychodynamic theories as a whole also recognize that anxiety is manifested in the smooth or striate musculature and in ideation.

One of the recent refinements in the study of anxiety has focused on the source of the stimulus for the state-trait differentiation (195). The concept recognizes the profound difference between suffering anxiety diffusely and chronically (trait anxiety), and suffering anxiety acutely and only in direct response to a specific stimulus (state anxiety). This formulation substantiates the traditional analytic view of diffuse or free-flowing anxiety versus anxiety bound in phobias.

Cattell summarized the formulation: "Anxiety is both a state and a trait. That is to say we all experience higher and lower states with changing circumstances, but there is also evidence that some people vary about levels which are typically different for them from the central tendency in others. We then speak of 'characterological anxiety,' i.e., a trait" (41, p. 114). He also indicates that there is

"...a simple anxiety factor, but different from the effort stress response and from well-known drives."

Trait anxiety is a generalized, diffuse, ongoing condition of relatively high level anxiety which can further increase in intensity when one is stimulated by a frightening event or even a pleasant, but "exciting" experience. Evidently, increased arousal for the trait anxiety person can evoke an acute anxiety episode. The stimulus for the increased arousal does not necessarily have to be a clearly identifiable stimulus. The trait anxiety person is highly prone to social and nonspecific stimuli such as open spaces, crowds, or social events. He is also highly susceptible to his own fearfulness (71) and any acute anxiety episode tends to become diffusely crippling.

Conversely, the state anxiety person is acutely reactive to fewer phobic objects and when the objects have been removed from his presence, his anxiety decreases relatively rapidly, not having diffused or persisted. Animals and objects common to state reactions are dogs, birds, insects, and snakes, and enclosed places, heights, and escalators. Animal phobias appear to be acquired in childhood and remit to treatment relatively easily. The social and diffuse anxiety reactions usually occur after childhood and are more difficult to reduce (129).

Diminishing state or trait anxiety and presenting symptoms are among the goals of any therapy procedure, although there are some disputes about the risks of symptomatic treatment. The analytic model of neuroses predicts symptom substitution as a consequence of reducing symptoms without resolving the internal conflict that presumably gave rise to and supports the symptom. In contrast, behavior therapy literature reports a striking lack of symptom substitution following symptom reduction.

A possible explanation for the contradictory views is that although behavior therapy literature on the whole does not specify that the anxiety supporting a symptom must be reduced along with the symptom reduction in order to avoid symptom substitution, nevertheless most behavior techniques that target such symptoms are applied to extinguish or countercondition the anxiety as well. With the inexplicable exception among the neuroses of conversion hysteria, when the anxiety and the symptom are both reduced in other neuroses there is no symptom substitution.

Symptom substitution may not occur for reasons other than success in reducing the anxiety. It is possible that all psychogenic symptoms do not necessarily originate in the context of internalized conflicts; some may well have been learned through the S-R model of symptom formation. Other symptoms may be autonomous behavior patterns that have persisted long after the resolution of any conflict, or learning, that precipitated the symptoms (220).

Differentiating the etiology of any given symptom whose onset cannot be precisely determined limits the validity of the treatment technique used to reduce the symptom. Symptoms that appear to be anxiety-related may also arise from biological defects, varieties of diseases, traumatic events, interpersonal relationships, and probably other sources. Classical psychogenic symptoms may also exist side by side with symptoms arising from psychoses, metabolic disturbances, or organic injury (216, 221). Applying symptom reduction techniques requires a careful discrimination of the symptoms that are appropriate for biofeedback.

Clinical experience has demonstrated that anxiety and symptoms can arise from causes other than internal conflicts, restricted self-systems, or other theoretically postulated etiologies. Perhaps a given symptomatology in a given patient at a particular time and context of his life may originate in a variety of causes. The evidence strongly suggests that all symptoms do not arise from a common source for all persons.

Clinical eclecticism in the diagnosis and treatment of learned fears, anxiety, neurotic symptoms, stress reactions, and exaggerated fears may be a useful frame of reference for the application of biofeedback techniques. The therapist would then assess the presenting problems in terms of the patient's restrictions on what he or she wishes to deal with—symptoms or self, and in terms of the specific treatment techniques within the treatment plan. The diagnostic studies and interviews would presumably establish the appropriateness of the technique selected. Needless to say, the therapist's theoretical orientation regarding the causes of anxiety and various symptoms would influence, if not predetermine, the development of the treatment plan and the particular uses of the biofeedback instruments and ancillary therapy techniques.

Relaxation

Relaxation is usually defined in the literature, if at all, as the absence of tension, stress, discomfort, anxiety, distress, etc. (11, 15, 22, 25, 27, 35, 72, 74). This is a common-sense view. Indeed, most people report that when they are not experiencing any of these states they are feeling relaxed. They also report not feeling any significant degree of alertness or readiness to respond, although their degree of receptivity may vary from low to very high. When relaxed, they appear to be in a mental and physical state of lowered arousal that they find palliative. They are not necessarily "deeply" relaxed, as in pre-sleep or sleep itself; nor are they always in an altered state of consciousness that has ablated sensory responsiveness. Sleep could be entered with ease, as could other, similar, hypnogogic or meditative states.

Diminished readiness to respond to internal or external stimuli, concurrent with the low level of mental and physical activity, are central characteristics of the psychophysiological state of relaxation. Both the experiencing ego and the observing ego are not making any demands on themselves other than a passive and diminished attentiveness. With the reduction of sensory input to the brain, afferent flow is also minimal. It is known that there is a decrease in cycles per second of brain wave forms, a lowered adrenal outflow, reduced heart rate and respiration, etc. That is, biological processes have slowed significantly and mental activity, other than effortless attention, has decreased.

Relaxation is defined here, in these descriptive terms, as *a generalized, psychophysiological, wakeful state of minimal activity or preparation for response to any demand placed upon the body and mind.*

There are apparent differences among the various states and methods of relaxation and among the altered states of consciousness that induce relaxation. The changes are manifested in either physiological or mental functioning, or in both parameters. Variations can occur in any one or more of the physiological systems, including sensory, somatic, biochemical, and in affect, degree of suggestibility to instructions, age regression phenomena, alertness of the experiencing ego, long- and short-term memory, transference, distortions of time and space, etc. (207). Most definitions of relaxation in biofeedback literature emphasize or are restricted to the physiological and bio-chemical parameters. The proposed definition includes psychic func-tioning, despite the obvious difficulties that generality raises.

Benson (16, p. 18) lists the physiological characteristics found in his study of relaxation achieved through the technique he developed in his studies of Transcendental Meditation (TM). "This response against 'overstress' brings on bodily changes that decrease heart rate, lower metabolism, decrease the rate of breathing, and bring the body back into what is probably a healthier balance." Benson includes mental activity as part of the procedure, as all methods do in some way or another, by advising use of words or by counting, and by maintaining a passive mental attitude. The technique is highly effec-tive as a stress reducer, especially with normal people.

Transcendental Meditation (TM) is a widely used relaxation method that aims, in the least, for similar hypometabolic changes. Many of the devotees also claim other extraordinary results, such as levitation, telekinesis and mystical experiences. These claims are heard more by word of mouth than as published or demonstrated revelations and are not possible to verify. However, apart from these questions, the method has value as a stress reducer.

Wallace et al. (213) define TM as a "wakeful hypometabolic physiologic state." He notes that the changes are not the same as in sleep, hypnosis, and autosuggestion. Generally, mental and meta-bolic processes slow down. The general physiological change also includes decrease in sympathetic tone and relaxation of both smooth and striate muscles. Mental content may seem to disappear in a fourth state of consciousness—"pure consciousness"—in which, according to TM proponents, the mind is aware only of itself (56).

Domash (56, p. 20) outlines the practice of the TM relaxation method in which the subject "simply sits comfortably with eyes closed and begins to use the thinking process, the mantra. . . ."

Evidently when one's attention is resting on a nonstressful, nondemanding, mental target, the mantra, other thoughts will be concurrently diminished in their potency to stimulate thinking and arousal. Counting sheep has that precise value for sleepless persons being disturbed by their own thoughts. Closing one's eyes increases alpha density, and relinquishing worries and other beta-producing preoccupations institutes the first phase of rest, preliminary to sleep onset, and evidently can also occur at the onset of the practice of TM.

TM has not been successful for every applicant (no method appears to be), and undesirable side effects are not posed as serious risks. However, a recent report by James Hassett (92) in interviewing Leon Otis about his survey of the effects of TM reveals that "seventy-eight experienced meditators who had been practicing TM for at least 18 months were far more likely to admit becoming anxious, confused, frustrated, depressed, and/or withdrawn" since meditating than the 121 people who had stopped (after an average of 7 months). Another report of 219 people who had been undertaking a 4-year training program in TM to be teachers had the "most frequent and the most severe side effects." Otis emphasized that about 52 to 64 percent of subjects who continued to practice had no ill effects. Perhaps the difference is in personality structures, or in the loss of repression.

There has always been some concern about the use of TM with schizophrenics who suffer from loose association. The possibility of exacerbating the poor ego controls would suggest that the technique is contraindicated in those cases. A project in which Gleuck and Stroebel (79) applied TM and EEG biofeedback to psychiatric patients did not report frequent exacerbations. Some patients found the experimental procedure of biofeedback and TM to be boring or anxiety-provoking and dropped out; but most patients completed the project. There were six schizophrenics among the treated group; and the authors report that "many of the patients" in the treated group who practiced TM consistently revealed on follow-up that the TM was a "valuable addition to their pattern of living" (p. 113).

Jacobson's progressive relaxation technique (101, 102) is probably the most widely used method in clinical biofeedback. Over many years of practice, Jacobson had been establishing its value in reducing muscular tension, anxiety, and physiological symptoms. The method, as he developed it, is extremely elaborate and time-consuming, and requires strong motivation for both patient and therapist. Most clinical and research reports indicate the use of some form of Jacobson's abbreviated method of progressive relaxation in preference to the prolonged method.

Jacobson defines relaxation as "the lengthening of muscle fibers following their contraction in effort states" (103, p. 62). The method includes the focusing of attention on the contraction of all possible muscle groups, progressively, group by group and by groups of groups, and at the height of contraction, allowing the sudden relaxation of the effort expended in maintaining the contraction. The principle of contraction-relaxation of muscle groups and learning to perceive the sensory signals of each end of the continuum is basic to the method. The relaxed muscles when returned to their lengthened state do not "feel" the same as tensed, shortened muscles.

Progressive relaxation requires mental activities of concentration on the procedure, and an increase in one's sense, or perception, of the self-control of one's mind and body. These characteristics might not be sufficiently appreciated by therapists who apply the relaxation technique. Yet, one of the distinct advantages of the method is that the learner must direct his attention to his mental control of a deliberately self-initated physical and mental act.

These mental actions, beyond the value of the physiological relaxation, are reassuring and psychologically beneficial in that they increase self-confidence and self-control, and provide coping acts to counter tension, anxiety, and intrusive, disturbing thoughts. These gains are oppositional to feelings of loss of self-control, helplessness in the face of tension and anxiety, and the diminishing of self-esteem. The inability to cope with undesired responses, such as phobias, diffuse anxiety, compulsions, sexual dysfunctions, or bodily tension, universally reduces one's sense of adequacy and self-esteem.

A major defect in progressive relaxation technique is the impossibility of exercising in public. It is hardly reasonable to contract muscles of the face, arms, or legs while sitting at a desk or on a bus. The technique is realistically confined to use in the therapist's office or the privacy of the patient's home. TM also suffers from a similar limitation in the risks of achieving a TM state in public.

The basic common denominators of therapeutic, relaxation methods are reduction of physiological activation levels and removing distressing thoughts from the mind. For some people, one of the two can be relaxing, at least ostensibly. Often a person can shift attention and occupy his mind with nonstressful ideation and find it recreational, though not necessarily physically relaxing. The two parameters interacting appear to be a more fruitful method in achieving both mental and physical relaxation.

The problem of selecting a given relaxation technique has not yet been fully solved, but some advances are being made. Davidson (48) reviewed some of the physiological variables relevant to research and recommends differentiation in application of relaxation techniques. He suggested that anxiety be viewed as cognitively based or somatically based, in relation to the patient's reports of the physical and mental manifestations. The former is essentially the mental or ideational form of anxiety and would be reflected in increase in skin conductance; the latter, somatically based anxiety, resides in striate musculature and is felt as tension. Consequently, techniques in reducing anxiety should be specific to the given biological system. The recommendation is to apply progressive relaxation to treat anxiety residing in the voluntary musculature. The effect of that technique on cognitive anxiety is minimal. Conversely, targeting thought processes and content should be most useful in reducing cases of cognitive anxiety. Meditation was considered of minimal use in either anxiety mode unless it utilized a mantra (a cognition) in the meditation. A comparison of meditators and physical exercises found the meditators to be low in cognitive anxiety and high in somatic anxiety; whereas, the exercisers were in the reverse.

Davidson's suggestion that treatment techniques be fitted to the residence of the anxiety is particularly relevant to biofeedback in view of the fact that biofeedback instruments target physiological systems. Adding imaginal methods of relaxation and other mental techniques in clinical biofeedback, during relaxation induction, targets ideational systems which are involved in cognitive anxiety, while the biofeedback procedure targets and enhances the physical relaxation.

In clinical biofeedback, relaxation is the standard precondition to biofeedback applications, as well as an end in itself. The relaxed state also provides the setting for the application of behavioral techniques to treat presenting symptoms that may be physically or mentally based, and usually both are implicated in the symptom formation. Deep relaxation is similar to hypnotic induction in that both states involve the narrowing of concentration and the focusing of attention. Hence, the patient can become highly receptive to suggestion by the therapist.

In the context of clinical biofeedback, the selection of an efficacious relaxation technique should meet several criteria: (1) simplicity in administration; (2) ready comprehensibility to most personality types; (3) ease of learning through self-demonstration; (4) targeting of both somatic and cognitive systems; (5) applicability to a wide variety of diagnostic groups, as well as to normals; (6) accessibility during practice to monitoring and to feedback through instrumentation; (7) suited to practice in whole or in part and in public settings; (8) sufficient flexibility to incorporate elements of other methods when required; (9) parsimony of time; and (10) being a stress reducer.

Very few patients report their tensions to be confined to one physiological system, or to exclude mental involvement. Therefore, a relaxation technique should target striate muscle tension, autonomic overarousal, depth and rate of respiration, and mental content and processes. Moreover, a relaxation method should involve practice in training one's concentration in order to develop useful mental coping mechanisms. Whether the physiological homeostatic dysfunctions presented are a consequence of learning or of innate susceptibility to abnormal variations, their retraining through biofeedback applications is not sufficient in and of itself to attain autonomous, normal functioning. The course of several psychosomatic disorders clearly demonstrates the need to acquire self-regulatory techniques in order to maintain any gains the clinical treatment may have achieved. Dysfunctions in healthy persons that are simply habits or are merely situational reactions are relatively easy to reduce and usually do not require self-regulatory practice over many months. Such patients form a small minority of referrals. The majority present significant disorders of long duration whose etiologies are complex and obscure and demand multiple therapies, some of which may be lifelong necessities.

Experience with a wide variety of complaints, diagnostic groups, personality types, and relaxation methods resulted in selecting one that best met the criteria listed above. The method consists of briefing the subject on the interactions of physiological arousal and mental distress, the use of biofeedback instruments to monitor and retrain the implicated physiological systems, and the psychological methods used during the application which could revise the interactions of the biopsychosocial matrix in which the anxiety and symptoms originate or persist. The value of stress reduction in ordinary living is highlighted, and the use of the relaxed state as a mental-physical state basic to the use of other therapy techniques in clinical biofeedback is explained.

Some precautions may be necessary for given patients. Dissociative phenomena of heaviness or lightness in the limbs or the whole body may occur, especially in patients with hysterical trends and in schizophrenics with a history of somatic hallucinations. It is wise to inform *all* patients of the possibility of sensory modifications in proprioception. Those patients whose psychopathology is liable to exacerbation should be monitored through intermittent verbal communication with the therapist over the course of the procedure in order to manage any disturbances in ego functioning that might occur in the relaxation procedure and before the patient's ego is overwhelmed by the diminishing of repression. Such reactions are quite uncommon in healthy, neurotic patients, and occur quite rarely among the schizophrenics. In the latter group, the patients obviously will have been stabilized before biofeedback procedures are applied.

During the initial training in relaxation and in subsequent sessions, particular instruments are used to target the physiological system that is dysfunctional. For example, in Raynaud's disease the thermistor is used to increase vasodilation at the periphery, as well as reducing sympathetic tone; in anxiety reactions manifested by sweaty palms, the GSR is used to reduce sympathetic tone and to decrease sweat gland production. That is, relaxation can be induced concurrent with the initial retraining in physiological self-regulation.

The relaxation method consists of guiding the patient's attention passively to various regions of his body, of regulating mental content and breathing, and the letting go of tension in the musculature (150, 219). The procedure usually takes 20 to 30 minutes and can be learned by virtually everyone quite easily. While sitting upright, both feet on the floor, hands in lap, or while lying supine, the patient is directed to allow his eyes to close and to bring his attention to his forehead. He is asked to recall a real life event during which he had experienced a state of calm, well-being, and adequacy. The specific details are recalled along with the subjective feelings. The feelings are reinforced by the therapist's encouragement. The patient is then instructed to place the event in the corner of his mind and to focus his attention on his forehead, to be aware of his forehead without attempting active concentration, or by expending any effort. This attitude of passive concentration is explained and offered as the sole mental approach throughout the relaxation procedure. Narrowing the field of attention to one's body in a calm and effortless fashion is the essence of the mind set to be developed.

Attention is then guided to the eyes, cheeks, and jaw, and the patient is told to let the face relax. The letting go of the facial muscles will result in awareness of a slight tugging in the cheeks and a dragging of the jaw.

If frontales placement EMG feedback is being used there is often a concurrent reduction in the feedback signal, especially at the upper end of the range. The feedback signal should also be listened to on the edge of awareness by the patient in order to develop the attitude of passive self-involvement and change in bodily functioning through *removal* of effort stress, rather than through striving to relax.

Attention to breathing can be introduced after the head region has been covered. Generally, it is most effective to draw attention to breathing after the rate and depth of respiration have lowered from baseline. When asked to be aware of their breathing, patients invariably take a deep breath. The therapist should be alert to whether the breathing is thoracic or abdominal in order to know if training in diaphragmatic breathing will be needed. In either case, at this stage of the procedure, the patient is told to pick up the rhythm of breathing by reciting to himself words appropriate to inducing mental calm: relax, tranquil, calm, peaceful, quiet; or the patient can count, also in rhythm with breathing, in and out, one—two, one—two. The procedure is then continued, directing attention to the right shoulder, upper arm, forearm, and hand, and suggesting that each region be relaxed by allowing the muscles to let go. Autogenic technique can be introduced after relaxation of each limb (184), by instructing the patient to recite to him or herself a few times, "My arm (leg) is heavy; my hand (foot) is warm." This is essential in cases of vasoconstriction. The remainder of the body is then covered in sequence in a similar fashion, slowly and calmly.

During the initial stages other comments should be made in order to assist the patient in developing mental coping techniques that enhance somatic and cognitive relaxation. "If your mind wanders off, just bring your attention slowly back to your breathing and to the body area you are focusing on. If thoughts run through your mind, just let them drift through. Don't try to remember any or try to do anything with them. Keep your awareness filled by the sensation of your body and your breathing. Let your thoughts slow down, let your mind relax."

In the event the patient experiences an eruption of anxiety, to any degree, the therapist can halt the procedure and analyze the event, or can direct the patient to recall his or her real life scenes of well-being, and after the distress has diminished to continue the relaxation. An occasional patient finds the method of letting go threatening because of a neurotic need to maintain continual vigilance. Jacobson's progressive relaxation can then be introduced, even with the eyes open. After a generalized relaxed state is induced. the patient should allow his or her attention to wander over the entire body to locate areas of tension. Finally, the patient is asked to open his or her eyes slowly and return attention to the environment.

Each patient reacts idiosyncratically to the procedure in terms of anxiety level, passivity, strength of the ego, the nature of defenses, and the level of psychopathology; transference and countertransference also influence the course of events. The use of the observing ego in self-monitoring one's physical and mental experience is a significant aspect of the training of concentration and attention, and becomes a chief agent in subsequent treatment procedures. The ability to empty one's mind of distressing thoughts is shaped by the practice of replacing them by other useful mental contents. Unwanted mental content can only be supressed or repressed, not removed, except by replacement with different thoughts. Patients are encouraged to practice the relaxation procedure a few times a day, even if only in part, such as relaxing the face. Patients are notoriously noncompliant. An audio tape of the procedure can be made for home use, which is often required to support practice sessions.

After the initial session the patient is debriefed as to the mental, emotional, and physical reactions experienced during the stages of relaxation. Most achieve quite deep, generalized relaxation and report it as restful and pleasing. The details of their experiences—images, associations, areas of tension, etc.—are incorporated in subsequent treatment sessions.

Relaxation often allows repressed material to enter awareness. One of the useful applications of biofeedback-augmented relaxation is to conduct the procedure adjunctive to intensive psychotherapy (219). While deeply relaxed, many patients increase their introspective ability and recall personal, historical experiences more quickly than while alert and vigilant. Patients may also spontaneously examine their more complex attitudes, values, and human interactions in greater detail, or with increased insight, as the defenses and anxiety are diminished. Since the biological component of the conflict are often expressed in physiological overactivation, the biofeedback technique can be used as a direct intervention in the mind-body interactions during the relaxed state. When the patient has been prepared to conduct internal searches under relaxation the possibility of free-association and of raising to consciousness preconscious material is sharply enhanced. The techniques can have the advantages of hypnosis without the disadvantages of hypnotic amnesias which may occur in deep trances.

Biofeedback-augmented relaxation has considerable efficiency in that the physiological system that is overactive and disrupting attention is targeted and reduced in intensity while applying relaxation technique. The procedure has two goals: augmenting general mental-somatic relaxation, and revising in the desired direction the physiological system in which anxiety resides. When both have reached criterion, the brain is less disrupted by input from overactive bodily processes and the ego is more capable of observing itself. This procedure is the preliminary stage used in clinical biofeedback application in the literature (7, 11, 28, 72,74, 219).

Budzinski and Stoyva (32) introduced the use of EMG frontales placement of surface electrodes as a method of inducing generalized relaxation. Other sites have also been proposed, such as forearm extensor muscles, but the forehead was adopted by many clinicians as the preferred site. The frontales are voluntary muscles over which we have very little control. They raise the eyebrows when contracted and in that motion participate in facial expression.

The assumption that biofeedback relaxation of frontales automatically leads to generalized relaxation has not held up in most research projects that controlled other variables. Alexander and Smith (4) reviewed much of the evidence and found that in "...the clinical use of single-muscle site (usually the forehead) EMG biofeedback techniques as an antistress or general relaxation intervention is largely without scientific justification" (p. 129). Clinical experience had already demonstrated that BFT through EMG applications was insufficient to establish a general, mental-somatic relaxed state (11, 17, 20, 28, 74, 76, 219).

In order to attain a significant degree of relaxation, both mental and bodily domains need to be targeted. The exceptions may be normal subjects who respond to single-muscle site EMG feedback with good success. Ohno et al. (147) reported BFT of frontales with 20 normal subjects who felt more relaxed after reducing mild spasticity in frontales. It is unlikely that persons suffering significant degrees of physiological overactivation, emotional distress, anxiety, or other psychopathological symptoms will achieve a generalized relaxed state by relaxing tension in only single-muscle groups.

The frontales do remain a useful site for monitoring private mental events during relaxed states and while applying various therapy techniques. Once the patient has become relaxed and any level of spasticity has been reduced in the frontales, the site can reflect emotional or arousal responses to ongoing therapies, or to the patient's own associations. Slight changes in the feedback signal can reflect clinically meaningful internal activity. Usually the patient is aware of the change in the feedback signal, and may also achieve insightful recognition of the internal event (memory, affect, or thought) as being connected with the problem under treatment. For other patients, other physiological systems may be the sensitive barometers and can be monitored in a similar fashion.

Generally, relaxation of physiological overactivation, along with mental quieting, is palliative for anyone. The ordinary stresses of normal living can be countered by daily relaxation. It is also used as the ground for applying psychotherapy and behavioral techniques for the treatment of a wide range of mental and physical complaints related to anxiety and stress, as a waking but low-defense state for depth therapy, and as a preconditon to the application or retraining in neuromotor impairments. Biofeedback instruments can accelerate the training in relaxation through providing concrete information about one's bodily changes, particularly in the physiological systems that are implicated in the presenting problems.

Part II

THERAPY TECHNIQUES

Chapter 7

INITIAL INTERVIEW

The initial interview sets the climate, the methods, and the goals of the course of treatment. As with any first psychotherapy interview, the fundamental task is to achieve a therapeutic, working relationship with the patient. The positive transference is the overriding consideration of the first session. Without a trusting alliance, the patient is handicapped in collaborating in the treatment plan. Biofeedback applications cannot be approached as though the machine-patient relationship is the crux of the treatment procedures. Confinement to that model should be the choice of the patient, as it is in some cases, rather than the result of the climate created by the therapist. It is most useful in engendering a patient-therapist, collaborative relationship that the patient be encouraged to voice any thoughts or affects that may rise to consciousness. Many patients are normally inhibited on first meeting a therapist who is a stranger in fact, or by other, more unreal, anxieties. They need to feel free to speak and to question any aspect of the clinical situation, equipment, and techniques. Extensive free-association is not appropriate, in contrast to the ordinary psychotherapy interview, inasmuch as the patient has come for symptom-oriented complaints that are to be treated through a straightforward therapy model. The therapist is therefore required to be more directive in structuring the interview than is ordinarily done.

The goals of the initial interview are to reduce the expected anxiety on first meeting, to understand the patient's complaints, to contribute to motivation for therapy, and to make comprehensible the methods and equipment of the biofeedback procedures. The time required is often more than one session; the introduction to the equipment can be easily carried over to the next session.

Most referrals in private practice originate with another professional who will have given the patient some explanation and encouragement concerning biofeedback. Often, the private patient has read the popular literature and has a general knowledge of the approach. The clinic or hospital patients are usually just as sophisticated but frequently present more serious and complex problems. Whatever attitudes and knowledge any patient presents, it is best not to assume that he or she is adequately prepared for collaborating in the procedure. These are among the issues to be assessed during the initial interview.

Biofeedback is used by the professional community most commonly as a symptom-oriented, time-limited, adjunctive technique (1, 3, 11, 17, 28, 219); with the exception of its use as the primary therapeutic agent for monosymptomatic patients who are otherwise in good health (127, 147). The patients referred for such adjunctive treatment will have had medical examinations and will be undergoing appropriate treatment programs. Determining the appropriateness of the referral and devising a treatment plan in all cases requires gathering a minimal amount and kind of basic data during the initial interview that may not have emerged in previous examinations.

The basic data include diagnosis, level of motivation and sophistication, the presenting problems or complaints, the activity of the various physiological systems, especially those implicated in the complaints, and the kind and degree of change that the patient expects. Anxiety and emotionality should be noted directly and indirectly during the interviews. Additionally, a brief series of questions can be asked covering the current life situation and life style, the use of drugs, previous illnesses, therapy and hospitalizations, and the developmental milestones from birth.

Some clinics and therapists gather much of the factual information through forms the patient can complete before or after the first interview (28, 74). Such forms and self-rating scales (Appendix B) can be filled out by the patient during the first phase of the consultation.

Any indication of anatomical involvements or diseases require specialized medical examination. As a matter of diagnostic accuracy, the patient should have appropriate examinations, including dental for head and face complaints, before one can assume that the complaints are psychogenic, or nonorganic in every respect.

The technical focus of the initial interview is on the presenting problem or symptoms. The nature of the complaint is the central issue to be identified. It should be described in detail: date of onset, circumstances of the first episode, possible precipitating events, frequency and contexts of occurrence, intensity levels, location in the body, physical manifestations, its relationship to any diagnostic condition the patient has been informed of through other examinations, what the patient has done about the symptom (drugs, sleep, diet, exercise, etc.), and the outcome of any other treatment or self-care that the patient reports undergoing. The emotional, social, mental, sexual and occupational concomitants of the symptom are also elicited. These are measures of the severity of the complaint and its diffusion into various areas of living; the elaborated responses provide information necessary to both diagnosis and treatment planning.

Specific questions regarding physiological processes are also prerequisites to treatment planning. Each physiological system should be referred to regarding homeostatic functioning even if the complaint reportedly resides in only one system. Among these are the cardiovascular, musculature, respiratory, gastrointestinal, genital, sweat gland and skin systems, and thermoregulatory. Sensations of pain or distress in any body region, sleep and appetite, and visual sensory processes are assesed, whether or not the patient has volunteered complaints concerning them. Some patients have limited insight or even forget chronic symptoms to which they have adapted or which are masked by the chief complaints.

The mental or cognitive aspect of the complaints need particular attention. The biofeedback procedure is essentially a mental-physical modality and it is rare that any bodily complaint does not reflect mental distress as etiological, or as a corollary symptom, to the complaint. Conversely, if the complaint is mental, a phobia or obsession, the physical and social domains are investigated in detail.

The life-style of the patient and of his closely related friends and family are of general relevance to biofeedback treatment, and of particular relevance in the psychosomatic arena. The driven personalities are rather common referrals for biofeedback therapies and their chronic, hyperaroused level of activity makes them prone to somatic disorders. Their stress disorders may be consequences of either the work they do or of how they do their work. It is often necessary to itemize their daily schedules, including days off, in order to locate and evaluate the effects of their hyperactivity. Some patients are not driven solely by internal pressures but have fallen in with the punishing schedules of their mates or friends without admitting to themselves that other people are a main source of their stress, and that their inability to cope with such people is a central problem.

The relevant details of the patient's existence in the biopsychosocial matrix is the conceptual model for the interviews and the treatment.

The diagnostic interview

A typical initial interview, with changes in identifying data and unessential exchanges deleted, is that of Kathy, a twenty-eight year old, single, college graduate, working as an administrative secretary. She was referred by her psychiatrist for high blood pressure, chronic anxiety with acute episodes, and airplane phobia. Her therapist reported that she was in psychotherapy for sexual anxiety, diffuse anxiety, difficulty in separating from her family, and had been diagnosed at age thirteen as having essential hypertension. However, she was not informed until age twenty-one and treatment was not required until age twenty-five. Blood pressure varied about 130/80, with increases to 140/80 when stressed. The psychotherapy was successful except for the tendency to general anxiety and for the phobia. There was no evidence of depression or thought disorder.

On interview Kathy was appropriate in behavior, coherent in reporting her history and problems, well motivated, and cooperative.

Therapist (T): Dr. M. has told me you were interested in dealing with the phobia and the tendency to elevated blood pressure.

Patient (P): Yes, and I'm anxious too much. But I want to get rid of the fear of airplanes—I'm afraid I'll panic. I did once on a plane, and I'm always anxious.

T: How long have you had this fear?

P: For 7 years.

T: Do you remember the first time?

P: Yes. Seven years ago my grandmother committed suicide and we went to visit the family. That didn't upset me, but my mother was injured in an accident while we were there. We'd been planning the trip as a vacation, but when she died we went anyway. I got anxious about losing her. (The patient thought the question had referred to the general fear, not the phobia.)

T: What kind of accident was it?

P: We were just walking and she fell and broke her leg. I got shaky in my legs and from then on I worried about her dying. She has angina. My father died when I was thirteen, and an uncle disappeared, or left, I don't know, and two years later my grandmother committed suicide. I know I'm worried about more losses.

T: I take it you've been dealing with these problems in your therapy.

P: Yes, and I've improved a lot but I still get anxious.

T: You want to concentrate here on the general anxiety, the phobia, and the high blood pressure?

P: Yes. But I'm going to Europe in a few weeks with my fiance and I'm afraid I'll panic. That's the big problem.

T: Can you tell me more about the fear of planes? When did it start? How long does it last?

P: I get nervous thinking about it. It's terrible when I'm on the plane and I just have to control it. Once I couldn't get on the plane.

The concrete details of the phobia in terms of the history and the time and space dimensions were elicited. It began when flying home 7 years ago. Currently, and for a few years, she begins to feel anxious when she's thinking about flying; the closer she gets to the date of the flight the greater the increase in the anxiety level; and the closer she approaches the plane, the more severe and immobilizing the anxiety would be.

T: In what ways do you feel the anxiety?

P: My face gets hot, flushed; my hands get tight, sometimes my whole arm. My heart palpitates and I can't breathe, like it's short breaths.

T: Anything else you feel?

P: My forehead gets tight and the top of my skull feels like pressure; and my neck.

T: Do you have these reactions at any other times?

P: Not much. Maybe mild ones. I used to have a lot of them before.

T: Do you have any other fears?

P: No, not really. When I'm anxious the subways make me nervous.

T: What part of the subway?

P: The noise, or the crowds. I don't know. I just get more nervous.

She was then asked about other physiological systems, sleeping, eating, history of illness, developmental milestones, traumas, illnesses, etc. All were negative except that seven days before onset of menses she suffered cramps, sometimes headaches, hypersensitivity to odors, or nausea. She occasionally gritted her teeth, usually had cold hands and feet, and had rare periods of motor restlessness. There were no complaints about her work, social life, or her engagement. She was on a maintenance dose of Valium and would increase the dosage whenever she was particularly anxious. A recent examination was suggestive of a kidney or adrenal tumor and she was to undergo further examinations within 2 weeks. These were negative.

Kathy manifested a 7 year history of moderate-to-severe chronic anxiety, reflected in the automatic and cardiovascular dysfunction, susceptibility to stress, mild obsessional thoughts and worries, recurrent spasticity localized in the jaw, head, and arm muscles, and which appeared to be reactive to episodes of stress; and a severe phobic reaction to airplanes.

Treatment planning

The treatment plan in clinical biofeedback is based on the clinical data, the assets and limitations the patient possesses, and the appropriate selection of treatment methods. The patient is briefed about the connections between the intervention techniques and the mental and physical manifestations of anxiety or dysfunction in physiology, and their relationships with the complaints. Relevant techniques in biofeedback training, relaxation, behavioral methods, desensitization, hypnotism, record keeping, home practice, etc., are described in terms of how each works, and how each would be applied to specific aspects of the complaint. The patient's and therapist's responsibilities in applying any technique to be used are specified as part of the explanation that the clinical approach is designed to modify the complaint and to teach the patient methods for self-treatment. The nature and extent of the patient's and therapist's responsibilities requires precise formulation and concrete understanding. Most patients actually expect to be treated, rather than to assume active responsibility in the treatment methods, regardless of their stated intentions. The more sophisticated, educated, and self-motivated patients are among the better candidates for biofeedback procedures, but even they need to be informed of the self-training.

With all patients, a tentative but explicitly stated plan should be outlined, with the understanding that no guarantees are being offered, and that the plan may need revision if new findings emerge throughout the sessions. It is essential that the patient have the fullest possible understanding of who will treat what (and what won't be treated), what methods will be used and the reasons for their use, the nature of the patient's commitment in and out of the office, the expected kind and degree of change predicted, the duration of the change, and the steps required to maintain any change.

Biofeedback is an approach of symptom reduction and change in psychophysiological functioning, conducted by the patient with the assistance of the therapist. The changes that require continual self-regulation are of no value to the patient if he is not clearly aware of his own necessary part in maintaining the desired change. The data of the initial interview, the training program, and the understanding of the ways the homeostatic balances are disrupted should be used to help the patient develop self-responsibility in maintaining his own healthy changes. This kind of attitude can be instilled throughout the early phases of the treatment procedure and continuously reinforced over sessions.

In Kathy's case, the goals of the treatment plan were reduction of autonomic overactivation and the various striate muscle spasms through biofeedback and relaxation methods, teaching self-regulation techniques for the peripheral vasoconstriction, and the desensitization of the phobias.

The plan involved EMG frontales placement, and hands and feet thermistor placement to augment relaxation training and to revise physiological processes, application of autogenic phrases during relaxation to warm the extremities, and desensitization to airplane flights. EMG feedback was also conducted from other sites to reduce spasms: the temperomandibular joints, the upper trapezius of the cervical spine region, and sternocleidomastoideus muscles. A wrist thermometer was provided for record keeping of hourly readings of hand temperature, day by day. Daily practice of relaxation and hand warming were included in the plan.

Kathy was treated over eight sessions with a satisfactory outcome. Striate spasms were found to be reactive to stressful situations, and the mild level of spasticity in all areas was reduced quickly through EMG feedback. The vasoconstriction was significantly reduced outside the office. Her hourly records were carefully noted and the variability in hand temperature ranged from the low 80s degree Farhenheit to the middle 90s. There was a gradual increase over weeks in stabilization of hand temperature, ranging from upper 80s to lower 90s. Kathy took careful note of significant decreases in vivo and was able to connect the increase with stress situations usually occurring at work and in moments of discord with her fiance. She also practiced relaxing to expected stressful situations and found she eventually experienced little anxiety at those times and that she could maintain vasodilation.

Office temperature readings for her feet were in the middle 70s with little increase within or over sessions. Hand temperature baselines varied from 80s to 90s and invariable decreased over each session, in contrast to in vivo levels. The reasons offered were her need to perform well which would raise sympathetic tone and an underlying tension that did not become subjectively noticeable during the sessions. She reported relaxing easily and deeply during the office sessions, despite the thermistor readings to the contrary. Evidently, the thermoregulatory process was highly sensitive to stress and effort, in contrast to other physiological and mental systems.

It is probable that the only significant change in hand temperature was raising the constant level several degrees, and warding off stress reactions in the stressful situation.

Two months after the last session Kathy reported that she had no difficulty boarding the plane, and during the flight out, when the plane entered an area of turbulence, she relaxed herself and fell asleep. Her extremities felt warm, her blood pressure was acceptable, and she had cut her medication 50 percent. We agreed on termination and that she would return if she needed to.

Chapter 8

THERAPY TECHNIQUES
IN SYMPTOM REDUCTION

Clinical biofeedback rests on the basic process of feeding back physiological information to the patient and applying appropriate therapy techniques. Physiological feedback is rarely sufficient in itself to revise complex disorders in mind-body functions. Consequently, therapy techniques have been incorporated in the procedure. These techniques come from areas of behavior therapy (80, 230), gestalt therapy (157), self-statements (136), hypnotism (110), and autogenics (184). Biofeedback itself cannot claim to have developed any radically new therapy methods other than the basic psychophysiological feedback procedure. The addition of psychotherapy techniques extended the biofeedback approach into the realm of treating attitudes and emotions, as well as physiological dysfunctions. The multimodality procedure could well be considered a newly devised clinical method in the field of psychotherapy (219, 232).

This chapter reviews some of the basic therapy techniques that have been adapted to biofeedback. These adaptations are applied before, during, or after the application of the instruments as the clinical situaton may require. Frequently, more than one technique is used. Selections are based on the diagnosis, presenting problems, and the patient's response to each technique. Specific uses of these techniques are illustrated in the case presentations of Part III.

Verbal psychotherapy

Verbal therapy is the fundamental skill of the clinician (11, 17, 28, 69, 84, 212, 219). Unless the patient's behavior and verbalizations can be comprehended and made use of by the therapist in a clinically useful fashion not much will be accomplished in changing complex attitudes and emotions.

Verbal exchanges reveal the internal, mental and emotional experience of the patient, regardless of what the biofeedback instruments may indicate. The patient's verbal revelations about internal experience, and the reactions to such experiences provide rich guidelines to areas of conflict or anxiety, self-images, origins of the complaints, etc. The therapist's inquiries about these private areas can expand the patient's consciousness of historical exeriences which are related to current symptoms, and assist in revising internalized attitudes and current behavior.

For example, a patient may complain of fear of women, or of his sexual feeling for women, and the biofeedback read-outs will confirm the presence of physiological arousal in an increase in sympathetic or striate muscle tone. Eventually, though, through a mutual, verbal search of his past and present heterosexual relationships, the fear might be identified as fear of his rage against women, rather than the fear of women. This kind of internal confusion is not always evident in the first interview, nor in the physiological processes. It can become evident through introspection and insight.

Generally physiological arousal reflects heightened homeostatic functioning, but not the specific thoughts and feelings that are causing the overactivation, patient to patient (93). Evidently, physiology can respond to internal, psychological stimuli in terms of each person's personal interpretation of the stimuli. Two men may both experience an increase in arousal when sexually stimulated, one of whom would associate the arousal with anger, the other with pleasure. Thus, as Schacter and Singer (179) have postulated, individual differences among people can exist in terms of their subjective interpretation of their changes in physiologically based sensation. Verbal therapy, employing introspection as a basic technique is a necessary treatment modality for many patients who undergo clinical biofeedback. Whatever theoretical interpretation of human behavior one may favor, the clinical behavior of many patients requires introspective searches of the history and meaning of the presenting symptoms. The expressions of the physiological component of the symptoms through the biofeedback instruments can provide the patient with direct evidence of the complex, underlying attitudes related to the symptoms. It is then possible for a patient to identify the interaction between thinking and bodily expression of thought. Many of the symptoms presented in biofeedback settings arise in that interaction and are attended to by the patient when he or she looks within.

Internal searches

Internal searches are among the introspective methods of looking within one's self. The simplist application is asking simple questions: What came to mind? What did you feel...recognize...recall...experience...think...visualize? The more complex applications appear in such techniques as age regression, free association, planned searches (of one's home, or a given age, or a series of activities), first events (loneliness, fright, onset of symptom, developmental milestones, losses, traumas). Ongoing, at this moment, internal thoughts, body sensations, and feelings that are identified serve to integrate the past and present in regard to the symptoms. Often, as the therapist applies any technique, some of the others may be used as the patient moves from the present to the past, from one event to another, from a memory to an emotion. The dynamic character of people's internal lives are manifested in this approach to the mind-body-symptom process in clinical biofeedback.

The complex searches are most easily applied after the patient is deeply relaxed or in an hypnotic trance (219). In these states, ego controls are diminished in defensive functions and preconscious material can be more accessible to consciousness.

Hypnotism

If the therapist should wish to include in the preliminary stage a greater degree of control over thought processes and response sets hypnotism can be applied at the onset or during some period of a session. Hypnotism (110) appears to be centrally related to the focusing of thought, thereby narrowing mental content and inducing selective inattention (62). Affects and attitudes of a response-set are not automatically revised from those the patient experienced at the onset of the induction. Whatever attitude was there will usually predominate throughout the trance, unless changed by the therapist or patient. Sometimes patients will deliberately change mental content or affect without being instructed to do so; and sometimes the changes are involuntary. The latter process may be interpreted as the release of repressed material which is frequently related to the symptoms being treated. That is, the patient knows he or she is there for the treatment of particular symptoms. This conscious attitude can assume a directing role, or response-set, during induction, and set off an associational chain, evoking the repressed experiences that are related to the symptom formation.

Combining hypnotism and biofeedback procedures is perhaps most justifiable when the therapist wishes to accomplish general relaxation and induce an hypnotic trace simultaneously. The biofeedback would be used to provide the patient with an attention-focusing device, as well as assistance in achieving bodily relaxation. With the patient's attention focused on the feedback signal an hypnotic induction can be instituted (219). Some patients who are quite susceptible to hypnotism will enter a trance state during relaxation without an induction being applied.

Hypnotism and relaxation are not identical or interchangeable. A trance can be achieved without any physical or mental relaxation. Some patients assume that they are the same and during an induction will relax themselves automatically. If the therapist wishes to use relaxation as part of the hypnotic procedure he or she usually must include that method in the procedure. Relaxation itself, however, often leads to an hypnogogic state, a twilight zone between full awareness of the outer world and increased, free-flowing awareness of one's inner world. In the event of a patient may seem to be vulnerable to the latter state, the therapist can minimize its release through hypnotic instructions that will maintain necessary levels of attention to the outer world, thereby supporting repression.

Imagery

Relaxed states and the narrowing of consciousness brought about by biofeedback or hypnotism permits the therapist to apply imagery (183) as a part of clinical procedure. Gestalt therapy (157) makes frequent use of imagery as a means of integrating emotion, body, and mind. Behavior therapy (80, 120) has emphasized the use of imagery in the systematic desensitization of fears and phobias. Wolpe and Lazarus (230) have specifically adopted "emotive imagery' in changing self-attitudes. The patients are instructed to imagine scenes of adequacy, accomplishment, or self-assertion instead of their usual, ineffective patterns of response.

Images can be abstract or concrete. They can be scenes of real or imaginary living, of events, objects, body sensations, people, emotions, and so on. Images are the mental representations of experience, and they can be used in the clinical process in changing thought, feeling, or behavior.

Certain images can be used for most patients, regardless of the complaints. Visualizing the image of a quiet, tranquil scene during relaxation empties the mind of distressing thoughts as well as inducing a tranquil mental state. The tranquil state can also be used as a mental mechanism to cope with expected stress, as a sleeping pill for sleep-onset insomniacs, or as a general stress reducer.

The patient is asked to recall a real-life experience characterized by physical and mental tranquility. The scene should not contain any exciting, happy, or otherwise stimulating elements. Lying on a empty beach or in a hammock, or visualizing a calm pool, are the common scenes. The scene has the function of an internal mandala that the patient is perceiving within the mind's eye. Attention is focused, other thoughts are diminished, concentration is practiced, and the technique provides the patient with a coping mechanism to allay anxiety if it should erupt during relaxation.

One cannot force a recurrent thought out of the mind; nor can one be aware in fullest attention of two incompatible thoughts at the same time. The most effective way to remove distressing thoughts and rumination is to replace them with other thoughts. This is particularly necessary for obsessional persons who must fill their minds and focus their attention constantly in order to avoid awareness of anxiety or of emotions that are saturated with anxiety. The compulsive need to control can be temporarily outwitted in the obsessive-compulsive neurotics by use of the tranquil scene, or similar imagery. There are others who cannot assume the attitude of passively concentrating on the feedback signal or on the relaxation instructions. They need preliminary experience or training in focusing their thoughts, in maintaining in their minds a desired scene. Deliberate and precise training in cognitive rehearsals of real-life situations while fully alert provides these patients with the needed control to undertake relaxation.

Other imagery useful in treatment include the recall and strengthening of an experience of adequacy, self-esteem, and well-being (219, 229). This imagery can be used, too, in counteracting feelings of helplessness or loss of self-control that may emerge during relaxation or hypnotism.

Cognitive statements

Human thought is composed mostly of verbal statements. Such statements relate to one's comprehension and interpretation of experiences, to one's judgment of the experience, and to the process of anxiety in events that evoke anxiety. Covert discussion with one's self is often used as a method for the increase or decrease of anxiety and a plan for subsequent behavior. What one says to one's self about current and future events gives direction to responses of the moment, thereby influencing one's actual activities over time. Many such statements are conscious or preconscious and automatically regulate desirable or undesirable behavior.

Behavior therapy utilized cognitions of these sorts to change, to increase, or to decrease various clinically identifiable responses (136). A person whose anxiety occurs in a given set of circumstances, such as a job interview, may be telling him or herself that he or she is unlikable or incompetent, with the consequence of communicating those impressions to the interviewer. The interviewer then justifiably concludes that the applicant would not get along with other employees and would not be able to handle the work. Rejecting the applicant confirms the applicant's self-statements. The rejection and the self-statements serve as negative reinforcers by removing the applicant from the anxiety-provoking situations of the interview. On more complex levels of personality, the patient's fundamental source of the interview anxiety may well be a matter of fear of social relations, separation anxiety by assuming an adult role, or some other powerful but obscure motivation. If that should be true, it requires eventual identification and treatment. In the behavioral model, that identification would be accomplished in subsequent sessions during wider explorations of the possible source of anxiety.

On the level of treating the interview anxiety through changes in cognitions, several techniques could be applied. One is to bring to full awareness the negative self-statements, in this case, "I am never liked. I'm not very smart, etc." These can be changed to positive, realistic statements, "I am likable; people have treated me as though they like me. I've learned how to do this work and I can do it, etc." The anxiety itself can be minimized concurrently through relaxation and biofeedback, if a multimodal approach is being applied. Changing negative statements to positive ones can also be applied in other kinds of situations identified by the patient as similar in pathology.

Cognitive rehearsal is a common, normal, imaginary process many people go through in preparation for coping with various future experiences. People fantasize the future event, what will take place and how they and others will act and speak. The neurotic often clothes others in the fantasy with distortions that arise from his or her own anger or apprehensions of being ill-treated. This rehearsal then prepares the person with a self-fulfilling prophecy of one's own ill treatment by others. Self-destructive fantasies can be brought to awareness and they can be deliberately changed by imagining a more realistic, productive rehearsal of the future event. Rather than rehearsing on the fringe of, or below awareness, rejection, coldness, disdain, or hostility from others, or self-defeating thoughts and acts by one's self, one can imagine ordinary and appropriate statements and acts taking place. These appropriate behaviors can then be practiced in vivo.

Systematic desensitization

Wolpe's method (229) of treating fears or phobias in the classical neurotic is probably the most widely used technique in the behavior therapist's repertoire. The structure and process of the method have also been adapted to assertive training with good results. Modifications of the method are useful, too, in treating the fears and phobias in other clinical syndromes in which bound or diffuse anxiety is a presenting problem.

The method does not presume to deal with complex issues of self-identity, intrapsychic conflicts, or the refined processes of human relationships (193, 229). The basic concept of the method is that the symptom is the neurosis, that the psychopathology is a learned behavior amenable to unlearning or deconditioning. Hence, the procedure is applied to the symptom about which the patient complains. Anxiety is viewed as a learned fear and that it is incompatible with relaxation. The general procedure is devoted to the induction of mental and physical relaxation and the presentation to the patient of elements of the phobia in gradations of their anxiety-provoking potency, as shown in Table 5 (220).

The hierarchy of items is a list of verbal statements constructed by the patient and therapist, starting with a lead item that evokes no anxiety when imagined by the patient. Each of the following items elicits increasing degrees of anxiety. The patient is deeply relaxed (Chapter 6) and when anxiety is elicited the patient counterconditions the anxiety by virtue of the relaxed state. In this fashion, degree by degree, the patient's anxiety response to the phobic object is deconditioned.

Wolpe used Jacobson's (229) progressive relaxation as the method to induce relaxation. He monitored the onset of felt anxiety

Table 5. Hierarchy of interview-anxiety items.

Frequency of Presentation*		Items	Sequence of Presentation
/	1	See interviewer	18
/xx	3	Enter office	17
///	3	Speak to secretary	16
///	3	At door of office	15
///x	4	Walk down hall	41
////	4	Leave elevator	13
////	4	Elevator ascending	12
////x	5	Enter elevator	11
/////x	6	Walk to elevator	10
//////xx	8	Enter building	9
////////	8	Leave cab	8
////////	8	Cab stops at building	7
////////xx	10	In cab on way to interview	6
//////////	10	Enter cab to go to interview	5
//////////	10	Thinking of going to the interview	4
//////////	10	Having name of potential buyer	3
//////////	10	Thinking of phoning a secretary	2
//////////	10	Thinking of making call next week	1

*The sign *1* indicates presentation of item; the sign *x* indicates that the item evoked felt-anxiety; presentation then discontinued; administration resumed from Item No. 1 in same or following session. Relaxing scene: image of symphony concert. Source: I. Wentworth-Rohr, Symptoms, insight, and behavior therapy. Reprinted from *The Psychoanalytic Review,* 1970, *57,* 1, p.57, through the courtesy of the Editors and publisher, National Psychological Association for Psychoanalysis, New York, New York.

by instructing the patient to raise a forefinger to signal the onset. Other relaxation methods are equally effective (Chapter 6), and when augmented with biofeedback instrumentation the depth and generalization of the relaxed state is increased. The biofeedback instruments are also used to monitor the onset of anxiety during desensitization by both patient and therapist. The physiological system monitored is selected on the grounds of the residence of anxiety or other clinical considerations. The frontales muscles remain a useful site for monitoring changes in the arousal level, expressed through striate muscles. Often the changes are quite small, less than 1uV, and must be carefully distinguished from an orienting reflex or the result of other stimuli. The patient's close, but passive, self-monitoring, after instruction in noting any changes in feedback signals, is a reliable index in tracking affectual responses to planned stimulation, such as the anxiety items.

In the treatment of a woman for acute episodes of tachycardia (up to 120 bpm) and high blood pressure (170/120), a significant increase of 1-2uV over the relaxed level of .50-1.00uV occured in the frontales muscles during the third clinical session. She reported that she had spontaneously thought of her upcoming professional examinations, the simultaneous experience of anxiety, and the awareness of an increase in the EMG audio feedback, even though the increase in rate of clicks was quite small. It then became clear to her that considerable apprehension about the examination, as well as her stated complaints, was contributing to the current stress. Desensitization of test anxiety evoked while imagining that she was being observed interviewing a patient was conducted. She also free-associated, covertly, to diverse, tension-laden situations while self-monitoring changes in frontales and would re-relax herself each time the frontales level increased. After several sessions of practice she reported significant generalizations of relaxation to several of the anxiety-provoking situations. Both heart rate and blood pressure returned to normal levels after 10 sessions.

Occasional patients decondition a fear, or stress response, by merely constructing the hierarchy. These are usually insightful people who have well-differentiated egos in the areas of life that the fears occur. They also can make healthy resolutions in their attitudes about how to cope with the stressors. Simply drawing their attention to the precise aspects of the fear-provoking situation, or object, during the construction of a hierarchy allows them to focus on the realities of their misinterpretations and to experience less anxiety.

Specific phobias (dogs, spiders, bridges, moving vehicles) remit most easily to systematic desensitization. The more global the stimulus (agoraphobia), or the response (diffuse anxiety or panics, regardless of the stimulus), the more difficult the anxiety is to treat (115). However, these assessments should be made for each patient. For some, a specific phobia may remit, but the underlying diffuse, chronic anxiety may not, or to only a limited degree. The patient who presents several phobias is likely to be suffering from more than neurotic psychopathology.

Desensitization of phobias in schizophrenia is best attempted after the patient has recompensated from an overt psychotic episode. The ego must be sufficiently intact so that repression is adequate and the patient is capable of conscious, appropriate cooperation in the application of the technique. Our experience suggests that if the therapist can identify an anxiety-related symptom in the recompensated patient, systematic desensitization is useful (Chapter 14).

Assertive training

Self-assertion is the expression of one's experience in an appropriate manner and context. It is not confined to the expression of anger or hostility, as is commonly misinterpreted. Assertiveness may be in opposition to others, or in moving toward others in a receptive and accepting mode. It may be in the form of giving, being available to receive, voicing one's needs and wishes, or merely expressing one's covert reaction to the acts of others.

Deficiencies in assertiveness are commonly reported in the dyadic and primary relationships with one's children, spouse, and parents. Difficulties also occur in the expression of emotions and sexuality, in resisting intimidation by clerks and other people rendering services, and with authority figures. Where anxiety is the disabling agent as consciously perceived by the patient, the treatment procedure is virtually identical with that used in desensitization. However, the more vital the relationship, such as in the primary dyads, the more complexities abound, and verbal psychotherapy is needed to clarify the complexities.

In adapting self-assertive training to the clinical biofeedback approach in treating phobias, the patient selects a person who evokes anxiety, which, in turn, blocks the patient's realistic self-expression. A hierarchy is constructed of items of verbal expressions of self-assertion in the context of that relationship. The patient is then relaxed and the hierarchy is applied systematically to decondition the anxiety response. The patient may also be guided in making initial and appropriate attempts at self-assertion in vivo (230).

Aversive conditioning

Aversive conditioning is the application of an unpleasant or punitive stimulus to a behavior that is undesired. Rachman and Teasdale (164, p. xii) state that "...aversion therapy is an attempt to associate an undesirable behavior pattern with unpleasant stimulation *or* to make the unpleasant stimulation a consequence of the undesirable behavior." Aversion therapy has rarely been used in biofeedback procedures, and strictly speaking the biofeedback has served only as a means of monitoring a physiological process while the aversive stimulus was applied. A classical use was by Lang and Melamed (118) in the case of a nine-month old infant suffering from ruminative vomiting. When food reached his stomach a reverse peristaltic reflex was stimulated resulting in regurgitation. The treatment procedure was placement of EMG surface electrodes to monitor regurgitation. When the EMG signals reflected the onset of the muscular spasms after the food reached the stomach, a mild electric shock was administered. The rumination was extinguished in six sessions. The technique has been successfully replicated by others. A similar use of aversion therapy in biofeedback was in the treatment of torticollis by Cleeland (43). EMG signals from the spastic sternocleidomastoideus muscles were monitored and electric shock was applied when the spasm reached an undesirable tension level.

Recordkeeping

Recordkeeping is remarkably useful in clinical biofeedback. The patient is instructed in maintaining a log throughout the day of the course of the symptom. The log may be simply a page a day in a small notebook, showing two axes, one for intensity and the other for time of occurrence. If vasoconstriction is being logged, hourly readings of a wrist thermometer can be charted of any changes in peripheral temperature. Insomnia, phobic episodes, eating habits, toilet functions, headaches, or any other symptom can be tracked. On the reverse side of the page, the patient can note where he was when the entry was made, what was going on, what was being felt and thought, and any odd associations to significant changes. Stressors are commonly discovered by the patient's careful attention to the symptomatic responses and the context of their occurrence. These stressors are then more manageable by the patient, as well as identified for treatment.

Varieties of record forms can be devised to track the patient's particular symptoms or patterns of behavior that are under treatment. Brown (28), Fuller (72), and Gaarder (74) have offered various recordkeeping formats that the therapist can use or adapt to clinical cases. Other examples are in Appendix A.

Recordkeeping by the therapist over each session is essential to the tracking of changes which can reflect internal processes. The precise logging over each session of baselines and changes in physiological parameters provides measurements of psychophysiological functioning, for both the therapist's and patient's knowledge and use. The basal and terminal readouts of the physiology are only the minimal records. In between, notations of changes in range of signal, averages of the signal over repeated time periods, changes in breathing, motor restlessness, and any verbalizations or expressions of affect, are noted as they occur. These mind-body manifestations are clinical data for further exploration, when appropriate, as well as measurements of the effects of the treatment procedure.

Autogenic therapy

Autogenic therapy consists of a series of phrases that the patient recites while relaxing and attending to his or her body (28, 125). Autosuggestion in the context of relaxation appears to be the effective agent. The method is divided into three categories of such training, beginning with the focusing on the body and the recitation of phrases that institute changes in afferent-efferent loops and in neuromotor activity. The first series of exercises are the ones most commonly adopted by biofeedback clinicians. They begin with autohypnotic kinds of phrases that result in relaxation, mental and physical: My arm is heavy. My hand is warm. I feel relaxed. My legs are heavy and relaxed, etc. These kinds of statements of heaviness, warmth, and relaxation are made about each area and part of the body, slowly and passively. Other self-statements abound after relaxation has begun in order to quiet thinking: I am at peace. My mind is quiet. My attention is turned inward. Warmth is flowing to my arms...my legs.

The autogenic method is routinely applied in biofeedback in treating vasoconstrictive disorders as a means of increasing blood flow to the extremities. Luthe and Schultz (125) also report successful applications in many other kinds of disorders of physiology, as well as in the cardiovascular system. Obviously, lowering sympathetic tone reduces the innervation of the smooth musculature; striate muscles also relax the patient lies quietly and slows cognitive activity through the repetition of the self-statements.

When included in clinical biofeedback, the procedure is usually voiced by the therapist during appropriate phases of general relaxation training. The bioinstruments serve to feedback changes in the physiology as in BFT. The patient is trained to apply the phrases during home practice of relaxation and to abort impending episodes of stress or vasospasms.

In summary, most biofeedback clinicians incorporate in their treatment plans well-established methods of psychotherapy. These are the operations that precede the machine operations, such as applying progressive relaxation, or they may be used during the machine operation, such as using autogenic phrases, or applied after the use of the machines have accomplished the desired physiological change, such as desensitization. This clinical procedure has a self-imposed limitation of not dealing with the complex, internalized domains of the personality in as detailed and as integrative a process as long-term, intensive psychotherapy evidently does. Rather, it is applied to narrowly defined symptoms, signs, or patterns of behavior with the goals of symptom reduction and overt change in behavior. Complex insight into one's human experience is not the goal of BFT, or of clinical beiofeedback either, when the procedure is applied under its own restraints. In this respect, biofeedback falls within the category of time-limited, symptom-oriented, ego-level treatment methods. When complex intrapersonal data emerge during biofeedback applications, traditional psychotherapy approaches are needed.

Part III

CLINICAL APPLICATIONS

Chapter 9

INTRODUCTION

The following chapters contain some representatives case studies and details of the clinical procedures used. The validity of the procedures is far from being experimentally validated, but sufficient clinical success has encouraged clinicians to apply them, especially in cases where standard procedures have had limited or no success. Many of the relatively simple and straightforward complaints and their treatment have been studied under controlled conditions more rigorously than those that are quite complex in diagnoses and symptom formation.

For the latter, treatment planning and applications and research designs are necessarily more difficult to formulate and justify within the paradigm of biofeedback. Almost without exception, these kinds of patients will have undergone conventional treatment procedures with poor or mixed results. Durations of the symptoms are usually measured in years, even decades. The poor remission rate and the years of suffering appear to have led the patients or their therapists to try clinical biofeedback for symptomatic relief. For some, the diagnosis is unknown, although the symptom may be relatively simple, such as episodic tension headaches. Conversely, the symptom can involve more than one organ system and to severe degrees. Clinical biofeedback may then be limited to contributing to the patient's health through reducing stress levels or the intensity of some of the symptoms.

Each patient, regardless of diagnosis, is approached individually, even if the presenting symptom is known to remit well to biofeedback. The clinical assessment and treatment planning include a large number of variables: age, sex, education, intelligence, diagnosis, life situation, motivation, energy level, and the integration of the biofeedback into any other ongoing treatment procedures.

Patients are approached in a prescribed series of stages; each stage is varied to fit each patient:

1. Diagnostic interviews, including referrals for specialized diagnostic examinations where indicated.
2. Explanation of the biofeedback procedure and ancillary techniques that might be used in the treatment plan.
3. Explanation of use of psychological tests and rating scales and recordkeeping by the patient.
4. Baseline studies of the relevant physiological systems.
5. Introduction and training in the use of the biofeedback instruments.
6. Training in general relaxation and stress reduction.
7. Application of the individualized treatment plans.
8. Continuous assessment of the patient's response to treatment and interpretation of the efficacy and consequences of each technique used.
9. Weaning from the instruments and training in generalization to real life of acquired skills.
10. Termination studies through repeat of baseline measurements and post-tests.
11. Follow-up assessments and surveys.
12. Refresher training when needed.

Some details of these stages have been described in previous chapters and are illustrated in the case materials. Particular attention is directed to the use of relaxation training, augmented by biofeedback instruments, for all patients as the foundation for the application of the treatment techniques. Usually the EMG, frontales placement, is the first instrument to be used in relaxation training (See Chapter 6). The EMG feedback signal serves as a concrete modality for the patient's use in learning the subjective nature of a relaxed state, and in reducing mental and physical levels of activity through self-intervention and regulation. When other physiological systems are implicated in the complaints or are the residences of the anxiety or stress, the appropriate feedback instrument is used in tandem with the EMG to augment relaxation training, as well as to retrain any dysfunctional physiological system.

The procedure is accomplished with considerable efficiency when the targeted physiological system that is overactivated and is disrupting thought and attention. is directly modified with feedback instrumentation in conjunction with relaxation. When the mental and physiological criteria for relaxation have been reached, the therapist can then apply specific treatment techniques for symptoms with each patient.

The need to transfer the training to real life is brought up in the initial interview and is restated frequently across sessions. The success of transfer is judged by the amount and kind of change occurring in the presenting problems under real-life conditions.

Progress in weaning from the therapist and the biofeedback machines can can be tested through charting use and success of self-relaxation at home and elsewhere. If progress outside the office is not rapid enough, resistance or dependency should be analyzed. Weaning from audio tapes is sometimes equally necessary. A few patients may shift dependency on the machines to dependency on a tape used in home practice. These patients can be weaned from the tape by setting a timer that rings just before the tape ends. The patient should complete the taped exercises as though he were listening to the tape. The timer can be retarded a minute or two every given number of runs of the tape, and occassionally a portion of the omitted part of the tape can be replayed to vary the schedule of reinforcement.

Criterion for success in biofeedback applications is based on one or both of subjective and objective changes. Objective measures of changes in blood pressure or muscle tone are examples of the latter forms of measurement. But even with that criterion met, the patient should have also changed stress reactions, improved in other home-ostatic functions, alleviated environmental sources of stress or whatever else was implicated in the complaints in the first place. Careful recordkeeping by the patient can provide objective measures of such progress.

In assessing other targeted physiological dysfunctions the patient continues to provide his own baselines, in addition to other criteria for assessing change. Bidirectional control of neuromotor dysfunctions can be used both as training techniques (139) and a criterion for success in training. Follow-up reports of at least 6 months after termination is a reasonable minimum of time to determine the durability of change in symptoms.

Various diagnostic categories of patients necessarily respond differently to clinical biofeedback. The patients who are least amenable, if at all, are those suffering from disorders of affect of psychotic proportions. Some reports have appeared (177,219) that described useful applications in patients diagnosed as manic-depressive. However, it is striking that the patients had also been diagnosed, at times, as schizophrenic. Endogenous depression does not remit to biofeedback treatment. Even reactive depressions are also not appropriate where the depression is a result of early loss—real or an interpersonal deprivation with a significant parent.

The schizophrenic populations are among the more complicated and variable patients in their symptom formation and success rate. But many of these patients have been responsive to the multimodal treatment procedures used in reducing some of their anxiety-related symptoms. The schizophrenia, of course, is not appropriate for biofeedback treatment.

One subgroup of schizophrenics which has responded poorly to biofeedback is the somatizer. Their complaint for biofeedback therapy is muscle spasms. The spasms travel from one region of the body to another as each spasm is reduced in biofeedback. Ego development is primitive in areas of relationships. Dependency on a parent or spouse is the central fact of their lives. They are unable to make any use of biofeedback training, relaxation methods, or behavioral techniques, and the poor response is evident within a few sessions.

Conversion neurotics require concurrent psychotherapy (219) to deal with the underlying conflicts. The few reports and our limited experience in treating conversion cases indicate that symptom substitution is inevitable when symptom-oriented biofeedback is applied without concurrent psychotherapy. It is possible that an occassional conversion case will have "outgrown" the conflict and the conversion sympton persists on the basis of habit. The symptom may then be treated with biofeedback methods with reasonable success. The diagnosis of conversion neurosis based on the symptom would then, of course, be in error.

Many patients in their sixth and later decades have great difficulty in revising physiological dysfunctions. If they should be successful they have difficulty in carrying the changes over to real life or in maintaining such revisions. The older the patient, the more guarded the prognosis. Our experience suggests that how "aged" the aged patient is is the diagnostic criterion to determine patient selection. We have treated patients up to the age eighty-one for headaches, insomnia, muscle spasms, anxiety, conversion symptoms, and phobias, with mixed results.

In selecting patients, the healthy, youthful, educated, intelligent, motivated people whose symptoms are psychogenic and well defined are needless to say, the most rewarding. These kinds of people are also responsive to any form of therapy, even if the symptoms are based on physiological dysfunctions that do not appear to be learned. They learn the techniques rapidly and develop excellent skills in self-regulation. When they practice their exercises and skills they control their symptoms satisfactorily.

Variations in technique and patient selection are currently reported in journals and at conventions. The accumulation of research data and clinical experience suggests that technique development will be a continuing process. As the usefulness and limitations of the procedure are confirmed, the approaches in the case materials presented here will be refined and improved. These approaches are in general use and may serve as guides for most clinical applications.

Chapter 10

STRIATE MUSCULATURE

Biofeedback applications in dysfunctions of striate musculature focuses on reducing spasticity, increasing voluntary control over viable muscle groups, and learning to control the interactions of synergistic or agonist-antagonist muscle groups. Voluntary muscle dysfunctions may arise from psychogenic causes, from central or peripheral damage to the neural channels, or to damaged muscle fibers. Biochemical imbalances such as low potassium level may also be etiological to muscle dysfunctions. Continual attention to diagnosis is essential in conducting neuromotor biofeedback in order to test the validity of the treatment procedure.

Technical issues in EMG machine applications (regardless of the diagnosis) includes the preparation of the skin for efficient electrode performance. Brisk rubbing at the site with an alcohol wipe is usually sufficient to remove the film of oils, dead skin, or makeup. A more refined method, after wiping the site, is to rub the site briskly with an abrasive skin cleanser. A Q-Tip can then be dipped in more abrasive

149

and twirled at the center of the electrode site. In order to have accurate readings of muscle output microvoltage, the electrode impendance should be below 30,000 ohms. Lower impedance is even preferred, say 5,000-10,000 ohms. Manufacturers' specifications recommend acceptable levels for particular machines.

Most surface electrodes are attached to the skin with double-adhesive collars. The collar is adhered to the face of the electrode rim surrounding the cup, and the cup is then filled with an electrode cream or gel. When the obverse protective covering of the adhesive collar is removed, the electrode is placed at the selected site. Ordinarily the two active electrodes are placed along axis of the muscle, each electrode abutting the belly of the muscle; the ground is placed in between or over a nearby bone. Basmajian (9) recommends 6 to 10 cm maximum distance between active electrodes. Distances will vary with the length of the muscle being monitored and the physical constraints of anatomy.

The electrodes should be firmly pressed onto the skin, and the exposed rim of the adhesive collar should also be carefully pressed to the skin. If any leaks out under the collar, the collar should be replaced. The close adhesion of the electrode to the skin prevents environmental signals from entering the cup of the electrode.

The signals picked up by the surface electrodes are a summation of muscle activity within the area of the electrodes. If the placement is over or near a pulse or artery, the output signal will contain a rhythmic artifact. Other normal and rhythmic muscle activity, such as in breathing, swallowing and peristalsis, can appear as in signals imposed on those of the targeted muscles. The therapist can accommodate the machine output signal by setting the upper end of the threshold to exclude those signals. For that matter, most patients can habituate to and ignore the unwanted signals during feedback upon being instructed.

Microvolt amplitude for most normal muscle, while the subject is awake and under resting conditions is quite low, below 2uV. Hig-

[1]Instruments used for all patients reported on are the Autogenic Systems, EMG 1500 or 1700, Thermistor 2000, and Biofeedback Research Institute, GSR 505 (Appendix C). Instruments from other manufacturers that were used will be noted in the text. Information regarding instrumentation is used in referenced cases appears in the references.

her magnitudes are suggestive of spasticity in the muscles being monitored.[1] The highest spasm we have encountered was over 250uV in the upper trapezius of a woman of multiple diagnoses and complaints (219). Generally, 1 to 2uV is mild tension level, 3 to 4uV is moderate, and above 4 to 5uV is considered significantly high and usually painful. Microvoltage criteria for determining when a muscle is relaxed vary with the construction of instruments by various manufacturers, and also by different standards of the users. We have had little difficulty in reducing psychogenic striate muscle spasms to below 1.5uV for most patients in most regions, and usually below 1uV. Combining the verbal relaxation technique with the EMG feedback perhaps accounts for the lower levels achieved than those reported by other clinicians (2, 17, 74). Most patients reach criterion during the first few EMG feedback-relaxation sessions, but require treatment of other problems or any other spastic regions before they can generalize and maintain low muscle tension levels in vivo.

The initial training in striate muscle relaxation can be done with frontales placement, which accomplishes the dual goal of reducing any tension level in the forehead and training in general relaxation. With the frontales placement, the contract-relax activity of muscles is demonstrated by instructing the patient to wrinkle-relax the forehead, close-open the eyes, and clench the teeth. Baseline EMG levels of contiguous areas should be monitored in order to discriminate the sources of the output signal, other than the frontales, when the initial training is being conducted. Frequently, the TMJs and the upper trapezius are spastic and the frontales readings are confounded. Tension headaches frequently include spasticity in areas contiguous to the frontales region. Frontales tension reduction itself is not sufficient to achieve general relaxation.

All motor training, increase or decrease, should include gaining voluntary control of the implicated muscle in *both* directions, and the success of the desired change in the dysfunction is measured in vivo, as well as in the office. Ocassionally, a desired change will be subjective without an expected corresponding physiological change. These successes may well illustrate placebo effects; or, after general relaxation has been achieved, the subjective distress of mild splasticity is no longer experienced as distressful. Low anxiety levels do appear to decrease the mental "painfullness" of pain.

Spasticity and Pain

Some patients will report pain in a muscle group which turns out to have low microvolt levels. The possibility of referred pain from another region should then be assessed. Chronic pain patients frequently have low tension levels in some of their areas of pain, suggesting that the pain is psychological, rather than originating in anatomical change.

Case examples: Carol was a fifty year-old writer who had been suffering cervical spine arthritis for several years. She complained of chronic neck and shoulder pain of some 2 years' duration, and being unable to raise her right arm above chest level or to turn her head to the right.

The initial interview revealed an appropriately dressed, cooperative, articulate woman. She described the complaints in detail, adding that the neck and shoulder pain was often exacerbated by sitting at the desk and writing. Intermittent episodes of pain also occurred in her right knee and lumbar region. She was mildly depressed in reaction to the pain and interference in her work.

The treatment plan was EMG frontales placement and relaxation training; EMG reduction of spasms in neck and shoulder regions; retraining in right arm elevation and head rotation; anti-pain training through visual imagery, and relaxation.

Basal tension level averages were: frontales 1.0uV, increasing to 12uV when suffering a headache; cervical spine muscles 7.5uV; right middle trapezius 14uV; right deltoids under 3uV. Initial basal levels across the early treatment sessions varied from 1-2uV to 7-14uV in relation to general tension levels, number of hours writing, and pain levels in her neck upon awakening.

Carol responded well to the relaxation training and the BFT of neck and shoulder muscles. Reducing the localized spasms through EMG feedback while relaxed was preliminary to gradually, over sessions, rotating her head and elevating her arm. Visual imagery was utilized to minimize pain. After nine weekly sessions the spasticity was reduced, she could turn her head and elevate her arm above her head without significant pain. Thirteen months after termination a follow-up found the changes to persist, provided she was practicing general relaxation to reduce reactive spasticity.

Neuromotor Rehabilitation

Gaarder (74) and Basmajian (9, 11) list various neuromotor disorders caused by injury or disease for which EMG biofeedback is an appropriate adjunctive technique. Among these are joint repair, foot drop, tendon transfer, flaccidity and spasticity encountered in stroke victims, and various neurological lesions resulting in loss of motor control which can be compensated through recruitment of other motor fibers.

Retraining in rehabilitation cases should be initiated on a healthy, easily controlled, muscle group, such as the forearm flexors. If the site selected is the muscle contralateral to the damaged muscle, the training also provides an ongoing criterion for the patient in learning to increase-decrease motor action in a similar but not impaired region.

Equipment should be flexible and adaptable to the presenting complaints. Re-establishing synergistic control over a joint is best conducted by a multichannel EMG so that each of the opposing muscle groups can be carefully retrained through negative and positive feedback simultaneously in precise amounts. Discrimination of proprioceptive input to the central system in neuromotor rehabilitation demands the best equipment available. Sensitivity level of the EMG should be at least 0.1uV to 1000uV, with response time settings of immediate to 100-second epochs, if not higher. Both auditory and visual feedback modalities are desirable in order to reinforce the patient's feedback information processing. Standard and miniature surface electrodes, as well as needle electrodes, are necessary for different procedures (9).

Providing biofeedback applications in rehabilitation is probably a speciality within the specialty. The diversity of conditions appearing, the endless variety of symptomatologies, and the wide range of competencies required to develop treatment plans using feedback instrumentation suggests that either the widely trained specialist should be the biofeedback therapist, or that a skilled technician under supervision of the specialist apply the technique. As Basmajian (11) suggests, the use of the EMG in rehabilitation medicine "expands the tools of the physical and occupational therapist."

Another specific contribution to rehabilitating patients is by applying clinical biofeedback to reduce stress levels (11). These patients can have marked stress reactions to their disabilities and even to their rehabilitation programs. Reducing the anxiety and overemotional reactions in these patients permits their rehabilitation therapists to conduct their established programs free of the psychological disruptions caused by stress. Cerebral palsy patients, for example, can become extremely frustrated by their poor motor control, and as they tense muscles to improve the control they can suffer increased stress levels. Applying relaxation tenchique with EMG feedback augmentation in patients who are overstressed can be a routine contribution to rehabilitation services.

> *Case example:* David was an active man of many interests who suf-
> fered a left-side cerebrovascular accident in his sixth decade,
> resulting in moderate right-side paralysis of both gross and fine
> movements. Recovery was limited to ambulation with a walker
> and poor fine-motor control in the right hand. Speech was clear.
> Referral to biofeedback was to decrease his general tension level
> and to increase neuromotor functions in his right arm and hand.
>
> On interview, the patient was articulate, highly motivated,
> and fully cooperative. His disability had interfered with his work
> and his life in general, and he was eager to continue the gains he
> had been making in his rehabilitation program. Other com-
> plaints were elevated blood pressure, irregular bowel move-
> ments, sleep disturbances, stomach spasms, and weakness and
> poor control over right arm and fine right hand movements.
>
> The treatment plan was to reduce the general tension level
> through relaxation training and to apply EMG training to the
> right musculature.
>
> Relaxation was taught with EMG frontales placement feed-
> back. Response was satisfactory and within 3 weeks he reported
> improvement in sleep, bowel functions, and absence of stomach

spasms. He practiced the relaxation regularly, as well as continued his rehabilitation program. BFT of voluntary control of right arm movements showed gradual improvement across sessions. He was able to place his right hand behind his head, and to perform other hand-arm functions that did not require much strength or fine control, within nine sessions. BFT in holding a pencil and in writing continued with feedback from wrist and hand muscles, alternating with forearm muscle training.

BFT of his right leg was conducted over the next 10 sessions to increase control and to reduce his complaint of stiffness. Movements included rotation, extension and flexion of the right leg and foot. Microvoltage levels increased gradually over several sessions, accompanied by mild improvement in voluntary control of the leg and foot.

At the end of 21 sessions he was able to manipulate his thumb with satisfactory control, handwriting was improved though still quite poor, and sleep was stabilized. He was more proficient in use of a walker, blood pressure was within normal limits and at the lowest level in several years, and his Valium dosage was decreased significantly.

Tension Headache

Tension headaches are caused by psychogenic spasms of the muscles of the head and neck regions (30, 140). Commonly, the temperomandibular joint (TMJ), the frontales, the scalp, or the cervical spine muscles are implicated in the complaint. Some patients report chronic pain, some report recurrent episodes. The latter are often related to environmental stressors (work, childcare, marital strife). Differentiating from intracranial tumors, vascular problems, malocclusions, or other serious etiologies is preliminary to treatment.

The routine application is the surface placement of each active electrode over each frontalis muscle with the reference in between. (32, 34), and application of the relaxation procedure. During the early sessions, other head-neck regions should be monitored, while the patient is relaxed, to rule out spasticity, especially in the TMJs.

Training in maintaining relaxation in the spastic muscle is also conducted while the therapist is describing to the patient the patient's stressors or phobias. These may be in the form of desensitization heirarchies (229), or merely by naming the stressors and allowing the patient to conduct his or her own counterconditioning. That is, the patient visualizes the phobic object or stressor while relaxed and reduces muscle tension and arousal levels when becoming aware of an increase in level.

Using an artificial stressor such as subtracting serial 7s is less effective and less reliable in counterconditioning than using the patient's stated stressors. The use of an impersonal stressor is applicable as a training device for patients whose severe, diffuse anxieties are evoked at full intensity by imagining their own stressors. After these patients have achieved some decrease in the intensity of anxiety and have good control in self-relaxation, the personal stressors are applied.

In treating tension headaches in women, the menstrual cycle must be carefully tracked in order to determine whether their headaches are directly caused by hormonal levels or are in addition to endocrine cycles.

Minor spasms that have been masked by severe pains can rise to awareness when the severe pains or tension levels have decreased. One patient reported throat constriction, another a slight tightness in the pectorales, a third in the middle trapezius. As with other such complaints in healthy patients, these mild spasms were reduced in one or two EMG applications concurrent with the general application.

> *Case examples:* Alice was a twenty-nine year-old married woman with two small children. The only complaint was chronic tension headaches for about 2 years' duration. Her history and other examinations were unremarkable. The possibility that her marriage was troubled was suggested by her lengthy denial of any marital stress. The treatment plan was EMG feedback to augment training in relaxation. Basal EMG frontales reading was severe (10 to 12uV). She could not respond to GSR relaxation training, probably because of a fear of letting go. Jacobson's progressive relaxation was then used with good success. Frontales level decreased consistently over the first several sessions,

and her record of headache frequency and intensity showed a corresponding decrease to about one a week. She learned to reduce the frenzy of her daily schedule to handle pressures with less anxiety and to assert herself with her husband more successfully. These latter gains were the result of listening to her gratuitously voiced complaints about her marriage during later sessions and to her own resolutions of the difficulties. After 16 treatment sessions she stated that she rarely suffered a headache and felt she could deal with her other problems more satisfactorily.

A more complicated referral was that of Diane, a forty-seven year-old single woman of borderline intelligence, suffering from multiple medical complaints which had been treated over the 30-odd years of clinical attendance. The complaints included skin disorders, cervical arthritis, episodic pain in her thighs and chest, nervousness, nausea, occasional vomiting, falling, dropping objects, insomnia and periods of drinking. Many of these complaints were recurrent and may have been related to anxiety and poor health habits. There was no neurological basis for the tension headaches.

On referral to biofeedback she was found to be rather poorly groomed, quite angry, and critical of hospitals, her family, and her former bosses. She demanded sleeping pills and pills for her headaches. Most of the first interview was devoted to alleviating her rage and attempting to explain biofeedback technique and muscle relaxation. Her history suggested an impulse disorder, characterized by violent outbursts when criticized or restricted. She was aware of these episodes and knew that she was "dangerous" but "couldn't help it if people push me."

The headaches began at about age sixteen. The pain radiated across her face and forehead, over her scalp, across the shoulders, and up her neck. The EMG placements were frontales, right and left TMJs, and upper trapezius to reduce spasms. All regions were mild to severe in intensity. There was a moderate level of tension in the left TMJ during relaxation, which responded well to EMG feedback. After several sessions of muscle relaxation and reduction of the spasticity, it was evident that the spasms were reactive to a dental disorder, aggravated by stress and rage at which times she would clench her teeth. Her emotional troubles also caused sleeplessness, nausea, and other, hysterical-like symptoms.

These relationships were explained repeatedly over the remaining sessions. She learned to recognize that during the days she was not enraged or anxious, she was free of pain, nausea, and insomnia. However, her impulse control was so poor that she would be enraged as often as not, and her pain would return. She had been referred to a dentist by the third session but never made an appointment. On termination, after 11 sessions, she could reduce most head pains by relaxing her jaw while she practiced general relaxation. Sleep also improved during her calmer periods.

Follow-up after several months revealed that most of the pains had diminished. She was unable to improve impulse control and quite angrily declined to return for biofeedback retraining or to re-enter psychiatric treatment.

Temperomandibular Joint Spasm

Bruxism (38,39,40) is the grinding of one's teeth and clenching of the jaw muscles, particularly during sleep. The grinding can lead to dental problems and to muscle spasms in the jaw and head region. Clenching the teeth is frequent reaction to pain, stress, fright, anger, hostility, and anxiety. The cliche, "grit your teeth and carry on," is well known to most people. In his detailed chapter on eitology and treatment of TMJ dysfunctions, Cannistraci (38) suggested that the "direct cause" is stress. A chronic, isometric contraction may be present.

Biofeedback treatment has been described in the previous case of Diane whose complaint was tension headache, and the etiology was left side TMJ spasm arising from malocclusion and aggravated by stress. The TMJ muscles should be routinely monitored, at least once, in all biofeedback referrals. Reducing a mild spasm, or determining that the muscle contractions are not equal in intensity in both joints, is helpful in treatment or disposition. Any persistence in TMJ malfunctioning should be referred for dental examinations. Spasms in the neck and head regions that arise from TMJ conditions can be reduced through EMG feedback but will soon recur if the causes are not treated.

The criterion for spasm in the TMJ, according to Cannistraci (40) is any level of microvoltage found, or as diagnosed by palpation. Our experience had been similar in that a wide range of tension levels is reported, whether or not the patient complains of clenching or bruxism. Evidently some patients with low tension level will suffer discomfort, while others report none.

Routinely, for TMJ complaints, the frontales, TMJ, trapezius, and sternocleidomastoideus muscles should be monitored for spasticity. One usually finds other muscles in the head-neck region in at least a mild spasm.

EMG electrode placement is determined by requesting the patient to clench his jaws. The masseter muscles knot conspicuously to sight or touch. Separate assemblies are placed at each TMJ so that each joint is monitored separately. The active electrodes are placed vertically over the joint with the ground on the mastoid process. The patient then leans the head back for support and relaxes the face, allowing the mandible to drop. Baselines are taken in the relaxed position and while the patient closes the mouth "normally." Commonly, one side has higher tension and is reduced first through feedback. When both joints are within 0.5uV of each other, the two assemblies can be fed back simultaneously.

After criterion is reached, the patient should visualize various stress situations while relaxed during feedback. Desensitization may be required to achieve muscular relaxation while stressed. Other contiguous head-neck regions should be monitored and any spasticity noted reduced through similar procedures. Occlusion should then be confirmed through dental examination.

Case example: A professional man, who was quite familiar with biofeedback, requested assistance in balancing contractions of the TMJs on recommendation of his dentist. Some 15 years earlier he had suffered a strain on the left TMJ. Subsequently, the left joint tended to slide loosely. There was significant difficulty in mastication or other movement until a few weeks before the referral when the joint slipped while he was chewing. There were no other complaints or homeostatic dysfunctions.

The treatment plan was EMG frontales placement to assist in training in general relaxation, concurrent with monitoring the upper trapezius and the TMJs. Frontales baseline was 1 to 2uV, the cervical area was 1.5 to 2uV, the right TMJ was 1.25 to 1.75uV, and the left TMJ was 0.70 to 1.0uV. Notably, the tension level was higher in the TMJ which was not the site of the injury. Evidently the right TMJ was compensating with mild, chronic spasticity to the malfunctioning of the injured, left TMJ.

During the first of two sessions all tension levels reduced about 50 percent. General relaxation was quite deep. The patient reported at the end of the session that he could feel the left TMJ moving into a more comfortable position as he relaxed his facial muscles. He also become aware of some mild pain in his right arm that he ascribed to cervical arthritis at C5 to C6 vertebrae.

At the beginning of the second session a week later, he reported that the left TMJ was improved in functioning. Pain was more obvious whenever he clenched his teeth, but he was monitoring that stress reaction throughout the day and deliberately relaxing his facial and masseter muscles. During chewing, his threshold for discomfort had heightened, he believed.

The session was devoted to relaxation and feedback from the TMJs. Baselines were about 25 percent lower with decreased over the session to below 0.50uV. The patient felt that he had reduced the complaint, had mastered a compensatory technique, and was not in need of further treatment. He said he would return upon recurrence of the symptom. Seven months' follow-up found him symptom free and maintaining his self-regulation.

Not all cases of TMJ disorders respond as successfully. Other patients require dental care, and some require intensive psychological treatment for stress or anxiety-related problems in living.

Spasmodic Torticollis

Spasmodic torticollis is a tonic, sometimes phasic, spasm of the muscles of the neck that are involved in the balance and position of the head. A spasm in the right or left sternocleidomastoidus muscle (SCM) will rotate the head to the ipsilateral side, while the contralateral SCM will remain flaccid. Other neck muscles are usually implicated as well, in particular the trapezius. Brudny and his associates (29,30) reported that the etiology is "elusive," and that most treatment procedures had a low remission rate. They applied

EMG biofeedback training as an experimental technique to determine its possible value. Surface electrode placements were on the trapezius and SCMs. Negative feedback procedure was returned from the spastic muscles to relax them and, alternately, positive feedback from the flaccid muscles was conducted to increase contraction level. This paradigm of differential EMG feedback training was coupled with self-practice at home and resulted in remission of seven of nine cases treated. The remaining two required follow-up refresher training and reinforcement.

The specific EMG procedure is placement of separate surface electrodes on each implicated muscle. The SCM is easily outlined when the head is lowered and turned to the side. The ground electrode can be placed on the mastoid process or the medial aspect of the clavicle. EMG training of upper trapezius is essential because they are usually involved in the syndrome. Desensitization of the patient to any fears, phobias, or stressors is useful inasmuch as spasmodic episodes can occur or intensify in response to emotional upsets or stress.

The initial sessions are devoted to training in relaxation and voluntary control of the EMG output signals. Training is best done at a site of healthy and easily regulated muscles, such as the forearm extensors or flexors. EMG relaxation of the frontales and BFT of the trapezuis reduce the complexities of the multiple flaccidity and spasms in the head-neck regions. Retraining of SCMs is then the major effort, using positive and negative feedback at each site. An additional treatment demand might be added. That is, criterion is reached when the patient can practice voluntary control of the SCMs, with EMG monitoring, while supine, sitting, standing, and walking. Frequency of sessions, in Brudny's project, (29) was three to five times a week, for an average of 10 weeks.

Cleeland (43) applied EMG feedback and aversive shock when a spastic SCM exceeded a given threshold in treating spasmodic torticollis. He reported good clinical improvement in 8 of 10 patients, with follow-ups revealing persistence in gains after 19 months.

Chapter 11

GASTROINTESTINAL TRACT

Some of the common referrals for biofeedback involving the gastro-intestinal (GI) tract are irritable colon, diarrhea, constipation, rumi-native vomiting, colitis, and psychogenic spasms of the stomach (11, 74, 76, 219, 232). The etiologies of these conditions are diverse and not always established (216). The usual disposition for biofeedback is the request by the physician for treatment of the stress or anxiety component of the disorders, and any possible reduction of homeostatic dysfunctions. These requests are usually used as adjunctive treatment techniques aimed at symptom reduction.

The patient is trained in general relaxation, desensitized to any fears and phobias, and trained in stress reduction as though one were treating a classical phobic or an overstressed patient. Frequently, psy-chogenic underlying sources of the disorders are not identified until several sessions have been conducted.

These patients are typically nervous, driven, tense, still engaged in adolescent resistance to significant relatives, and quite fearful of their dependency needs. Ocassionally, a precipitating event marks the onset of the disorder, but there are clear, pre-existing conflicts and traits that appear to provide the soil for the growth of the disorder. These traits need to be taken into account in the treatment procedures.

Irritable Colon

Patients reporting irritable colon syndrome reveal obsessive-compulsive personalities with poor use of the obsessiveness as a means of self-examination. They isolate much of their affect through their obsessive mechanism and lead rather rigid, overorganized lives that lack efficiency and self-satisfaction. Preoccupation with bowel movements eventually dominates their daily living. They tend to become involved in many rituals in bathroom routines to the annoyance of everyone, and they abuse drugs and enemas.

A combination of relaxation, change in life styles, and stress reduction appears to be the most effective, short term treatment approach. Biofeedback itself has not been established as efficacious, and is usually a part of a multimodality procedure (217, 219).

> *Case example* is that of a forty-eight year-old male, married, senior business executive, under medical care many years for irritable colon. His response to conventional treatment had been minimal. He also complained of tension, overwork, inability to socialize on the job, rectal spasms, and excess gas. He was quite tense, mildly depressed due to the chronic constipation, but strongly motivated. The treatment plan was to reduce the general tension, retain bowel habits, and to revise the compulsive life-style.
>
> The first few sessions were devoted to EMG frontales feedback to augment training in general relaxation, training in stress reduction techniques, EMG placement over the abdomen, and discussions of his morning routines and work habits. Baseline forehead and upper trapezius were around 2uV, with reduction to below 1uV when relaxed. Forehead increased to 2 to 3uV when instructed to think of morning routines; abdominal increase was insignificant. He was desensitized to bathroom routines during the next session with good results, according to both subjective and objective assessments. The basic procedure of EMG augmented relaxation and desensitization was reapplied each session, along with monitoring the ANS through the

dermogram, and brief discussions of current activities, such as lunches, work habits and home practice of relaxation. Skin conductance level was low and not affected by stressors.

By the sixth session, he had become less compulsive about morning bowel movement, which he would complete when he sensed the need rather than forcing them. Office routines were being changed, such as eating lunch with members of his staff, being more talkative and at ease in various settings, and less compulsive in doing his work. The week had passed without any constipation, although his bowel function was irregular.

Over the next several sessions he continued his progress in these areas but began to complain of the discomfort due to gas and the occasional rectal spasm. His wife was becoming impatient with his changes in routines, evidently releasing a great deal of suppressed hostility. EMG relaxation of the masseters, sternocleidomastoids, and the larynx were conducted with good results. He had become aware of some tension in these areas when he was deeply relaxed. He had been advised to check with his physician concerning the gas and an intestinal parasite that was found was treated with antibiotics.

By the fifteenth session, he was free of constipation but complaining about the irregularity of his bowel movements, the excessive gas, and the rectal spasm which usually occurred after a bowel movement. His physician had prescribed various medications for the gas, providing temporary relief. He was offered a referral for direct treatment of the rectal spasm, which he declined. During the remaining two sessions the presenting complaints and methods for dealing with them were reviewed. At termination he stated that the goals of treatment had been reached and he would continue medical care for the gas and rectal spasm.

During the 18 weeks of treatment the patient had sustained several personal blows. His brother's manic-depressive psychosis recurred, his mother-in-law had died suddenly, and his daughter had contracted a serious neurological infection that had threatened paralysis and had not responded to intensive treatment for several weeks. She eventually recovered and was then injured slightly in an automobile accident. The patient reported managing these traumas not only without his expected severe stress, but also with more appropriate emotional responsiveness than he thought he possessed. These events were among those analyzed during the course of the treatment.

Chapter 12

CARDIOVASCULAR SYSTEM

The cardiovascular system's susceptibility to psychosocial variables (160) is a major premise in biofeedback applications. The applications do not presume to alter anatomical properties that are basic to the normal or abnormal functioning of the system. Rather, the interactions between mental-emotional and biological processes is the central issue in treating cardiovascular dysfunctions (11, 16, 19, 27, 72, 117, 161). The goals are generally of two kinds: the retraining of homeostatic imbalances in the cardiovascular system, and the reduction of stress or anxiety that aggravate or may cause the dysfunctions. Biofeedback training itself is not yet fully determined to be the effective agent in treating cardiovascular disorders (16, 19, 20, 27, 28, 74, 76, 232). As in treating other psychophysiological complaints, a multimodal approach is applied.

The thermistor is used principally to monitor increase in blood flow to the periphery (176, 185), in treating vasoconstrictive disorders or in lowering sympathetic tone. The standard placement of the sensor is on the pap of the end of the middle digit (or toe). Other placements are at the wrist or the small finger. The latter has been suggested as particularly sensitive to blood flow changes related to emotional activity. Wherever the placement, the mental task of the patient is to think of warming the hand —*the whole hand*—or foot.

It is best to place the tape (Dermacil or other paper tape) along the longer axis of the finger or toe, rather than to encircle the member as most manuals instruct. Encircling may restrict blood flow.

The thermistor is also used to reduce sympathetic tone through peripheral feedback placement. The sympathetic nervous system regulates vascular muscle activity at the periphery and a decrease in sympathetic activity is required in order to vasodilate. Any patient whose usual hand temperature is below 90 °F should receive thermistor feedback training at least one session. And if cold hands occur reactive to phobic stimuli or to stressors, the patient should be desensitized with thermistor feedback to those stimuli.

Ordinarily, the hands can be warmed up rather quickly, the speed varying with the severity of the disorder or the symptom. Reducing vasospasms in the feet and toes requires considerably more time. Unless contraindicated, training to criterion for the hands is sufficient to learn the general procedure for both hands and feet. The patient then continues practicing after termination to reach criterion for the feet.

Notably, the biofeedback clinician's view is that both change in the symptom and related psychosocial stressors are the goals in treatment. The biofeedback machine is effective in the treatment program in changing the physiologically expressed symptom, but the remainder of the program requires use of intervention techniques from the realm of psychotherapy. Much of the recent research has caught up with clinical experince in finding that changing physiology alone, in isolation from the person, is not always sufficient (11, 72, 74, 219).

Raynaud's Disease

Raynaud's disease is characterized by constriction of the peripheral blood vessels in mild to severe degrees. The patient may also be peculiarly sensitive to particular substances such as tobacco, to cold weather, or to stressors. Severe cases can result in excruciating pain, or even ulceration and gangrene at the periphery. The anatomical basis of the sympathetic system regulating vasospasms suggests that the reduction of sympathetic tone, increase in blood flow to the periphery, and therapeutic interventions in any anxiety or stress that may be present are the treatment goals. Remission rate is generally high under these treatment programs, particularly if the patient maintains, in vivo, the practice of handwarming and relaxation. Some patients require refresher training after a year or so.

Case example is that of a sixty-four-year old single business woman who was referred with the diagnosis of borderline Raynaud's syndrome of about 2 year's duration, although she had always had cold hands. Her fingers were chiefly affected, episodically becoming intensely cold and turning white regardless of weather conditions. Her middle fingers and large toes were especially susceptible. Family history revealed her father had suffered chronically cold hands and her mother had died 20 months previously, following a CVA and gangrene in one leg resulting in amputation. She believed that her mother's death may have aggravated her complaint, but that she had otherwise dealt successfully with the loss. Developmental history was normal; there were no other complaints except for cervical arthritis and stiffness in her neck.

She approached the consultation in a businesslike fashion. She had heard about thermistor feedback and wanted to learn to warm her hands and feet using the thermistor and had no interest in any other therapies or instruments.

The treatment plan was to train her in general relaxation and hand warming, using appropriate biofeedback instruments to augment the training, and in antistress techniques.

During the first of six treatment sessions thermistor feedback was applied with relaxation and hand warming. Basal temperature at the right middle digit was 92.4°F and left 96.4. Feedback was started from the cooler area, as a routine, and when it was within 2° of the left digit, the temperature from both were combined and fed back via machine averaging. After 30 minutes she appeared to be deeply relaxed and hand temperature had stabilized at 95.1°F. Similar readings were found at her large toes. She subsequently reported that while relaxing she felt tense, her mind raced at times, her hands got sweaty, and she felt her heart palpitating. These responses were discussed in terms of anxiety caused by her fear of letting go and her need to control her environment. The usefulness of using the EMG and GSR instruments in order to target the spasms and automatic overactivation was suggested. She was receptive and agreeable.

The following sessions incorporated EMG feedback from the frontales, TMJs, upper and middle trapezius, and GSR palmar feedback. Thermistor monitoring of her hands and toes, without feedback, was continued. Most muscle areas manifested some tension, ranging 1.50 to 3.50uV, with quite quick reduction to below 1uV. Palmar tonic conductance level was within normal ranges, with a significant decrease as she relaxed. Her increase in sweat production and heart rate were evidently reactive to her apprehension about letting go and her fear of failure. She confirmed those possibilities, relating that she always felt she could not afford to fail at anything. Her distrust of others was not analyzed. She was simply reassured that the biofeedback procedure was under her control and the therapist was functioning only as a teacher and guide.

By the fifth session she reported warming her hands at work, at home, while driving, and during any stress situations. Evidently she did not experience anxiety while relaxing when alone. She also realized that upon losing her fearful anticipation of a vasospasm she was not inducing any episodes. The stiffness in her neck was virtually gone, and the more consistently she practiced relaxing her mind and various muscle groups, the better she could relax physically and keep her hands warm.

The termination session was devoted to reinforcing blood flow to the periphery through autogenic phrases, imagery of a tranquil scene, and imagining herself in stress situations but feeling at ease. She then went on a lengthy vacation and upon returning put her life in order for retirement. She reported continual progress in dealing with the complaint and was essentially free of tension.

The patient's chief character traits were crucial elements of her treatment plan. She was not given to leaning on others and was even fearful of it. Her defensive need for control of anything happening to her alleviated her anxiety and was used clinically to enhance her training in self-regulation. So long as she knew what to do, and how to do it, and could predict the consequences, she was an excellent candidate for clinical biofeedback.

Migraine

Migraine is classified into classical and common types (28,31). The former is characterized by periodic episodes and preceded by a prodrome, or aura, of visual disturbances, and changes in other sensory systems. Ordinary sounds or smells may cause intense irritability or pain and nausea. These reactions extend into the episode itself which can be one of unbearable pain. The throbbing pain begins on one side of the head but before the attack has subsided the entire head may be in pain, accompanied by loss of appetite and vomiting. Common migraine is distinguished from the classical essentially by the absence of the prodromal stage.

When migraineurs suffer their episodes of pain they react with bracing the shoulders and gritting the teeth. Consequently, spasticity in the head and neck develops, adding to their pain. They may also have high sympathetic tone, vasospasms at the periphery, or sweaty palms.

The condition is a vascular disorder that is stress-related and more common in females than males. The distension of the superficial temporal artery may be a site of the pain, but the intracranial arteries are also implicated. Many imbalances in body fluid occur, along with increased outflow of epinephrines, and changes in level of neurotransmitters in the brain.

Biofeedback technique for treating migraineurs was initiated by Sargent, Green, and Walters (174,175) when one of their research subjects raised her hand temperature and aborted an episode. The procedure they devised is basically unchanged to this day: relaxation, feedback of hand temperature to increase vasodilation, and training in autogenic handwarming. Green and Green (85) reviewed some of their work in biofeedback, thermal in particular, and reported adding EMG and breathing exercises to the basic program, as most clinicians have done. Recordkeeping by the patient of frequency and intensity of headaches, and context of occurrence is essential in determining progress, as well as identifying and reducing stressors.

The effective agent in the clinical biofeedback program for treating migaine is not clearly established, although relaxation appears to be a necessary element (85,219). Whether the biofeedback training itself is necessary in revising cardiovascular dysfunctions on the symptomatic level is a moot question—as far as the patient is concerned. Undoubtedly, it remains a crucial question and, probably, valid answers will be found in the careful and extensive investigations of the research scientists. Meanwhile, the bioinstruments are excellent training devices in training relaxation and self-regulation of blood flow.

> *Case example*: The patient, Vera, was a thirty-six year-old single nurse, neatly dressed, slim, self-referred for migraine. She was an only child. Her father and his mother had had life-long migraine. The mother's grandfather had suffered a brain tumor and had committed suicide.
>
> Vera's migraine began at age twenty-five, initially diagnosed as sinus headache. She could not relate the episodes to anything in her diet, life experiences, or menstrual period, except that she had been involved in a "self-destructive love affair with an alcoholic." She had been a heavy drinker during that relationship in her attempts to keep up with his drinking. She had often awakened with a hangover and a severe headache and ascribed both to the drinking.
>
> Currently, migraines occurred about once a month, with no regular relationship to her menstrual cycle. Previously, she suffered episodes two to three times a week that were evidently related to stresses in her work. Upon changing work assignment to a less demanding hospital situation, the frequency decreased significantly. Occasionally, she would wake up in the early morning with a severe attack; or upon awakening at her regular time, she would experience mild pain.
>
> The episodes varied in intensity. Usually they followed an aura of visual disturbances of black or white dots crossing her visual field, hypersensitivity to light, and mild dizziness and lightheadedness. The aura would precede the attack by as much as 24 hours, although an attack did not always follow an aura. She believed that many episodes were delayed reactions to crises, such as the death of her father.
>
> There was a history of allergies to dust, grass, and most antibiotics. She suffered asthma from childhood until she left home for college. She attempted to regulate her diet as prescribed by her physician, but she still used liquor and consumed up to five cups of coffee a day.

When stressed or anxious, she experienced cold hands and feet, stomach spasms, frontal headaches, increased sweating on the right side, and occasional diarrhea. She was mildly claustrophobic at times in crowds, elevators, and at parties. Anxiety was dealt with by talking with a friend, smoking marijuana in the evenings, or drinking liquor. She had recently stopped the marijuana because it made her more anxious and suspicious of the people around her.

Vera also complained of difficulties in her social and professional relationships. She tended to remain on the fringe, participating only if necessary. Conflicts with others made her quite anxious, and she had to push herself in order to exert her authority. For several years she had been feeling quite depressed and helpless about her problems, and withdrawal was increasing. Medication for the migraine and tranquillizers for the anxiety had minimal effect.

The treatment plan was general relaxation training with thermistor and dermogram feedback to lower autonomic arousal levels and to increase vasodilation. Spasticity in the head and neck regions would be assessed and EMG feedback applied where indicated. Recordkeeping of headaches and stress reactions were to be maintained for desensitization and self-assertion training.

The first session consisted of EMG frontales feedback and relaxation training. The hands and feet were monitored for temperature level. EMG baseline was 2.5 to 3.5uV with reduction over the session to 1.5 to 2.5uV. Hand temperature was 94.7 °F; feet were 77.3 °F. Although she reported feeling deeply relaxed by the end of the session, her hand temperature had fallen to 89.6 °F. Commonly, patients are apprehensive and striving to succeed, which increases sympathetic tone and lowers peripheral temperature. She reported becoming aware of tension in her throat, forehead, lower back, and buttocks.

The treatment procedure was varied over the remaining 11 sessions. Usually Vera's hands were between 85 to 90 °F at the beginning of each session; and they were highly responsive to imagery of stress situations. As such, her hand temperature was used to monitor the desensitization to varieties of social, familial, and work situations. The dermogram was also applied to monitor sweat gland production and as feedback to reduce sympathetic tone. Recordkeeping revealed a relationship between alcohol and migraine attacks. Other EMG placements to reduce spasticity were the upper and middle trapezius.

As the anxiety remitted in the office and in vivo she became more at ease and more responsive to others. There was an improvement in self-assertion in these areas, as well as a decrease in the strains of supervising others. Bodily tension decreased significantly as she learned to relax herself, to warm her hands and feet, and to be less stressed throughout the day. The anxiety-ridden relationship with her mother became clearer over the course of the treatment, as well as her use of alcohol to reduce anxiety and loneliness. When these problems were conceptualized she decided to enter psychotherapy.

By the end of treatment, the migraines had reduced in severity and duration, and she had been able to abort two through relaxation and hand-warming. Twelve month follow-up found her to be maintaining the gains.

Hypertension

Hypertension is variably responsive to clinical biofeedback in symptomatic expression (20, 27, 28, 74, 152). Evidently relaxation training is a necessary ingredient of the treatment, and may well be the effective agent in any behavioral or biofeedback program. Other methods of relaxation through hypnotism (160), meditation (16), and autogenics (125) are also successful in reducing high blood pressure (HBP). Pressures over 140/90 are suspect and some estimate that 10 to 20 percent of Americans are hypertensive. Stress and anxiety exacerbate the cardiovascular response, in addition to improper diet, lack of exercise, smoking, and alcohol. About 90 percent of hypertensives are without known cause (essential hypertension). A great danger of HBP is that the sufferer cannot be subjectively aware of dangerous increases in blood pressure (20).

The standard clinical biofeedback approach in treating HBP is to reduce physiological arousal levels in all systems, daily practice of relaxation, diet, medication, exercise, relieving fears and phobias, and developing a stress-free life style. The more serious the hypertension, the more the patient has to do to avoid HBP. During the course of biofeedback therapy, it is necessary that the attending physician be aware of any changes in blood level in order to monitor medication. Also, a decrease in medication during the day does not automatically remove the need for nocturnal use in many cases.

Case example is of a thirty-two year-old physician who, within a period of a few months, had completed training in her specialty, married, opened a private office, assumed a supervisory position, and suffered great apprehension about her family which was caught in a revolution in her native country. Her blood pressure ranged between 165/116 to 170/120 and her heart rate was often 100 to 120 bpm. Insight was excellent and she had agreed with her cardiologist that before they attempted medical interventions she would try biofeedback. She was undergoing tests for an adrenal tumor, which were negative. Since she had taken an introductory seminar in methods of clinical biofeedback she was familiar with the approach.

The initial interview revealed complaints about muscle tension in the upper trapezius, generalized body tension, and stress at work. There were no other physiological dysfunctions or personal difficulties.

The treatment plan was EMG applications in the head region to reduce any spasticity, training in relaxation, and desensitization to stressors in her work life.

During the first session, the EMG was placed on the frontales and the right and left upper trapezius. Baselines lines were 2.50 to 3.50uV, 1.50 to 2.00uV, and 1.75 to 3.00uV, respectively. Relaxation was applied with feedback from the frontales. Termination levels were frontales 1.75 to 3.00uV, right trapezius 1.50 to 2.00uV, and left trapezius 1.25 to 2.00uV. She achieved a deep state of mental and physical relaxation. Heart rate decreased from 100 to 72 bpm.

In the next session she reported her pulse that morning of 100, with occasional readings between 100 to 120 during the week. She was practicing relaxation twice a day. The procedure was repeated. EMG baselines were about at the level of the termination readings of the previous session with small decreases occurring over the session. Pulse was 76 on termination.

Over the remaining nine sessions, the procedure of EMG feedback was continued with placements on the TMJs during two sessions and on the frontales and trapezius during all sessions. Heart rate was usually high at the beginning of the early sessions (80 to 100), decreasing to 62 to 76 by the end of each session. Desensitization hierarchies were applied concerning specific stressors in her work life. By the final session BP had stabilized at 135/90 both at home and in the cardiologists's office, and heart rate was consistently between 68 and 80 bpm. She reported feeling generally relaxed and there was a significant decrease in stress levels in the stressful situations. Seven-month follow-up found the changes persisting.

A more complex case, a posthospital referral was that of a forty-five year-old twice-married woman, with a 20-year history of alcoholism and agitated depressions, both under remission when seen (219). Her history also included hypertension, migraine, multiple phobias, chronic insomnia and severe morning nausea. The insomnia was evidently related to the severe headaches. She had been hospitalized twice for acute, agitated depressions with three courses of electroshock therapy and had had a sympathectomy for the migraine. During her hospitalizations she had been diagnosed as manic-depressive and schizoaffective. Her medication levels were at their limits and the symptoms were not responding to psychotherapy. Her psychiatrist was particularly concerned about reduction of the pain, the general agitation, and medication level. She was not clinically depressed, nor were there any signs of thought disorder.

Pain level in the forehead, neck and shoulders was extreme. She could not use hairspray because if any fell on her forehead the skin constricted and she would suffer excruciating pain. She slept poorly and awoke with nausea and fatigue. The agoraphobia interfered with her social life, and she could not stay alone. Blood pressure was 150/92.

The treatment plan was biofeedback augmented by relaxation, hypnotism, hand-warming, desensitization of separation anxiety, and changes in her daily routines. In the first session she was hypnotized during the application of the relaxation technique which focused on breathing and visual relaxation of muscles of the head and neck regions. Response was satisfactory. She felt considerably calmer and less hopeless after the session.

During the dozen sessions conducted, the patient was routinely relaxed using GSR feedback and EMG placement at the upper and middle trapezius to reinforce the relaxation and to reduce autonomic overactivation and striate muscle spasms in the head region. GSR was variable but stabilized over the sessions. The large knots in the cervical spine region registered above 250uV at 100 to 200 Hz setting. The pain in her forehead prevented any placement there. Termination readings at the neck were below 10uV while relaxed, rising to 20 to 30uV while alert and with her head supported by the chair. During later sessions, while relaxed, she was desensitized to separation anxiety and diffuse agoraphobia. She began to be less anxious when alone, the head pains diminished dramatically, sleep improved, the morning nausea disappeared, medications were reduced, and her blood pressure returned to near normal limits, 120/80. Follow-up revealed continued progress with a few relapses in insomnia. She learned that home practice was crucial in maintaining the gains.

Chapter 13

CENTRAL NERVOUS SYSTEM

Alpha-Theta Enhancement

The enormous complexity of the brain is the first apparent diffi-culty encountered in EEG biofeedback. Brown (27,28) makes this most evident in her reviews of the research and clinical arenas. The difficulty surfaces when attempts are made to relate psychological states with particular electrical activities of the brain. There are some general brain waveforms that are present when people introspect and report their mental-emotional states (Figure 4). However, that the waveform can be brought under volitional control has very little and very restricted verification in the literature (112). There is a world of difference between *monitoring* and *controlling* a physiological process and its accompanying natural mental state in humans.

Kamiya's (107) original postulation that increase in alpha led to increase in tranquillity can be viewed as a naturally occurring corre-late between brain state and mental state. Alpha does increase natu-rally with the eyes closed, over the eyes-open condition, during a relaxed state. And a mental task will attentuate alpha rhythm. Some investigators have found that alpha cannot be increased beyond the eyes-closed level (152). The probably effective agents in EEG alpha feedback are those described by Plotkin and Cohen (162): body relaxation, mental relaxation, and tranquillity. This state is equiva-lent to the alpha state, but it is not brought about by the control of alpha rhythm. Cause and effect appear to be misstated. Evidently the reduction of stress and anxiety through relaxation is palliative, but the claim that one can volitionally increase alpha, thereby leading to relaxation, is yet to be proven. In order to induce an increase in alpha while under EEG feedback the subject must lie still, close the eyes, and be calm. The authors logically proffer the explanation that "...the major contribution that alpha feedback makes to the attainment of meditativelike experience is to supply a setting..." for relaxation.

This explanation was demonstrated by patients several years ago while monitoring (without feedback) their EEG changes during relaxation training through the method described in Chapter 6. As they relaxed mentally and physically alpha-theta would predominate, suggesting that the relaxation technique was the effective agent.

Consequently, EEG feedback was discarded as a principal agent in conducting clinical biofeedback. The simplicity of EMG electrode attachment and the direct relationships between EMG and muscle tension, GSR and sympathtic tone, led one to believe that these machine operations would be more reliable and clinically more manageable than use of the EEG in treating psychogenic disorders, anxiety, or stress. Combining any of these machine operations with general relaxation resulted in the increase of alpha rhythm.

Control of Epileptic Seizures

Sterman and his colleagues (197, 198) first reported the use of EEG feedback as a method of reducing the severity and frequency of seizures in epilepsy. They noted the blocking of movements in cats increased as the 12 to 16 Hz rhythm over the sensorimotor cortex increased. This came to be known as the sensorimotor rhythm (SMR). They postulated that increase in SMR in the human brain region analagous to the cat's might decrease epileptiform movements in humans. EEG feedback of 12 to 14 Hz did appear to decrease the frequency and severity of seizures in epileptics. Further research subsequently indicated that the specific area and brain-wave frequencies were not the effective agents. More likely the normalization of brain waves, as such, in EEG training resulted in a decrease in seizures.

Kuhlman and Kaplan (112) reviewed the evidence as well as replicated and varied the treatment procedure and concluded that normalization did, in fact, appear to be the effective agent. They point out that relaxation ordinarily achieved by patients frequently aborts seizures. Clinical experience has also found that seizure onset can be precipitated by stress, anxiety, traumas, etc., and seizures can often be aborted by stress reduction or even normal movement intervention.

Clinical biofeedback approaches include standard stress reduction or relaxation procedures, and appropriate psychotherapeutic techniques that deal with conflicts, anxiety, and the impact of being epileptic. The EEG is added to reinforce normal brain-wave activity. Probably the only help biofeedback has to offer is EEG normalization and relaxation techniques. Depending on the needs of the patient, other soures of treatment are necessary for most patients.

Applications in pain cases, sleep-onset insomnia, obsessiveness, and drug abuse have been attempted with mixed results (19, 28, 74). Many of the successes appear to be confounded by the use of ancillary techniques, relaxation in particular. Perhaps different combinations of bioinstruments and particular therapy techniques will be found to be of primary effectiveness in various complaints.

Chapter 14

PSYCHIATRIC DISORDERS

A wide range of disorders of behavior that are treated in psychiatry, and some in other specialties, have been reported as amenable to clinical biofeedback. Table 1 lists several of the diagnostic groups and symptoms that are targeted. Summaries of research and treatment procedures can be found in Basmajian (11), Birk (17), Brown (28), Fuller (72), Gaardner and Montgomery (74), Gatchel and Price (76), Wentworth-Rohr (219), and in the Aldine yearly readers (189). There is considerable variation in the literature in describing the symptoms treated, the diagnoses, and their relationships. Differences in instrumentation are obvious, and probably subtle differences in the applications of the psychotherapy techniques are present as well, though not as obvious. One is often left with the impression that the biofeedback instruments are not the effective agents, but that they are the tools of the psychotherapy techniques. In this model, they are quite helpful in the efficacious application of therapy techniques in the treatment of significant degrees of disorders of personality.

As reiterated throughout most of these chapters, the multimodal approach in clinical biofeedback is widely accepted among clinicians as the necessary procedure in attaining satisfactory remission rates in these populations. It is probable that the separate techniques of the multimodal paradigm affect separate but interactive parameters of the personality, and that no one technique is sufficient. Moreover, when applied in concert or in sequence, each technique may enhance one or more of the others. Identifying individually effective treatment variables in the clinical biofeedback approach is much like the problem of identifying the individual variables of verbal psychotherapy. The complexity is enormous and no one treatment variable appears to be sufficient.

The complexity of many of these disorders requires attention to mental-emotional-social-physical parameters, especially on the behavioral and symptomatic levels. The treatment procedure rarely presumes to treat the basic disorder; rather, the goals are essentially the reduction of symptoms. Probably the symptoms are not the direct expressions of the disorders in most cases. They may be defenses against conflicts, learned habits in the model of behaviorism, or symptoms that are persisting after the causes have been resolved through other therapeutic interventions or simply through growth.

Some presenting symptoms in the schizophrenic populations may be ego defenses against an overt psychosis. This is a difficult determination to make, even though therapists have been making it for years under the conditions of traditional treatment procedures (220). An adequate diagnostic screening interview, especially for schizophrenics, is essential to this determination.

Symptoms referred for treatment may range from a single learned habit to complex patterns of behavior that disrupts virtually all of the patient's life. A detailed search of the history and functioning of the symptoms can clarify the etiology in most cases. All symptoms do not have the same etiologies (Chapters 5 and 6). Some may have multiple etiologies; others may exist without known causes; and still others may be learned habits that have no relationship with anxiety, conflicts, chronic stress, or biological disorders. The symptom may arise merely from a conscious act. The case histories to follow are examples of the varieties of disorders of behavior that have been treated in clinical biofeedback.

> A *case example* of a simple learned habit, a tic, is that of a young woman who shrugged her shoulders frequently and inappropri-

ately.She had undergone surgery to reduce the size of her breasts and had become unnecessarily worried about the loss of sensation in her breasts. Her surgeon had informed her that sensation would return in due time. However, her worry caused her to shrug her shoulders frequently because she had discovered the movement would create some sensation. After a few weeks she was distressed to find that the shrugging had become a habit, even though sensation had returned to normal levels. The habit had also generalized to a few situations that were ordinarily, and normally, stressful in her work and private life.

The treatment plan was relaxation, EMG retraining of the implicated muscle groups, recordkeeping, and the desensitization to the stressors reported.

The first of three sessions was devoted to training in general relaxation, EMG feedback from the deltoids, trapezius, and pectoralis muscles. Baseline EMG values were 1.00 to 1.50uV, with quick reduction to below 1uV for all regions through feedback and relaxation. Obviously, the tic was episodic and had not yet resulted in chronic spasticity. During relaxation, the patient complained of cold hands, which had cooled further when asked to visualize a recent stressful event that had induced shrugging. There was also an increase in EMG values of about 1uV, and her thoracic respiratory response was more noticeable. She was subsequently taught diaphragmatic breathing. Homework included recording the time, place, and situation of the occurrence of the symptom, practicing relaxation and diaphragmatic breathing, and making a conscious effort not to shrug.

At the next session she reported compliance with homework assignments and that she had not responded with the tic in two or three stressful situations. She also monitored her hand temperature which was generally around 88 °F. The session included thermistor feedback from the hands. EMG values were low and temperature baseline was 87.6 °F.Within 10 minutes of relaxation, averaged hand temperature increased to 95.2 °F.She was then asked to visualize three different stress situations, one at a time, and re-relaxed when the EMG readings and hand temperature varied from the desired levels. Response to the desensitization procedure was satisfactory. She finished the procedure with low EMG values and hands at 94.8 °F.

Preceding the third session, the patient reported continuous progress. The only significant episode was awareness of tightening her shoulders and torso during her routine piano practicing. The previous session's techniques were repeated and included visualizing practicing the piano playing.

Twenty-two month follow-up revealed no recurrence of the tic, except for the expected two or three brief regressive episodes that often recur immediately after termination. She was no longer stressed by the reported stressors and she used the relaxation technique to reduce stress levels arising in work and social events. However, she was quite derelict in practicing diaphragmatic breathing, as most patients are.

Phobias

Anxiety is the central affect in phobias and avoidance responses are the manifestations of the anxiety. The patient's complaint of a subjective awareness of the unpleasant character of anxiety and the attendant disruptions in living comprise the overt clinical data. The goals of clinical biofeedback in treating the phobia are to reduce the frequency and intensity of the anxiety, and to assist the patient in reducing the phobic disruptions of his life.

Wolpe's (229) contribution of desensitization procedure is the bedrock of biofeedback applications in treating fears and phobias. There is little doubt that counterconditioning or deconditioning a classical phobia is the treatment of choice. The use of the state of physiological and mental relaxation as the precondition for the relief of the anxiety is fundamental to clinical biofeedback approaches. The precise kind of relaxation technique used, and when and how applied, and the addition of other treatment techniques, are matters of clinical judgment, patient to patient.

The standard clinical biofeedback procedure in treating phobias is general relaxation augmented by biofeedback training, lowering of physiological overactivation with particular targeting of the implicated physiological systems, the application of desensitization, and the acquisition of effective responses to the phobic object or situation. Innumerable variations of and additions to this general treatment plan are devised in accordance with the clinical data and the unique characteristics of each person being treated.

Case examples: The patient was a twenty-seven year-old single male professional, who presented a fear of flying. The fear was experienced when the plane began to take off, and on landing, and became severe when any turbulence was encountered; otherwise he was calm aboard the plane in flight. The acute onset was about one year earlier when his plane had flown through a lengthy stretch of turbulence. He suffered heart palpitations, general body tension, trembling, and sweaty palms. There was a history of mild apprehension 10 years earlier during a flight during bad weather; and at age ten he had had to return by rail from a visit because the outbound flight had been too distressing. Over the years, until the recent acute episode, he managed to suppress his moderate anxiety reactions to lifting, turning, and landing.

The history was otherwise unremarkable, and he had no other complaints

The treatment plan was EMG frontales feedback to augment general relaxation, supplemented by GSR application, and desensitization to airplane motion, in particular, lifting, turbulence, and landing.

Response to EMG frontales training and relaxation was excellent. The basal EMG was about 1.75uV, with reduction to below 1.00uV within 15 minutes. The patient was asked to visualize a parked airplane, and frontales level increased to over 1.00uV. When re-relaxed the tension decreased. This sequence of imagery-relaxation was repeated three times. By the third trial, his forehead level remained below 1.00uV when stressed. Baseline for the second session was .90uV with decrease to .60 when relaxed. A hierarchy was then presented. Whenever his forehead level exceeded 1.00uV, he was re-relaxed. The 22 items began with "in your apartment, thinking of flying," continued through dimensions of leaving the building, riding a cab, approaching plane, boarding, lifting, flying, plane banking and bouncing, and ended with "smooth flying." Tension level increased to 2.00uV with the images of boarding the plane, lifting, and banking.

The fifth and last session was devoted to the standard procedure, with self-statements added: "I will remain calm. The plane is like a boat keeling in the wind." Frontales level began at 1.00uV with increases to 3.00uV with some images, particularly flying through turbulence. He reported feeling relaxed during the session, as in the previous three, despite the increase in muscle tension.

The patient was leaving town by car the following day and planned to return by air. He said he would phone if the flight distressed him. He did not phone, and a seven month follow-up found him flying without anxiety.

The success of the treatment plan, even though the physiological component did not change, was probably due to a change in his mental expectation of the dangers of flying. That is, the anxiety was not chronic, as he himself reported, and emerged when he thought of being in danger. The coping mechanisms of relaxing himself while on board and thinking the various coping statements probably combined to allay physiological arousal previously evoked by the frightening thoughts which had evidently been the prelude to an anxiety attack.

A somewhat more complex phobia patient was a thirty-three year-old recently-married business woman who complained of a 10-year fear of driving a car. When behind a wheel she would become acutely anxious and paralyzed. Her hands would become clammy as she clenched the wheel, feeling nauseous, short of breath, and lightheaded. She had once attempted to drive but upon stopping at the ingress to a main highway she was again paralyzed with anxiety. The police had driven her home. As a passenger in a car she was always tense and nervous, and tended to be a back-seat driver.

Her father died suddenly of a heart attack when she was twenty-one, and 14 months later her mother also died of a heart attack. The patient was left without any relatives, little money, and became the guardian of a younger sister and brother. Soon after, her brother suffered grand mal and her sister petit mal seizures. The patient remembered being terrified after her mother's death and considered committing suicide, but persevered grimly.

Her history had been uneventful before the father's death. She presented other complaints of cold, wet hands when in a demanding work situation, and would feel intimidated, weak, and confused. Medical examinations were negative.

The physiology implicated was the sweat gland and circulatory systems and visceral organs, particularly the stomach and respiratory apparatuses. The treatment plan was to lower autonomic overactivation through GSR and thermistor feedback concurrent with training in general relaxation, hand-warming, desensitization to automobile driving and stressful work situation, and self-assertiveness through other than grim and hostile behavior patterns.

The first two of 17 sessions focused on EMG frontales augmented relaxation. The patient was repeatedly reinforced for the development of passive concentration and comprehending the feedback procedure as a nondemanding, neither pass nor fail learning process. The GSR was used to monitor arousal level after 10 minutes; the EMG auditory signal was nulled while she received the GSR signal. Both signals decreased until she was asked to visualize herself sitting behind the wheel of a parked car. The EMG and GSR increased and she was relaxed using an image of lying in a hammock in the shade. She was then desensitized to driving.

The thermistor was introduced in the third session. Right and left middle digits were about 84.4 °F and feedback was applied. She raised temperature level to 92.7 ° in 12 minutes of self-relaxation, then the level began to drop The feedback was ended after 7 minutes at 82.0 °F. She reported that when she had been relaxed she became afraid that the therapist ''would spring a fear scene'' on her. She also had no subjective discrimination of hand temperature at any time. Evidently, she would be aware of having cold hands only when they were intensely cold.

To offset that problem and to train her in hand-warming she was provided with a liquid crystal wrist thermometer and instructed to keep frequent and careful records. Over the following 2 weeks she practiced hand-warming and partial self-relaxation whenever she recorded a temperature below 90 °F and whenever she was about to enter a stress situation.

The fourth session was opened with the patient's declaration that she wanted to talk. The substance was about her husband's attitude to marriage and her mother-in-law's prolonged visit. Her husband felt that his wife was making enough money to support them well and he had no need to work. He suggested that he stay home and maintain the house and his hobby in horticulture. The mother-in-law was an interesting and active woman but one who pried and interfered in the marriage. The following session she reported that she held a lengthy, detailed talk with her husband and they reached a mutually satisfying arrangement.

The remaining sessions were taken up by continuing the application of the various parts of the treatment plan. There was a gradual lessening of anxiety when she rode in a car; she was less aggressive and more successful in asserting herself on the job; she began driving a car in the neighborhood and finally on the thruways. She had not experienced cold or wet hands for several weeks, even when under strong stress. Her marriage was more satisfying, and she felt generally less helpless and threatened. One of our sessions had dealt with the period following her mother's death when she was feeling helpless, abandoned, and threatened by her fear of filling her mother's shoes.

The treatment was terminated as satisfactory. She phoned 2 days later to tell me that when riding with her husband on a crowded, high-speed road, their car had been sideswiped. "Nobody was injured, but my husband and the other driver were hysterical. I couldn't believe it, but I was the only one not panicked."

Follow-up of 12 months revealed the gains to have persisted and to have generalized to other parts of her life.

Insomnia

Insomnia has been among the most widely studied symptoms in the biofeedback literature (3, 11, 17, 28, 72, 74, 219). Evidently, sleep disturbances are suffered by millions of people, and, as Adler and Morrissey-Adler point out (3), the etiologies are manifold and diverse. Anxiety appears to be the most common cause of insomnia, especially sleep-onset insomnia, and the most appropriate for biofeedback procedures. Early wakefulness is often related to depression but it is not unusual in older people. Reduction in muscle tension does not appear to be sufficient to reduce insomnia.

Many patients who present sleep-onset insomnia are also suffering from other difficulties, which may or may not be the direct cause of the insomnia. One patient's trouble was sleep apnea; another's was chronic bitterness about the daily lack of personal satisfactions which he then stubbornly daydreamed about for many, many minutes upon retiring. Some persons are not even aware of how much sleep they need, most of them being convinced that they must have 8 hours every night. They then go to bed too early.

Each patient reporting insomnia should therefore be carefully interviewed regarding the symptom itself. Records should be kept by the patient, to be reviewed by the therapist. A clinical precaution is not to offer a definite opinion as to the cause of the sleep disturbance until 2 to 3 weeks of recordkeeping has been completed to avoid misleading the patient with mistaken cause-effect relationships. Often it is most effective to reduce other presenting problems first, such as tension headache, back spasms, sexual anxiety, obsessions, lack of exercise, overeating before bedtime, etc.

Case example: The patient was a forty-nine year-old married woman mother of two grown children, referred for a 7-month history of sleep-onset insomnia, with occasional wakefulness. She stated that she had been happily married for 28 years and had a happy relationship with her two grown children. History was negative. She viewed her life as being satisfying in every way.

The only problem she could identify in her current life was that of her daughter's difficulty in conceiving. They had an excellent relationship and the patient understood her daughter's wish to have a child, and shared the apprehension about the infertility.

The treatment plan was to apply EMG biofeedback-assisted relaxation, to assess tension levels in the neck and head region, and to record self-experience preliminary to bedtime. It was also suggested to the patient that she might be experiencing, for the first time within her memory, a problem that she could not solve or simply avoid. She was quite struck by the possibility of her insomnia being caused by feeling frustrated and helpless over her daughter's inability to conceive.

The patient was seen over 9 weeks for 7 sessions. Moderate tension levels were found and reduced in the frontales, the right upper trapezius, TMJ, and sternocleidomastoids. Response to relaxation training was excellent. Recordkeeping made her aware of her excessive concern about her husband's distress over her insomnia and her own overconcern about her daughter's problem. The chronicity of the insomnia began to alleviate within 3 weeks and by the sixth week she was almost symptom-free.

The foregoing uncomplicated case is an example of the impossibility of determining one effective agent, if there is only one, in the multimodal procedure. Perhaps the interpretation of the patient's virtually unique experience of helplessness in a life-time of successful management of any significant life problem was the central treatment agent. Or, perhaps the acquisition of a method of putting aside, through mental and physical relaxation, the helplessness and frustration was sufficient to reduce the insomnia. One might wish to compare this case with the forty-five year-old hypertensive presented in Chapter 12 who had not had a normal, sucessful, nor satisfying life. Yet the insomnia was alleviated in her case as well and the improvement persisted for both women.

Dysphagia Spastica

Dysphagia is a difficulty in swallowing that can arise from several organic causes as well as from the dysfunctional contraction of throat muscles. Dysphagia spastica is related to the constriction of the esophageal and pharyngeal muscles as a result of chronic stress or as a response to a stimulus that evokes the throat spasm. Haynes (93) treated a chronic case in which the young woman reported a 2-year history of tightness in her throat, especially in stressful situations. Swallowing was a problem during eating and frequently she couldn't eat during periods of stress. He applied EMG frontales feedback, supplemented by home practice of relaxation once a day and whenever tense. Over the 20 sessions of biofeedback her general stress level gradually diminished and the dysphagia was minimized. Six months' follow-up revealed that the improvement was maintained.

It is inexplicable as to why the EMG placement was not on the throat. We have treated several cases of chronic or acute throat spasms by placement of the electrodes lateral to the larynx, with good results.

> *Case example* is that of a young married woman who was referred because of an inability to swallow pills. She would gag at each attempt. The situation was critical because she was suffering from hypoglycemia, malnutrition, cardiac arrhythmia, profuse sweating, fainting spells, outbreaks of blisters, insomnia, allergies, and blurred vision. Most of these symptoms resulted from years of an improper diet. Her physician had placed her on a strict program of medication, diet, and diet supplements in pill and capsule form, some 40 per day. She reported normal

development except for late onset of the menarche, followed by 2 years of amemorrhea. She also complained of cold hands and feet.

She was extremely apprehensive about what would be done to help her, but she was willing to cooperate in any recommended technique. The treatment plan was EMG frontales placement to augment general relaxation, hand-warming phrases, laryngeal EMG placement to reduce the spasm, and hypnotism to implant post-trance suggestions.

She responded extremely well to relaxation which then led into deep induction. Tension level in her throat was moderate even when relaxed. While in the trance during the first session, EMG feedback reduced the throat spasm and she was told that her throat became soft and comfortable upon being stroked. She said her throat seemed to "open." Guided imagery was used, when she was asked to extend her tongue and told that a very tiny pill was being placed on it and that she would be able to swallow it. Her tongue was touched by a toothpick to enhance the suggestion. She managed to swallow the simulated pill. Several more simulations were carried out, each followed by the patient swallowing. The procedure was repeated in the second session. She was then asked to bring all her pills and capsules.

During the third session the basal tension level in her throat was low. We lined up about 10 pills, using the smallest sizes in the batch. She was hypnotized and relaxed deeply and the smallest pill was placed on her tongue. She drank some water with the pill which went down without difficulty. She gagged momentarily on the fourth pill but managed to swallow it. While still hypnotized, she was given the following instructions. "You are standing in front of your mirror, about to take some pills. You let your face relax; you allow your breathing to slow down; you feel your throat softening and opening; you can see yourself calmly and slowly selecting the pills you are to take, and, one by one, you swallow each with a sip of water. You will experience this calm and ease whenever you are in front of your mirror."

By the third session she was reporting an improvement in her sleep, less tension in her job, and successfully swallowing a few pills a day. By the sixth week she had been able to swallow about half of her medications. She then wanted assistance for test anxiety and social anxieties experienced when at home or out. Desensitization was applied to the test phobia. She terminated, stating that she could continue the procedures on her own. A 6-month follow-up found that she had continued to improve and was recovering well from her difficulties.

Conversion

Conversion symptoms are manifested in sensory, motor, and mental systems. In the sensory system, common symptoms are blindness, deafness, paresthesias, anethesias, and hypesthesias. The motor system reflects tics, spasms, tremors, and paralysis. Mental conversion symptoms are usually fugues, amnesias, trances, and somnambulism.

Diagnostic considerations are not restricted to the possibility of an organic basis for what appears to be psychogenic symptom formation, but includes two other possibilities: first, that particular symptoms may no longer be supported by a psychogenic base and that they are currently autonomous and do not serve any psychodynamic defensive function. The original conflict may have been resolved but the physiology of the symptom remains in its altered state. The second possibility is that *all* symptoms presented by conversion hysteria, or as part of any other psychopathological disorder, for that matter, are not necessarily formed out of the conflict of the given disorder. A person may have acquired a symptom as a result of learning before, during, or after the onset of a classical psychiatric disorder or disease. A learned symptom might be easily become intertwined with the primary complaint, and even aggravated by it, but it is not necessarily a direct manifestation of the complaint.

Precise and valid methods for accomplishing these refined discriminations of symptom formation and etiology are not readily available. Often the discriminations are established or confirmed, over the course of treatment.

Conversion symptoms, as such, as rarely appropriate for direct symptomatic treatment without concurrent psychotherapy for the conflict and anxiety supporting the symptoms. De Witt and Palacious (51) appear to have used the combined approach in the treatment of two cases of conversion neurosis. They applied EMG feedback to flexion contractures of the hands and fingers in "a learning theory model psychotherapeutically.'' They also spoke of their approach as combining the ''strengths of both a physical and emotional treatment plan.'' The treatment consisted of EMG placement and feedback that began at the frontales and then moved to the forearm extensors. The procedure lasted 3 months, and 4 to 6 months after completion the patients were still free of symptoms.

Case examples: The patient was a sixty-four year-old widow who was chairbound due to 7 years' spasticity in her legs. She was also liable to general body spasms during which her knees would be drawn up to her chest. She usually awoke in a fetal position. The left ankle was in severe contraction, with the foot twisted to a sharp degree. All examinations had ruled out neurological pathology and the diagnosis on referral was conversion hysteria.

She was interviewed in her hospital room and attempts to motivate her were based on the observation that the severe contractions might be reduced and she would then be able to return home for outpatient psychiatric care. As much as she did not wish to relinquish her disability, she wanted more to leave the hospital.

The initial session consisted of instructions in relaxation, the use of a tranquil image, and biofeedback instruments. The second session was devoted to right forearm flexor placement of EMG surface electrodes in order to self-demonstrate the feedback procedure, and to emphasize the *self-regulation* of the treatment procedure. The following session introduced frontales placement to augment the training in bodily relaxation. Nine of the next 11 sessions focused on EMG placements on the implicated muscle groups of her legs, especially the left leg and ankle. The other two sessions included frontales placement in order to reinforce the general relaxation.

Within a few sessions, the left leg and foot had straightened as the chronic spasms diminished, and she began standing and walking a few steps with assistance. Her psychopathology involving the loss of her husband became more accessible to consciousness, although she could make little therapeutic use of the recollections. She practiced the relaxation technique fairly diligently and soon the morning spasm of the fetal position remitted.

At this point of the treatment the patient suffered an accidental trauma of mild proportions and regressed to her previous morbid level of functioning and symptom formation. There was also a recurrence of her intermittent episodes of asthma, making her breathing and relaxation exercises more difficult to conduct. *La belle indifference* returned in full force. On discharge, she had lost all gains except the reduction of the severe spasm at the left ankle.

The quick reduction of spasms in the voluntary system is not unusual, nor confined to the hysteric who characteristically loses and acquires symptoms easily. Perhaps a slower reduction of conversion symptoms should be considered in the symptom-oriented treatment of such cases, thereby permitting concurrent psychotherapy to integrate any gains within a more durable change in personality. In the event the symptoms appear to be autonomous, direct treatment could be appropriate. The following case illustrates some of the difficult clinical situations the clinical biofeedback therapist can encounter.

The patient was a sixty-eight year-old woman, separated from her husband for over 40 years. She married at twenty, had two daughters within a few years and left her husband, with his concurrence, after the birth of the second child. She stated that she had suffered much anxiety in her marriage, indicating that the problems had been caused by her husband's drinking and his frequent absences. He continued to support her generously after the separation, and visited his children fairly frequently. Evidently, they had had a friendly, platonic relationship following the separation. The patient did not enter into any intimate relationship with other men throughout her life. She reared her daughters successfully with the financial support of her husband.

The patient was referred for biofeedback and psychotherapy by the consulting psychiatrist who examined her after she had undergone extensive examinations and multiple traditional treatments for her motor complaints. The problem was ataxia of increasing severity over the preceding 5 years. She had suffered unsteadiness in gait for over 25 years with long periods of remission. The symptom gradually worsened over the last several years with a significant exacerbation occurring 5 years ago while she was en route to her weekly visit with her father. She recalled feeling weaker and weaker each trip, sometimes to such a degree that she would have to lean on something for support. She continued the weekly visits but soon had to be driven to his house. When he died about 2 years ago there was no remission of the symptom. On the contrary, her anxiety and her unsteadiness in standing and walking increased in frequency and intensity. When asked about her reactions to her father's death, she said she had been expecting it for years and she had prepared herself to deal with it.

Currently, she walked with a broad gait with her knees slightly bent. She could not balance on one leg nor stand for several minutes without support; and, intermittently, she would be unable to walk at all. Her legs and body would tremble, her knees would "lock," and she would feel as if she was falling. At times, when walking in public and a number of people were heading toward her, she would become acutely anxious and the spasms would occur. She was leaving her house less often and had to have a companion because of the danger of falling. She could not recall any thoughts or emotions, other than apprehension, during the acute episodes. There was no understanding of the cause, nor was she interested in exploring any areas of her life.

The impression was that the muscle spasms and disrupted motor coordination had a psychogenic origin and had become habitual in response to her lifelong attempts to control and compensate for the chronic but adequately defended anxiety. The treatment plan was to teach the patient relaxation to counteract the heightened anxiety, to apply EMG feedback to the lower limbs to reduce any spasticity, to retrain muscle coordination for standing and walking, and to desensitize her to various stress situations. Attempts at insight therapy would be minimal, though attempted where appropriate, in view of the patient's history of her adequate management of her conflicts and her life. Moreover, she obviously did not want to engage in any explorations of her internal life or significant relationships. The symptoms were therefore approached as though they were autonomous.

Nine sessions were held over a period of about 4 months. During the first six weekly sessions, EMG frontales placement combined with relaxation technique were preliminary to EMG placement on the quadriceps and gastrocnemius. She was surprisingly responsive to the initial relaxation training. Basal forehead was 2.50 to 3.00uV; terminal was 1.25 to 1.55uV after 30 minutes. She complained of feeling poor control over her legs when, upon being relaxed, she had been instructed to tighten and lift her legs off the footrest of the lounger. She was asked to record episodes of acute attacks during the coming week and to practice relaxation and lifting her legs while supine several times a day.

At the next session she reported having practiced often, that there had been no acute episodes, and that she felt less shaky. EMG assemblies were placed midthigh, anterior surface, to monitor tension levels. Both areas (quadriceps), were low, although the right thigh, at 1.50uV, was double the left. Feedback for relaxation of the region was begun on the right thigh and when it reduced 50 percent the assemblies were averaged for feedback. After 15 minutes of feedback she was instructed to visualize herself standing with support, then without support. There was only moderate increase in microvoltage during the imagery.

The procedure was continued in the following sessions. Additional applications were the thermistor to monitor and feed back the temperature of her feet, EMG placement on the gastrocnemius and proneus brevis, and desensitization to crowds, stores, and being alone in her house. These scenes were suggested to her while she was relaxed, without using hierarchial steps for every scene.

By the sixth session she reported feeling consistently calm and that her visitors also remarked on the noticeable change. She had suffered one acute episode in a department store. As she approached an escalator she suddenly got worried about getting off and froze for a few minutes.

Thermistor basal readings varied between 78° and 80°F, and she was unable to raise the latter above 84°F. She did faithfully practice hand and feet warming during her relaxation excercises.

The last three sessions included standing and walking a few steps with EMG feedback from the thighs. She complained of having poorer control over her right leg, especially after standing awhile. She threw most of her weight on to her left leg.

The patient was not seen again. She suffered an episode of elevated blood pressure and was diagnosed as migraine with possible arteriosclerosis. When she had stabilized it was decided that she would transfer to a clinic nearer her town, which provided the same services, in order to obviate the long trip into the city. A 30 month follow-up revealed that the improvements in walking, standing, general anxiety, and agoraphobia had continued. She still experienced occasional acute episodes. She had not continued the treatment because the clinic she had been referred to did not apply the same procedures, but had used verbal therapy. She withdrew after a few sessions.

Both of these patients had undergone various treatment procedures in rehabilitation, chemotherapy (for motor dysfunctions), and attempts at psychotherapy. The procedures had limited or no effect on the motor dysfunctions. Undoubtedly, similar patients have presented the same complaints and have responded to traditional treatment approaches. The issue is not one of determining the treatment of choice, but the description of an approach that can be used early in many cases, and tried in some when other procedures have not been efficacious, or have been rejected by the patient.

Anxiety-Related Symptoms in Schizophrenia

Reducing anxiety-related symptoms in schizophrenics through a biofeedback-behavioral paradigm was conducted with 45 patients referred from various out-patient clinics of a metropolitan psychiatric hospital. It was assumed that schizophrenics manifested symptomatic behavior or responses that did not arise from the primary or secondary symptoms of schizophrenia (128). The "personality" of the schizophrenic, rather than the psychosis, was the structure and process of human functioning that was to be treated. In addition, anxiety was viewed as a personality characteristic that would also be targeted. Various affects, attitudes, ego processes, and defenses (15, 18) would necessarily require diagnostic considerations, and treatment procedures would be adapted to the variations in these factors among the patients treated. Simply put, the concept of the treatment paradigm was to treat the person's symptoms and not the underlying schizophrenia (18).

Diagnostic discriminations were made between symptoms that would be categorized as neurotic or psychophysiologic in nonpsychotic patients, and those that were classified as disorders of thought or affect in schizophrenia. Virtually all of the patients who had suffered secondary symptoms of hallucinations or delusions had recompensated. A few were maintaining relative success in the suppression of delusional systems.

Basic considerations of the treatment paradigm included general mental and physical relaxation through the application of the verbal relaxation technique (Chapter 6), biofeedback reduction to overactivation in autonomic and striate muscle systems, without the loss of conscious control of the ego. Avoiding regression was a primary issue in the treatment procedure. The loss of ego boundaries or the removal of defenses would risk the eruption into consciousness of ego dystonic thoughts and affects, or the possibility of derealization occurring (15). The loss of the executive and defensive functions of the ego in schizophrenics can lead to regressive states.

To counteract regression or derealization and depersonalization, the patients were informed in detail about the possible changes in interoception. EMG forearm or frontales feedback was demonstrated on the patients with meticulous attention paid to their questions and apprehensions. Although the patients rarely verbalized more concern than nonschizophrenics, extra time was devoted to verifying their clear and concrete understanding of the source of the signal of any bioinstrument used. The relaxation technique and the imagery used were carefully explained as "taking one's attention and mind and placing them where one wants to." Through the relaxation method, the patient's observing ego was directed to body relaxation and the development of self-control of attention. Letting the mind go blank or empty was discouraged throughout all sessions, and free-association was minimized. Every attempt was made to remind the patients to maintain their attention (passively) on their body regions, rather than to allow their minds or attention to drift off. Recollection of an experience of self-adequacy and a sense of tranquility were used. The point was to maintain activity in both the executive and observing egos. For most of the patients that formulation was unique as an experience of one's own mental-physical functioning.

The relaxation method was that described in Chapter 6 for 40 of the patients. The others responded to Jacobson's method. The depth of relaxation was restricted through intermittent communications of the therapist when indicated in order to support relative alertness during the relaxed state. If frontales microvoltage level fell to below

2uV at 100 to 200 Hz, and the patients' respiration became noticeably slow and shallow, they were instructed to recall the scene of adequacy (Chapter 8) or other imagery in order to lessen the depth of the relaxation. However, as long as the patient's attention is definitely engaged by focusing on the body there is little likelihood of sleep or ego regression occurring during relaxation.

The relaxation should permit the patient to relinquish some degree of defensiveness but simultaneously to maintain self-control, or the integrity of the regulatory ego. In psychodynamic theory, Waelder (212) describes the process of regression in the service of the ego in that the "watchfulness of the 'ego' is temporarily diminished." Relaxation may well be added to his list of parapraxes, dreams, and jokes, in which healthy regression takes place.

The mental and somatic functioning of the patient during relaxation is significantly altered and the ego's observation of these alterations must necessarily be free of anxiety. The schizophrenic's susceptibility to ego dysfunctions and the low ego tolerance for anxiety requires the maintenance of ego controls to a greater degree than in the neurotic patients. Hence the need to avoid anxiety as well as regressive episodes in the treatment of schizophrenics with these methods.

Lowering physiological overactiviation without the loss of the ego's executive functions during relaxation permits application of cognitive and behavioral methods aimed at changing attitudes and in strengthening ego processes.

Under the conditions of this kind of relaxation state it was possible to apply some standard behavioral techniques to treat the anxiety-related presenting problems. Among these techniques were desensitization, self-assertion rehearsals, self-statements, and other cognitive-level communications (Table 6).

There is little literature on the use of biofeedback procedures with schizophrenics. An early case study in 1971 was by Nideffer, et al. (145) who attempted to increase percent alpha and to apply behavior techniques with a good premorbid schizophrenic. The patient left the hospital before the treatment was completed, despite its apparent usefulness. Wentworth-Rohr (219) also reported detailed treatment applications to several cases of schizophrenics who presented many symptoms. They were both in- and out-patients and

Table 6. Frequency of use of biofeedback instruments and behavior techniques

Techniques	f
Attentional relaxation	40
GSR	37
EMG	31
Desensitization	28
Imagery	22
Cognitive statements	12
Record keeping	11
Thermister	8
Thought stoppage	7
Assertive training	6
Progressive relaxation (Jacobson)	5
Aversive conditioning	3
Hypnotism	2

Note: 42 of the 45 patients underwent two or more techniques; 2 received none; 1 received one.

were among many treated over the last decade. They had been referred for symptom-oriented treatment. Satisfactory progress had been accomplished and they were significantly less disabled in living by the symptoms that were treated. The treatment model presented here was used with these patients.

Sarris et al. (177) presented the case of a severe depressive who decompensated during the procedure and was re-diagnosed as schizophrenic. They applied psychotherapy, relaxation, EMG frontales feedback, and recordkeeping to alleviate her migraine headaches and tension. She responded well and also lessened in paranoid ideation; there was improvement in her social relations and most medications were discontinued.

Gleuck and Stroebel (79) used TM and EEG alpha feedback to treat a variety of psychiatric inpatients, six of whom were schizophrenic. Improvement was reported on termination and on follow-up for "many of the patients" who continued to practice TM.

Acosta and Yamamota (2) recently applied EMG frontales feedback to groups of six schizophrenics, five neurotics, and three tension headache cases. After 10 weekly sessions of EMG feedback, and being instructed to relax and to reduce the feedback tone, analysis of variance showed a significant decrease in forehead tension levels for all groups.

Evidently, the use of these symptom-oriented, short-term methods with schizophrenics can be efficacious. Although the foregoing studies are not explicit about the mental status of their subjects, one assumes that all were recompensated from any psychotic episodes they may have suffered and that they were capable of appropriate kinds of cooperation. We find that to be a prerequisite for such treatment procedures.

An evaluation study was conducted of 45 cooperative schizophrenics who had been referred by various out-patient services for biofeedback-behavioral therapy. All patients seen are included in the study. Sixty-six had been referred over several years, but 21 were not seen at all due to their refusal of the service, or their not being available after the long delays on the waiting list. Each patient was phoned in order of referral for the first session. If the patient was not available, the next was called, and so on. They were referred for the short-term, symptom-oriented treatment procedure because their symptoms had not remitted to other, standard procedures.

All the patients seen were currently in individual or group therapy; 35 were taking psychotropic medications. It was not possible to control for medication due to the wide variations in kinds and dosage. There were 20 males and 25 females, ranging in age from sixteen to sixty-nine, with a mean age of 36.36. Years of education ranged 8 to 18, with a mean of 12.73; occupations were varied and 28 were unemployed. Of the patients, 30 had had one or more psychiatric hospitalizations, totaling 81, and ranging 1 to 12. The average for these 30 patients was 2.70. Twenty-eight had been hospitalized one to five times, one eight times, and another 12 times; only 13 had been hospitalized only once. Of the patients, 27 were single, 10 married, and 8 divorced or separated.

Duration of schizophrenia ranged from one year to 38, the average being 13.38 years. The duration of presenting problems, those complaints selected for biofeedback-behavior therapy treatment, ranged from 10 months to 40 years; the average duration was also 13 years. The range of the number of presenting problems was 1 to 5, averaging 2.93. Only five patients presented one problem for treatment. The number of sessions totaled 522 and ranged 1 to 32, averaging 11.6; and 29 of the 45 patients (64 percent) were seen nine or more sessions. Treatment sessions were conducted by 13 different intern and staff psychologists, and by five psychiatric residents.

Table 7 shows the frequencies of the problems in 27 categories presented by the patients for treatment. The most common were diffuse anxiety (35), obsessions (13), phobias and fears (13), insomnia (11), generalized muscle spasms (7), depression (6), and general muscle tension (6). These comprised 90 (68 percent) of the 132 problems presented.

Chi-square using 1 df was applied throughout in testing for significant differences. It was anticipated that few symptoms would be improved by the treatment procedure, inasmuch as none had remitted to other therapies. However, expected frequency for change in symptoms was set at 50 percent of the observed frequency. The 50 percent improvement by chance was selected in order to establish a highly stringent criterion to test significance.

The criterion for improvement in presenting problems consisted of a reduction in the intensity and frequency of the problem so that it no longer interfered appreciably in the patient's functioning. Both patient and therapist judgments were used to assess the degree of change, supplemented by records kept by some patients.

Further inspection of Table 7 shows that on termination, for the 45 patients, 64 of their 132 symptoms had improved, 68 had not. The difference is not significant. For the 29 patients who came nine or more sessions, 63 of their 85 symptoms were improved, 22 symptoms were not. The difference by chi-square falls below the .001 level. For the 22 patients who came 12 or more sessions, 43 of their 63 symptoms were improved, against 20 not improved. This difference is also significant (p. <.005). There was an improvement in symptoms for different patients in 21 of the 27 categories, although no one of these reached significance.

A follow-up survey was conducted 6 months after termination. The patients were interviewed by phone or in person concerning the status of their presenting symptoms. The time period of the follow-up ranged from a minimum of 6 months to 46 months; the average was 14.9 with an SD of 10.03. Table 7 shows that 31 of the 45 patients were found. They had presented 87 symptoms, 48 of which had not remitted. For 22 of the 31 patients who had had nine or more sessions, 43 of their 64 symptoms had changed, which is significant below the .007 level. Of the 31 patients who were treated 12 or more sessions 16 had presented 46 symptoms, 29 of which had improved on termination and had held for 6 months. The level of significance was below .077.

Generally, the treatment paradigm was efficacious with regard to the reduction of symptomatic behavior for the group of 45 patients, as measured on termination and follow-up, provided the patients received nine or more treatment sessions.

The foregoing discussion dealt with the number of changes in symptoms for the group of 45 patients. Table 8 reports on the *number of patients* who improved in one or more symptoms, worsened in pathology, or who developed new symptoms on termination or on follow-up. The criterion for dividing the 45 patients into improved versus unimproved was established on the basis that improvement in at least one symptom would constitute improvement for any patient.

Of the 45 patients, 27 improved in one or more symptoms on termination, which is not a significant change for the population. Of the 29 patients who had 9 to 32 treatment sessions, 26 improved; and 19 of the 22 who had 12 to 32 sessions were improved. Improvement in one or more symptoms on termination of treatment for each of these groups was significant at below the .001 level. No patient developed new symptoms during the course of treatment, but four patients of the unimproved group suffered an exacerbation of their psychopathology. They will be discussed shortly.

Follow-up data on 31 of the patients who were located revealed that 22 of the 31 had maintained their improvement in at least one

Table 7.
Frequency of presenting problem and improved-unimproved rates on termination and follow up

Frequency of Presenting Problems

Presenting Problems	Termination (N=45)			Follow-up (N=31)		
	f	imp	unimp	f	imp	unimp
Anxiety	35	20	15	23	15	8
Obsessions	13	4	9	7	4	3
Phobias, fears	13	6	7	9	5	4
Insomnia	11	5	6	6	3	3
Muscle spasms (general)	7	5	2	5	2	3
Depression	6	2	4	6	2	4
General tension	5	3	2	3	3	0
Smoking	5	2	3	5	2	3
Tension headaches	4	1	3	2	2	0
Sexual dysfunction	3	3	0	3	3	0
Muscle spasms (localized)	4	1	3	1	0	1

					p<					p<
Vasoconstriction	3	2	1			2	1	1		
Respiratory dysfunction	2	0	2			1	0	1		
Bruxism (TMJ)	2	1	1			1	0	1		
Compulsions	2	1	1			1	1	0		
Drug abuse (marijuana)	2	1	1			1	1	0		
Dysphagia	2	1	1			1	0	1.		
Nail-flesh biting	2	2	0			1	0	1		
Social anxiety	2	1	1			2	1	1		
Separation anxiety	2	0	2			1	0	1		
Allergies	1	0	1			1	0	1		
Motor restlessness	1	0	1			1	0	1		
Anorexia	1	0	1			1	0	1		
Sweating	1	0	1			1	0	1		
Pain	1	1	0			1	1	0		
Neurodermatitis	1	1	0			1	1	0		
Excessive medication	1	1	0			1	1	0		

Sessions	$\bar{X}$	N			p<	N				p<
					.728					.335
1-32	11.60	45	132	64	68	31	87	48	39	
9-32	16.34	29	85	63	22	22	64	43	21	.007
12-32	17.59	22	63	43	20	16	46	29	17	.077

p< .001   .005

Table 8.

Number of patients improved - unimproved in one or more symptoms, worsened, or developed new symptoms on termination and follow-up according to number of sessions.

No. of Sessions	Termination (N=45)						Follow-up (N=31)					
	N	Imp	Unimp	p<	Wor	New Symp	N	Imp	Unimp	p<	Wor	New Symp
1-32	45	27	18	.250	4	0	31	22	9	.025	2	3
9-32	29	26	3	.001	3	0	22	19	3	.001	2	3
12-32	22	19	3	.001	3	0	16	13	3	.025	2[a]	2

[a] One symptom a recurrence of a treated symptom (dysphagia).

Note: Nineteen of 45 patients improved in all symptoms on termination (p.=.75); on follow-up, 12 of 31 (p.=.50).

symptom that had improved on termination, regardless of the number of sessions. The level of significance fell below .025. Of the 31 patients, 22 had come nine or more sessions and 19 had similarly improved, the level of significance falling below .001. And for 13 of the 16 who had come 12 to 32 sessions, 13 had sustained any improvement achieved on termination. Again, the level of significance was below .001.

Four patients are noted on Table 8 as having worsened on termination in symptoms or diagnosis. Inspection of their clinical records revealed that they had presented 14 symptoms, four of which worsened. These symptoms were agoraphobia, obsessions for two patients, and exacerbation of the schizophrenia for the fourth patient who was being treated for anorexia nervosa. She had been treated for her inability to experience tactile sensation through an increase of exteroception by means of her touching different areas of her body and noting the hardness, softness or the quality of the tactile sensation. There was mild improvement in appetite, but it accompanied the emergence of psychoticism. Evidently, her dissociation of bodily sensation was a defense against the psychosis.

In the follow-up of the four patients only two were located; the agoraphobia and obsessions for one of them had improved. The other obsessive patient had been hospitalized after 12 sessions because of an increase in suicidal thoughts. She was not located on follow-up. The second of the patients who were worsened on follow-up was one whose moderate hyperphagia had improved on termination but had recurred on follow-up.

Three new symptoms were reported on follow-up by three patients. One was a loss of appetite which was diagnosed as being related to a long-standing gastric ulcer; the second was obsessions about being emotionally hurt by others; and the third was acute anxiety attacks. The last patient's record suggests that she has suffered anxiety attacks periodically for several years. Only one of these new symptoms appeared to be substitutional for a previous symptom—the obsessions. In that case, the patient had previously suffered from ego dystonic, homosexual preoccupations which had lessened significantly over the course of treatment. Evidently, the preoccupation later acquired a paranoid direction.

Chemotherapy was not controlled throughout the treatment of any patient. Thirty-five of the patients were on a variety of psychotropic medications. The variety and combinations of drugs made it impossible to inspect subgroups according to type of medication. Also, many of the patients had been on medication for extended periods of time. Only one patient was taken off all medication during his period of treatment and he became quite anxious and suffered a recurrence of suicidal thoughts (see case example of the twenty-three year-old male).

Inasmuch as the 35 patients had been on chemotherapy *before* undergoing the biofeedback-behavior therapy and that a significant number of patients, or number of symptoms for the group, remitted upon adding the treatment procedure, it is possible to assume that the procedure was efficacious. However, one must consider the possibility that the combination of chemotherapy and the treatment techniques contributed to improvement in the presenting symptoms.

The possibility is demonstrated in Table 9 which listed numbers of patients according to their number of sessions and comparing the 27 patients who improved with the 18 who did not improve, as well as subdividing these groups into categories of medication and previous hospitalization. Hospitalization was inspected in view of the probability that it is a measure, along with medication, of severity of psychopathology. Perhaps the number of sessions varied with hospitalized versus nonhospitalized, or medicated versus nonmedicated.

Results of analysis of variance examining the effect of sessions and hospitalization of improvement (Table 9) indicated that only the main effect of the number of sessions had a significant influence on improvement $F_{3,41} = (8.926,$ p $<.001.$). Regarding medication, the lack of cases in cells prevented testing for any effect on improvement. The possibility of medication acting on the rate of improvement remains to be determined. There may well be an interaction between sessions and medication in the form of the treatment procedure being necessary, but not sufficient, to reduce the anxiety-related symptoms while the medication minimizes the ego-disorganization resulting from the schizophrenia.

Figure 7 illustrates the scatter of 45 patients along the axes of improvement in symptoms for each patient over sessions. The vertical axis is composed of weighted scores of improvement derived from multiplying the number of symptoms times the number of symptoms improved for each patient. The horizontal axis is number of sessions from 1 to 32.

Table 9. Number of patients improved-unimproved in one or more symptoms according to hospitalization, medication and number of sessions.

No. of Pts.	No. of Sess.	Improved (27)[a]					Not Improved (18)				
		Hospitalized[b] Medication[c]		Not Hospitalized Medication		Total Imp	Hospitalized Medication		Not Hospitalized Medication		Total Unimp
		Yes	No	Yes	No		Yes	No	Yes	No	
10	16-32	7		1		8		1	1		2
3	15	2	1			3					
1	14				1	1					
3	13	3				3					
5	12	2	1	1		4	1				1
2	11	1			1	2					
3	10	1		1	1	3					
2	9	1			1	2					
2	8			1		1	1				1
1	7								1		1
1	6						1				1
4	5						4				4
1	4								1		1
7	1-3						2	1	2	2	7
N=45		17	2	4	4	(27)	9	2	5	2	(18)

a. Only one patient improved who came less than 9 sessions.
b. At least one hospitalization previous to biofeedback therapy.
c. Psychotropic medications.

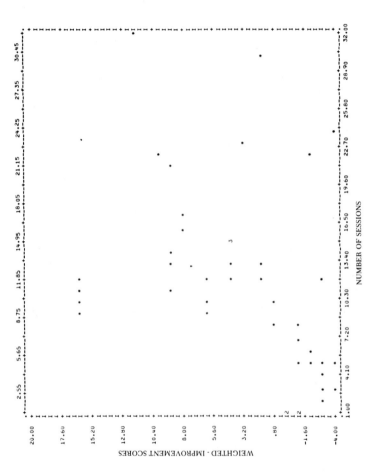

FIGURE 7. Scattergram showing individual, weighted-improvement scores as a function of number of sessions (N = 45).

Inspection of the scattergram indicates that as sessions increased rate of improvement increased, especially between sessions 9 to 21. As shown in tables 7 and 8, there is little relationship between improvement and sessions below session seven. Moreover, there is some tendency in Figure 7 to a fall-off in rate of improvement after session 21.

Generally, then, applying controlled processes of relaxation, keeping the patient in touch with body awareness and the mind occupied with imagery that counteracts anxiety, applying appropriate therapy techniques that reduce physiologically based anxiety and diminishing anxiety-provoking attitudes, such as phobias, can result in a wide variety of changes in anxiety-related symptoms in chronic, ambulatory schizophrenics. The changes persist as determined on follow-up for an average of 14 months. The treatment procedures require about nine or more sessions, once a week, to be effective.

Severity of psychopathology as measured by duration of schizophrenia or of the symptoms treated and whether or not previously hospitalized, did not relate to remission of symptoms. Most of the patients were on psychotropic medication, and a large majority on medication improved in one or more symptoms. The small number of patients in cells grouped according to medication versus no medication and number of sessions treated precluded statistical comparisons of the subgroups. Medication, therefore, confounds number of sessions treated. Moreover, in view of present clinical experience, one should not predict usefulness of the treatment procedure until at least 7 to 9 sessions have been conducted.

Case example: Judy was a forty-nine year-old, attractive, single, unemployed secretary, diagnosed as a chronic undifferentiated schizophrenic. Her early history was uneventful except for her "miserable and bad" family life. Her father was an alcoholic who physically abused his wife and abondoned the family when the patient was six. The mother was described as "sick and disgusting," as hating the patient who reminded the mother of her husband, and who beat the patient frequently. Judy left home in her middle teens for a large city where she worked as a dancer for ten years. After being unable to continue dancing, she worked as a secretary.

At age thirty-seven she became physically ill and experienced episodes of derealization. She entered psychiatric care manifesting flat affect, hyperactive motor behavior, concrete thinking, loose associations, and feelings of helplessness. She was hospitalized briefly, receiving multiple treatment procedures including electroconvulsive therapy. Progress was satisfactory and she continued in outpatient therapy. She was hospitalized several times over the following five years but was adequately successful in maintaining herself with the assistance of medication and psychotherapy when needed.

Judy was referred for biofeedback and relaxation therapy for severe headaches of some five years' duration and for Tylenol abuse, 10 to 14 per day. She rated her headache pain upon awakening at 10 (on a 1 to 10 scale), and immediately took two Tylenols. In the afternoon the headache lessened, increasing to 7 to 8 in the early evening.

The onset of the headaches followed a return from an eventful vacation. But the patient attributed the headaches to an auto accident, 10 years previously. All examinations were negative. There were no other complaints appropriate to biofeedback treatment.

The treatment procedure consisted of 13 weekly sessions of EMG, frontales and TMJ feedback to reduce the tension headaches and to augment general relaxation. In the first session, EMG frontales basal was around 20uV (100 to 200Hz), with considerable variations in the meter readings. She was apprehensive and tense throughout the session, with no significant change in EMG frontal output. The verbal relaxation technique was applied over the session. She stated that she felt more relaxed at termination, dropping from 8 to 3 on a subjective scale. This procedure was the primary treatment of the 13 sessions, along with monitoring and keeping records of the use of the analgestic and her home practice of relaxation.

In the second session the EMG basal was still high and variable. However, reduction to 2.0 to 3.0uV occurred within 20 minutes. At the end of the session she again reported being relaxed even though she was disturbed by the loud noises of a group therapy session from the adjoining office. Fingertip placement of a GSR machine had also been used but was unchanged across the session. The third session was replicated without the GSR, and the patient responded well. Her subjective report of general tension level at the beginning and the end of the session was 7 to 3, respectively. There was no change in incidence or frequency of headaches or use of analgesic during the previous week.

Over the following 10 sessions a gradual change in the complaint took place. Basal EMG frontales consistently fell to a usual level of 1 to 2uV, and when relaxed to below. TMJ monitoring was conducted during the 8 to 11th sessions, with the mild tension levels responding well to feedback. There were no complaints about other head or neck regions. On occasional sessions, the patient discussed some aspects of her personal life.

By the last session she had reduced the analgesic to 1 to 3 times per day and was essentially free of chronic headaches. On follow-up, 12 months after termination, the patient reported that her general tension level was usually around 3, she was having headaches only in the morning and taking only one analgesic pill, and she had cut her other medication in half. No new symptoms had appeared.

Another patient treated was a twenty-three year old single unemployed male, referred for severe anxiety and social phobias. He had been a brilliant high school student who dropped out of school due to his diffuse anxiety and phobic reactions to social situations. At age eighteen he used mescaline and LSD and became overtly psychotic. He suffered depersonalization and ideas of reference, and since that acute episode he was mildly paranoid and convinced that people could read his thoughts. He had been hospitalized following that episode and rehospitalized several times over the next 4 years, each time for an acute exacerbation of the schizophrenia and for suicidal gestures.

He had been a sickly child from birth to age seven. Both parents had suffered poliomyelitis leaving the mother paraplegic and the father hemiplegic. He described his mother as a "domineering warhorse," and his father as "submissive and nonsupporting." His relationship with his older brother had been one of mutual dislike and harassment by the brother.

The patient's last hospitalization followed a decompensation after feeling rejected by some female friends. He slashed his arm and appeared at the emergency room. On admission to the psychiatric hospital he was reported as being fully oriented, appropriately dressed, and cooperative. Mood was depressed, affect was restricted, associations were loose, tangential and circumstantial with a flight of ideas and mildly paranoid thoughts, and he had feelings of depersonalization. After inpatient treatment and considerable improvement, he was placed in the day hospital where his progress continued.

On referral for biofeedback-behavioral treatment of the anxiety and phobia he was highly motivated and responsive to the suggested treatment plan. His complaints were chronic and diffuse anxiety, experienced as general tension and nervousness, inability to assert himself in his family and with peers, a marked rise in tension in any interpersonal situation, and occasional severe stomach spasms. The treatment plan was to train him in relaxation and to desensitize him to the social phobia.

During the first few sessions of relaxation, augmented with GSR and EMG forearm feedback, he was extremely restless and distracted. He gradually learned to use the GSR feedback and the relaxation technique and began to lower the autonomic over-activation and his subjective feeling of fearfulness. He felt his life was becoming more "orderly." There was then a change in the medication, resulting in an increase in anxiety and a recurrence of suicidal thoughts. Upon returning to the neuroleptic drug, he stabilized and was able to continue the treatment procedure. The remaining seven of fourteen sessions were devoted to reinforcing the relaxation technique and to desensitization of the social phobia, using the GSR to augment the relaxation training and to monitor his autonomic changes to the desensitization hierachy. Progress was satisfactory, including an increase in self-assertion. Six-month follow-up revealed that the gains were being maintained.

An example of a "somatizer," the kind of patient who has a poor response to the treatment procedure, is forty-one year-old male who had a symbiotic relationship with his mother. He was referred for obsessive preoccupations with somatic complaints concerning dying from a heart condition or a respiratory ailment, diffuse anxiety, and multiple phobias. There had been four hospitalizations over the previous 8 years, and numerous consultations with medical specialists. He had been in private psychiatric care during those years with intermittent periods of remission of his symptoms. There was no known reason for the recent exacerbation which led to his last hospitalization.

He was a single, high-school graduate of high-average intelligence, homosexual since age thirteen, unemployed, and living at home with his mother. His father had died 8 years previously. He was being carried in a day hospital facility, participating in several occupational and therapy groups, and on psychotropic medication.

In the first interview he was fully oriented, self-preoccupied, quite restless, but cooperative in discussing possible treatment techniques. He smoked and chewed gum incessantly. Associations were intact though quite mobile; affect was appropriate; mood, mildly depressed. He complained chiefly of somatic difficulties. The onset was about 8 years previous, although he was uncertain as to whether the complaints occurred before, at the time of, or after his father's death. He recalled walking down the hospital corridor after the death (he had not been present), and feeling " the walls shifting and I had to lean over." His skin felt "numb," while shaving the following days.

Currently, he describes his problems as getting numb and being convinced he has a brain tumor. The numbness "is all over my body; and my breathing isn't working. A better way to put it is I feel like a deflated balloon; like I have no substance. I feel the air in my nose but I don't feel like I'm breathing." He also suffers fearfulness on the street, when with relatives, and on the subway. Two weeks before he had vomited at the subway entrance. He felt weak before and after eating, not while eating, and never felt satiated. At times he'd feel that he was falling off his feet, his throat would constrict, and he'd think of having a brain tumor. There were fears of flying and of having any of the attacks described above. The smoking and gum-chewing made him "feel himself."

There were no complaints of striate muscle spasms or vasoconstriction, even though his hands were cool, and he did not perspire excessively.

The tentative treatment plan was to apply relaxation technique, thermistor feedback from the hands, and to attempt desensitization to the subways and the mild agoraphobia. In the event the procedures were helpful, desensitization to separation anxiety (from the mother) and to work situations would be added. The prognosis was poor. Reassessment of the procedure would be done in 2 to 3 sessions.

The first session consisted of EMG frontales placement and application of general relaxation. Frontal levels were low and variable (1.5 to 5.0uV) with some reduction of the upper ranges over the first session. He persisted in interrupting the procedure with restless movements and several comments. The session was ended early in order to let him talk. He rambled on about his family, his father's death, and his symptoms. He did add that his parents had divorced when he was born, that his father was schizophrenic and had lived out his life with his own parents, dying of lung cancer. When the similarities with his own heart complaint and his lfie-style was pointed out him he merely ignored the interpretations.

The second session was a continuation of the first. Frontal levels were similar but fell to below 1.0uV within 10 minutes of relaxation. He complained about a family gathering that had taken place and his reluctance to attend it, but upon taking extra medication the anxiety decreased. He was out ill the next week. In the third and last session, thermistor feedback from the hands was applied. The right had was 87.5 and the left, 90.1°F. The output was averaged for feedback. Within 15 minutes, with relaxation and the feedback, the temperature increased to 95.0. He was asked to recall any recent stressful experience, but there was no change in temperature. After the session he reported not feeling any anxiety during the recall.

The patient was not seen again. He was discharged from the day hospital to another outpatient facility, with the arrangement that the biofeedback procedure would continue if he and his next primary therapist requested it. He said he didn't think he'd return, that he really needed a brain operation, and that there was no change in any of the symptoms.

Chapter 15

RESPIRATORY SYSTEM

Asthma

Asthma appears to be the most commonly reported respiratory condition that has been treated by clinical biofeedback (1, 11, 28, 47, 72, 74). The goal of the biofeedback is to reduce stress levels, susceptibility to stress and muscle tension, and to gain some control over bronchial spasms. Asthma is a complex of factors involving allergies, stress, endocrine changes, genetic disposition, and psychological traits. Dependency and fear of separation or rejection are present in a significant number of asthmatics (216), with a wide variety of idiosyncratic defenses used to deal with anxiety and the symptom. Secondary gain is a characteristic development. Asthmatics may also have breathing difficulties while asleep, resulting in sleep disturbances. The disruption of the natural progress of the stages of sleep interferes with the production of growth hormones in children, as well as resulting in fatigue and poor attention. The severe bronchial spasm can be a life-threatening event; and even if the asthma is not considered severe enough to be lethal, episodes of loss of one's breath feel as if it is life-threatening. These episodes cause anxiety in both the patient and family, which often increases stress level and dependency problems.

The clinical biofeedback program concentrates on reducing physiological overactivation in any implicated system, training in relaxation augmented by appropriate bioinstruments, desensitization of fears and phobias, and proper breathing. Diaphragmatic breathing is taught or improved when required (see below). Particular attention is paid to the possibility of the patient's fear of shallow breathing, or of any change through training in breathing habits. Often anxiety erupts because the patient has experienced his breathing as a dreadful threat.

Abdullah (1) reported good results in using feedback of bronchial spasms during relaxations. The patients were taught to recognize the spasms and they then relaxed and attempted to reduce the spasticity through stethoscopic feedback. Abdullah did not report any details of his population, which leaves open the question of appropriateness of use with regard to age, sex, or severity of illness.

Davis et al. (74) had qualified success in treating 24 children suffering fron intractable asthma who were under treatment in a residential center. Twelve of the twenty-four were between ages six and ten, and the rest between eleven and sixteen. One-half of the twenty-four were considered, for purposes of the study, to be severe by virtue of being on maintenance dosages of cortiscosteroids. Those not on medications were considered to be nonsevere cases. The 24 children were divided into three groups, matched according to age and severity of asthma. One group received Jacobson's relaxation technique augmented by frontales EMG feedback. A second group received only Jacobson's relaxation; and the third group, the controls, were instructed to read and to relax. Pre- and post-expiratory flow rates were recorded at each session. Baseline measurement periods lasted 8 days, the treatment period 5 days (one session per day), and the post-treatment period 8 days. The outcome was good for the nonsevere cases, regardless of age, for both treatment groups, with a more significant degree of improvement found in the biofeedback-relaxation group. The reduction in peak expiratory flow rates did not persist for any of the subjects. The authors evidently did not require the subjects treated to practice daily relaxation after the project was terminated, which may account for the lack of generalization. The few—only five—sessions of treatment may also have provided insufficient training.

In clinical practice, the patients are instructed to practice daily and informed that they would probably have to maintain low activation levels so long as the asthma persisted.

Diaphragmatic Breathing

Proper breathing is a rehabilitaiton aspect of treating asthmatics. Training in diaphragmatic breathing can be included in their treatment programs, as well as in the program for any patient seen in clinical biofeedback who is breathing incorrectly.

Diaphragmatic breathing uses fewer muscles during the breathing cycle, provides more oxygen at a lower expenditure of energy, and is an efficient method of respiration whether one is sitting, walking, speaking, singing, or running. The diaphragm is a large muscle below the organs of the chest and is teepee-shaped when relaxed. It flattens when contracted, allowing the lungs to drop and expand, permitting an increase in air volume in the lungs.

Training is done by having the patient stand erect, place one hand over the upper abdomen, or just above the navel, and "push" the area out. Do not instruct the patient to breathe in; he would merely repeat habitual thoracic expansion of the costals of the chest and become confused about what to do. Ignore any errors in breathing, and reinforce the correct movement with approval. When the EMG is used to train breathing the ground is placed above the navel and each active about 4 to 6 inches from the ground, on a horizontal line. Sessions in positive feedback are conducted sitting and standing. The sensitivity gain is set to exclude the maximum amount of noise but to allow the appropriate feedback signal through. The training goal is to increase the signal during each inhalation; the amplitude should co-vary with depth of each inhalation. Home practice is of course essential.

> *Case example:* A complaint of a functional problem of shallow breathing in a seventeen year-old high school girl who also complained of an inability to stay awake while studying. She was extremely intelligent, cooperative, and motivated. Her breathing problem was "life long." She occasionally gasped for breath for no cause, and when exercising she would become quite short of breath. Mild attacks of asthma occurred when close to dogs and cats. She also reported amenorrhea for which she was under medication and was experiencing a side effect of skin eruptions. Development and health were otherwise normal. She did not suffer vasoconstriction, sweaty hands, or other physical dysfunctions.

The treatment plan was EMG frontales and GSR augmented relaxation, diaphragmatic breathing with EMG feedback, and record-keeping of complaints.

Baseline tension level in the frontales was moderate (2.25uV), and skin conductance low. There was little progress in the first session due to the patient's difficulty in staying awake while relaxing. Diaphragmatic breathing was taught in the fourth session after she had learned to relax herself in the office to a deep level. She had added breathing exercises to her home practice in relaxing. By the ninth session she was breathing easily from the diaphragm. In some sessions, frontales would be initially high (4.0 to 2.0uV) with reduction to (1.5 to 2.0uV) over 30 minutes. She reported that she could become tense by striving to relax and being worried about succeeding.

After 12 sessions she reported no difficulties with breathing, even when exercising. Her concentration has improved, she did not fall asleep while studying, and her menstrual cycle had recurred.

Follow-up at 1, 3, and 4 years found her to be symptom-free

Chapter 16

SEXUAL DYSFUNCTION

Biofeedback instrumentation used in the treatment of sexual dysfunctions is a recent addition to the techniques of sex therapists. Perry (158) reviewed the literature and surveyed both biofeedback specialists and sex therapists in 1978 and found that "sex-specific" instrumentation has come to supplement the usual treat procedures of psychotherapy, behavior therapy, relaxation, and sexual exercises. The value of the bioinstruments has been their direct and precise measurements of genital blood volume, temperature levels, vaginal and rectal myotonia, and concurrent physiological processes involved in sexuality but can also be used to reintegrate body-mind-emotions in cases of over-repression that result in decreased sensuality (219).

The biofeedback literature in the arena of sex therapy tends to concentrate on the physiology (95). This particular approach may well be appropriate and useful for person's whose personal relationships and sexuality on the mental-emotional levels are not impaired. It is not surprising to find that many cases of psychogenic impotence, frigidity, and vaginismus originate in childhood and adolescence, and that the dysfunctions persist into adulthood even though the adults had revised their attitudes about sexuality. The dysfunctions remain as learned, physiological states that the sufferers cannot revise as easily as their attitudes. Repeated attempts to overcome the physiological handicap through repeated sexual activities are as likely to reinforce the dysfunctions as to reduce them. Failure, embarrassment, and frustration would add to the tension and come to increase the probability of failure. In these cases, where serious conflicts no longer exist, or where growth and knowledge have minimized puritanical attitudes, the application of a symptom-oriented biofeedback paradigm is a sensible treatment procedure.

Instances of significant underlying conflicts or serious degrees of psychopathology in patients are inappropriate, *initially*, for biofeedback treatment. Kaplan (108) reviews many such cases in her volume on sex therapies and emphasizes the importance of both psychosocial and medical assessments preliminary to treatment planning. Generally speaking, when both organic and psychopathological etiologies have been ruled out, the clinical biofeedback procedure is quite useful in treating functional disorders of sexuality.

Many patients present classical autonomic hyperarousal responses in the sexual situation—cold hands, sweaty palms, increased heart rate, etc. The increase in sympathetic tone results in vasoconstriction in many of these people and the blood flow to the genitals is diminished. Sexual arousal then cannot take place. Some patients report serious spasms, usually in the pelvic region, occasionally of sharp loci. Spasticity reported as painful or an interference in sexual activity for males or females are targets for tension reduction with EMG feedback.

Since sexual stimulation normally heightens arousal, response stereotypy can occur if the person is susceptible to such generalization of responsivity. The stereotypic response along with general stress reduction should be alleviated before focusing on the sexual dysfunction. This procedure sometimes leads to a spontaneous remission of the specific symptom itself. Similarly, treating social anxiety, or the fear of rejection that may be the basic apprehension, or other mental complications reported by the patient, may also result in spontaneous symptom reduction. Sexuality in humans includes a cortical or mental state and in many instances the physiopathology is a *response* to thoughts and emotions, rather than an isolated dysfunction of biology.

Most often, though, the sexual dysfunction presented requires treatment of the physiological component of the symptom, as well as the psychosocial components. By the time the patient appears for therapy any physiological response may have become fixed and would need direct intervention through biofeedback applications.

The male sexual sequence of erection-ejaculation is not regulated by a single neurophysiological mechanism. Erectile adequacy is the end result of vasocongestation of the penis through vascular flow. The flow is regulated by involuntary reflexes, but is susceptible to central mechanisms that can be modified by mental-emotional states. Anxiety, fight-flight sympathetic overactivation, disturbing thoughts, shame, etc., can disrupt blood flow to the genitals. Parasympathetic fibers are directly involved in the dilation of genital blood vessels. Conversely, the phase of *emission* which is preliminary to orgasm in the male is regulated by sympathetic nervous system activity. These fibers also innervate and contract organs participating in the sequence: the prostate, vans deferens, seminal vesicles, and the internal urethra (108).

Ejaculation is necessary for normal male orgasm. Erection is not. Obviously, in the act of coitus, the erection is essential to the male's performance. Orgasm is the end result of the contractions of the voluntary muscles of the bulbar urethra expelling the bolus of sperm and prostatic fluids from the penis. The complete process is an involuntary reflex, but is mediated by the voluntary nervous system. Therefore, it can be modified by central activity.

Lack of orgasm is failure in the ejaculatory mechanisms, for the male; and, in the female, failure to reach contractile level in the circumvaginal muscles. These are the perineal, bulbar, pubococcygeal, uteral, and some related muscles. In these anatomical structures the male and female are orgastically the same: both groups of muscles appear to be the particular physical agents producing orgasm.

The male and female initial (excitement) phase of sexual arousal are also physiologically the same: vasocongestion of the sexual apparatus, leading to tumescence in the female and erection in the male. In the female, the dilation causes engorgement of the uterus, labia, the perineum, the bulbs of the vestibule, the lower third of the vagina, and the pelvic area. Vaginal lubrication simultaneously occurs in preparation for penile insertion. As in the male sexual sequence, dysfunctions can occur at various psychological or physiological levels of sexuality.

The male ejaculation biologically guarantees orgasm through its reflexive mechanisms. The female orgasm is not biologically analogous in that respect and constitutes a major difference between the sexes in their experience of sexual pleasure and adequacy. Women report sexual pleasure through the vasocongestive phase and do not always require orgasm to feel satisfied. However, if orgasm is not achieved sufficiently often, women then experience the same frustrations as the man who has become aroused but does not ejaculate.

In general, most patients who undertake clinical biofeedback for psychogenic sexual dysfunctions are provided with relaxation training, biofeedback for any physiological complaints, desensitization to sexual anxiety, reduction of any other symptoms appropriate for treatment, and sexual counseling and exercises. Couples therapy is not always necessary, but when it is, it is crucial.

The initial interview for biofeedback should assess the mental-emotional-social aspects of the patient's complaint, as well as the physiological. The minimum data needed for treatment planning (Chapter 7) is sufficient to institute relaxation technique and to target implicated physiologies. As the patient reduces defensiveness and masking-symptoms, any others not reported rise to consciousness and require appropriate treatment.

Functional Impotence

Kaplan (108) lists three general forms of male, dysfunctional syndromes, naming impotence "erectile dysfunction." The others refer to states of retarded and premature ejaculation. She emphasizes that there are innumerable variations of erectile difficulties relating to internal and external causes. Many attributes of these environments can be influential in erectile inadequacy: unconscious conflicts, choice of sex partner, problems of self-assertion and dominance, attitudes toward women in general and individual sex partners in particular, situation-specific reactions, conscious or unconscious hostility, and so on. Some men are impotent periodically or chronically; some partially or wholly; some with wives but not with other women; some in terms of position in intercourse, etc. There are also fluctuations over time in these possibilities for some men. A common denominator among cases of psychogenic impotence is the physiological failure in adequate blood flow to the cavernous sinuses of the penis. This homeostatic dysfunction can be caused, among different men, by disruptions of any stage of the heterosexual sequence of activities. There may be a specific historical experience that disrupted the normal vascular reflex mechanisms at a particular stage, in the sense of learned response, that results in an insufficient or blocked blood flow, and a partial erection or none at all. Response stereotypy may be present in the form of spasms in the perineal or adjacent muscles. The onset, or the sequence, of sexual arousal may evoke anxiety, which in turn triggers homostatic dysfunctions of the normal physiological sequence of sexual performance. These precise discriminations are not always obtained during the initial interviews, but will emerge over treatment sessions.

As indicated above, stress reduction to lower chronic or acute over-activation is the preliminary stage of any treatment plan.

> *Case example:* Carl was an applied scientist in his late twenties, unmarried, living with his parents. His complaint was functional impotence. For the several years of his active sex life he had been impotent periodically, and rarely fully potent in intercourse. During the previous year he had been unable to maintain his erection at the onset of coitus. He usually dated sexually naive young women and seldom attempted sexual activity beyond petting.
>
> He had tried verbal psychotherapy briefly with two different therapists, several visits to a sex surrogate, behavior therapy, acupuncture, and hypnotism. He derived some benefits in self-understanding from the psychotherapy, but none from the other procedures.
>
> Additional complaints were episodes of autonomic overactivation, mild tachycardia, clammy hands, recurrent stress at work or in the company of women, excessive shyness with women, an inability to express emotions, and a chronic "feeling that my pelvic muscles, deep down are tight and the blood flow

to my genitals is not full.'' The area of tension covered the anterior aspect of the lower half of his torso to the middle of his thighs. There were specific loci of painful spasms: right and left groin, above the pubic bone, and in the perineum posterior to his genitals. Various medical examinations had been negative.

Birth and developmental history were uneventful with the exception of his severe shyness with girls and his almost total absence of sexual information until well after puberty. His parents were pictured as "good parents but they never talked to anyone; and they never expressed any emotions. I grew up the same way. They did not interfere in my social life—or in dating, which I never did until college. My mother would get very worried when I dated. She was always afraid it would ruin my grades. When I started going out with girls in college, I didn't know what to say or what to do. I'd get anxious and worried and tense. Then I began feeling like this vise clamped down on my waist and thighs, a paralyzed feeling.''

Attempts at sexual intercourse usually failed due to the loss of his erection. However, a few of the times that he had remained sufficiently potent to intromit he had suffered varying degrees of difficulty in ejaculating. He would suffer marked spasms in the pelvic region to the point of painfulness, and when an erection or ejaculation was impossible to achieve he suffered loss of self-confidence and self-esteem.

The treatment plan was to train him in general relaxation, apply EMG feedback from the pelvic area to reduce the spasticity, GSR feedback to augment the relaxation, and desensitization for the heterosexual anxiety.

Carl was treated in this model for 25 weekly sessions. He responded well the first session to EMG frontales placement and general relaxation. Frontal microvoltage basal level was 1.00 to 2.00uV, with reduction to below 1.00uV within 5 minutes. In view of his good response, a hierarchy of a social-heterosexual content was applied the last 10 minutes of the session. He reported feeling deeply relaxed and that "everything was flowing through me without any blocks.'' He was instructed in diaphragmatic breathing and advised not to attempt intercourse until the treatment was well advanced. Several weeks later he volunteered that his steady improvement had encouraged him to attempt intercourse with a sex surrogate with discouraging results.

The second session replicated the first. Basal frontales was below 1uV and remained low througout the session. The hierarchy was reapplied with additional items of sexual activity from foreplay through intromission. He was instructed to fantasize the coital stage by himself. As expected, he felt no physical tension until he was about to intromit. His pelvic region then began to tense. He also began to "lose self-confidence. This is the point I always get nervous and afraid I'll lose my erection" he reported.

The following session was devoted to reinforcing relaxation through GSR feedback. Micromho level was low and did not vary significantly when the previous hierarchy was presented. He reported feeling relaxed except for his thighs and pelvic region. He also mentioned that that region would relax while jogging but tighten up as soon as he stopped. Clearly the stereotypic response was located in the pelvic region and was in chronic spasm which would intensify when he was stressed.

The treatment program then concentrated on reducing any spasms in the quadriceps (by bridging the right and left thigh with one active assembly on each thigh), the adductors of the thighs, and other regions of the pelvic area, particularly the groin. As various placements were monitored at rest and while visualizing intercourse, the implicated muscle groups in the pelvic area were relaxed through EMG feedback. Most of the placements revealed basal levels of 2uV or more at 100 to 200Hz. The final, principle loci of spasms were in the perineum and over the left pectineus. The perineum placement was an active electrode on the right and left sides of the region (or the raphe), just posterior to the genitalia. Criterion for reduction of spasticity for all placements was maintaining tension level below 1uV while visualizing a tranquil scene and while visualizing a few common stressors at work.

By the eighth session the chronic spasm in his groin was reduced, recurring only when he was highly stressed. Over the remaining sessions the program was applied with variations of imagery of social heterosexual scenes and of sexual intercourse. Progress was generally steady, with intermittent occurrences in vivo of spasms in the implicated regions, particularly in the perineum and left groin. The change over time was in the decrease of the frequency and intensity of stereotypic responsivity. The GSR was occasionally added for feedback in the few sessions that he manifested moist palms. The thermistor was applied twice; both times his hands were above 90° F and remained stable. The GSR level decreased in correspondence with increased relaxation, but did not vary significantly with the administration of stressful imagery. Evidently, the vasospasms and the palmar sweating were reactive to stress situations.

Carl changed his job and residence after some 20 sessions of treatment. These new situations aggravated his spasticity during the initial week of relocating. Otherwise, there was continual progress in the alleviation of the spasticity, his erectile inadequacy, and the heterosexual anxiety. The pain in his groin and perineum had remitted; he was experiencing successful intercourse on most of the occasions; when he awakened in the mornings he no longer felt depressed and strained; and the numbness in the pelvic region occurred only when he was severely stressed. He could usually reduce most stress reaction through self-relaxation.

Carl's impotence appeared to involve early life constraints of emotional expression, the development of anxiety attached to seeking gratifications at the presumed expense of success in goals emphasized by his family, and the displacement of the anxiety to the circulatory and striate musculature of the erotic zone of his pelvic region. The previous treatment procedures had probably failed because no one of them was sufficient to intervene in the multiple causes of his sexual dysfunction. Direct EMG retraining to reduce the chronic spasms was as necessary to treatment as was the reduction of sympathetic tone and changes in the intrapersonal dimension of his personality. There were no significant experiences of insights or abreactions over the course of the treatment.

Vaginismus

Vaginismus is the involuntary spasm of the vaginal introitus. The sphincter muscles contract, preventing intromission. Not all women suffering from vaginismus are sexually unresponsive or inactive. Usually, the women are unable to allow penile penetration, despite the fact that many have resolved their sexual anxiety or fear of mutilation. They are simply unable to be relaxed enough to permit intromission. Some extremely anxious women who are fearful of sexual arousal and are without any experience in genital exploration or stimulation do not discover their vaginal spastic reaction until their first attempt at coitus. The shock is traumatic to the man as well as the woman, with the same reaction of embarrassment and frustration that occurs in impotence.

The women who fear mutilation should be helped through psychotherapy to resolve that profound fear before other therapeutic measures are attempted. Physical causes of vaginismus must also be ruled out. The etiology may also be of such a severe unconscious conflict that behavioral, hypnotic, or biofeedback techniques should not be applied until the conflict has been adequately resolved.

The most frequent cause of vaginismus is psychosocial. In such a case, the rearing of the girl was in an atmosphere of sexual anxiety, or hearing stated fears of sex, childbirth, or of the brutality of the sex act, fears of pregnancy, or by developing pervasive guilt and tension over sexuality.

The usual treatment plan is the reduction of general body tension, desensitization to coitus, and, when necessary the use of the Masters and Johnson procedure. Reducing spasticity is, in our experience, consistently achieved through these methods, in one or more of their combinations.

> *Case example*: Thelma was a thirty-seven year-old single woman who had undergone intensive psychotherapy for 2 years, terminated by the death of her therapist. She had entered therapy in order to deal with several recurrent problems. Chief among them were vaginismus, morbid sexual guilt, and feelings of helplessness in her intimate relationships with men. The psychotherapy had alleviated much of the sexual guilt. She developed a fairly satisfying social life with both men and women and had gained a good deal of insight into her attitudes toward herself, her sexuality, and toward men. She had lost her fear of men, she believed she was fully knowledgeable about male and female sexuality, and was normally interested in a love relationship. The vaginismus remained as a major problem, along with a general feeling of body tension, ''like I'm in a strait- jacket.''
>
> The treatment plan was to focus on the mental-physical interaction in the sexual sphere of her life. She was agreeable to

learning relaxation and biofeedback reduction of the bodily tension, and the use of hypnotism to investigate the childhood sexual abuse.

The first session was devoted to EMG frontales placement feedback to augment general relaxation. Frontales level was moderate, 2.50 to 3.00uV, with an expected reduction to 1.50 to 2.00uV after applying the relaxation technique. Hypnotic induction was instituted, and she was instructed to increase her body awareness in a passive and calm frame of mind. After the session, she reported feeling deeply relaxed with one moment of sudden, general tension sweeping her body at the conclusion of the relaxation instructions. Apparently she had relaxed her defenses and had a sudden fear of loss of control. After the anxiety passed, she felt a "rushing up my torso; not unpleasant." Her relaxing imagery was that of floating on water.

Over the next seven sessions, the relaxation and hypnotic trance were applied preliminary to each session. The early sessions concentrated on body searches (219), such as entering her body and exploring internal organs, and in increasing direct, mental awareness of her erotic zone, in which the patient is instructed to visualize pleasant sexual foreplay while deeply relaxed. Areas or acts that increase tension are avoided during the early use of the imagery. Desensitization hierarchies outlining the sexual act from first embrace through coitus to climax are applied in the later sessions.

By the third session the patient began to spontaneously associate her current male friend with an older male relative who had engaged her in childhood sexual activities. She would then be asked to recall the early scenes, while in trance and to speak freely. Over several sessions she described the sexual scenes and would abreact strong mixtures of emotions. Moment to moment, she re-experienced anger, eroticism, anxiety, hate, fear, and longing. She would recall her childhood thoughts about being responsible, or would be accused of being responsible, for the sexual acts. The past memories would be mixed with recent ones of sexual activity and how her body would tighten when aroused. The anger began to predominate and to be expressed verbally more directly as her bodily tension level decreased over sessions.

During the seventh session she became aware of the similarities between her early and current sexual experiences; both were exploitative and lacking in affectual qualities. She also realized the nature of her internal conflict, that developed with the onset of puberty, between her own sexual pleasure and the guilt that she had experienced over the years. These abreactions and fantasies were worked through during and after each session.

The treatment procedure was terminated gradually as the time between sessions was extended. Most of the final sessions were devoted to reintegrating the unconscious material through standard psychotherapy discussions.

The clinical biofeedback approaches for both Carl and Thelma were based on the use of physiological feedback through bioinstruments in order to reintegrate the biopsychosocial matrix of their functioning. In Carl's case, the precise reduction of focal spasticity was essential in alleviating the chronic stereotypic, physiological response that he had developed. He was not lacking in insight nor was he isolating his affects from his thoughts. For Thelma, the general bodily tension was supporting her obsessive defenses against her anxiety and required reduction in order to allow the emotional aspects of her insight to rise to consciousness. Once the conflict was resolved, the vaginismus remitted. These applications are illustrative of the biofeedback paradigm in treating varieties of complaints of sexual dysfunctions that have a psychogenic etiology.

Chapter 17

BIOFEEDBACK AND PSYCHOTHERAPY

Psychotherapy techniques have been used with most of the biofeed-back applications discussed in this text and illustrated in the case materials. It is a rare case that does not require some clinical management of thought and feeling that emerge during biofeedback therapy. As Rickles (167) has pointed out, "Even though biofeedback appears to be a promising treatment for various psychological and psychiatric disorders, many researchers and clinicians acknowledge that biofeedback is not often a treatment in and of itself." He notes, further, that biofeedback is more "a treatment of the symptoms rather than the etiology." This has been the treatment model outlined here, in that biofeedback combined with appropriate psychotherapy techniques can stand as a useful clinical procedure for symptom reduction.

The use of biofeedback adjunctive to intensive ongoing psychotherapy or psychoanalysis is also a fruitful technique in various respects (221). Clinical experience indicates its usefulness. However, the model raises endless questions of transference and countertransference, the nature of ego functioning and defenses, the problem of resistance and transference cures, the role of placebo effects, the psychophysiology of mental and somatic symptom formation, the risks of regression and symptom substitution, and the danger of quick but superficial remission of signs and symptoms of the disorder under treatment.

Conversely, there is the possibility of enhancing the processes of introspection and insight, the acceleration of therapeutic regression, the deepening of transference, and the removal of bothersome symptoms that block analytic progress or remain intractable after prolonged psychotherapy. Moreover, for those patients who have detached their feelings from awareness, for those who are unable to conceptualize internal events or to free-associate, the physiological or somatic pathway of biofeedback can begin the reintegration of bodily sensation and emotionality and the ideational awareness of these processes.

Intensive psychotherapy is based on internal searches through verbal interpersonal and intrapersonal communications. The "classical" psychoanalytic patient is highly adept in making use of the verbal procedure. The patient's ego is strong and flexible, emotional experience is neither alien nor disorganizing, introspection is more frequently used than not, insight is present and highly generalizable to past and present experiences, and the somatic background of affect is reasonably discernable.

There are, nevertheless, many healthy, analytic patients whose enhancement of these personality parameters can be assisted by special techniques, such as clinical biofeedback (219).They present various symptoms during psychoanalysis that are appropriate for clinical biofeedback. Some of the symptoms may not have arisen from an internal conflict, or are no longer supported by a conflict, or are simply learned responses (Chapter 5). Their persistence is bothersome and they do not respond to insight therapy. The symptoms can take the form of muscle activity, such as mild tics. For example, one analytic patient at the end of analysis thought to mention his mild, localized throat constriction. One session of EMG feedback from the implicated muscle area reduced the chronic spasm. The symptom probably originated in childhood when he was thoroughly trained not to speak back to his parents nor to express his emotions freely.

Phobias are sometimes behavioral responses that emerged from real life experiences, particularly animal phobias acquired in childhood. Most afflicted adults have outgrown such specific phobias completely or to a significant degree. Those whose phobias persist are either generally anxious patients and need more than simple BFT and desensitization, or those who have an autonomically based, phobic reaction to the fearful object which is isolated from any other psychological conflicts that may be present. Usually these phobia can be reduced in these analytic patients in several sessions and no longer clutter up the analytic work. Chronic tension headaches, migraine, constipation, test and interview anxiety, and other circumscribed, physiological or attitudinal symptoms are better reduced, if analytically appropriate, within a few weeks of direct, symptomatic treatment than repeatedly analyzed as though they are direct reflections of internal conflicts.

Applying biofeedback interjects another kind of interpersonal event in the psychotherapy process and has an impact on both the reality and transference aspects of the therapy. The therapists's offer of a presumably quick method of reducing a symptom is an obvious change in the original, analytic agreement. The patient needs to understand the precise limits of biofeedback therapy in that it is confined to the treatment of the specific symptom and does not treat the complexities of personality. If the symptom is caused by a disease or dysfunction, such as vasoconstriction in Raynaud's, the reason for the use of biofeedback is easily explained to the patient and separated from the usual modality of verbal psychotherapy.

Nevertheless, the transference is inevitably stirred up by the therapist's close proximity to the patient upon applying the sensors of the bioinstruments. There is typically an increase in the patient's anxiety about emotional, and probably sexual, closeness to the therapist. The consequences of the intensified transference reactions—withdrawal, dependency, anxiety, reaction formation, tension, or whatever—may well be taken for granted and affects both the verbal psychotherapy and the biofeedback procedure itself. Intensity of reactions varies with the intensity of anxiety and transference and the strength of the defenses. The impact on the transference can be analyzed much the same as it would be if the changes occurred during verbal therapy. However, the realities of the use of the biofeedback applications regarding the issue of the patient's self-treatment needs to be emphasized. Patients can view the biofeedback as another form of being taken care of, with a resultant increase in dependency operations. Others can become aware of the independency of the procedure and become more self-responsible. These and any other reactions to using biofeedback are clinical data for the analytic work.

The relaxation technique (Chapter 6) used at the onset of biofeedback diminishes defensive strength, can institute regression, and provides conditions for accelerated free-association and insight. In this context, transference can be intensified, deliberately or inadvertently, and made more accessible to consciousness. In the event the therapist wishes to avoid regression, the relaxation depth can be minimized and conscious contents can be regulated by the therapist by continuous direction of the patient's mental contents during the course of relaxing. However, patients do not always maintain a mild stage of relaxation or focus their attention completely on the therapist's running instructions. Often enough, patients spontaneously undergo some degree of loosening of defensive ego functions and will experience the eruption, or seeping, into consciousness of emotions and recollections that have been repressed. Needless to say, those patients who suffer ego defects or weak defenses require particular care in preparation and during the procedure to counteract disabling episodes of regression. (Chapters 6, 14).

The present stage of experience with biofeedback applications in conjunction with intensive psychotherapy is reflected in the case of Kathy (Chapter 7) who was referred concurrent with her psychotherapy, with satisfactory results in reducing a phobia. The case of Vera (Chapter 12) illustrates a fairly common course of events during which a patient develops insight, reduces anxiety, and clarifies the nature of the psychological problem so that entering psychotherapy is a natural step to take. As more experience accumulates in the use of clinical biofeedback, it is possible that the paradigm will be useful to a wide range of patients for whom verbal psychotherapy is not efficacious as the sole treatment modality.

CLINICAL DATA FORMS

Recordkeeping forms in biofeedback appear in the literature and manufacturer's manuals in endless variety. They are most useful when adapted to the clinician's particular patient population, instruments used, and purposes for collecting the data. Precise records are necessary to permit an objective within-sessions and across-sessions assessment of the patients' progress. The bioinstruments provide quantified scores (of muscle tension, temperature, etc.) that allow for objective measurement of psychophysiologic activity. There is hardly any point in using bioinstruments without noting the changes in signals.

Additionally, both therapist and patient can provide subjective measurements of feeling states, mental content, relaxation response, anxiety levels, etc. These measures are as vital to clinical assessment as the objective measures.

The purpose of collecting clinical data is to chart normal and abnormal mental-emotional-biological processes that are affected by the treatment procedures, and to revise and integrate these domains of functioning. Recordkeeping attends to the normal variations in physiological activity from normative baselines, as well as from the patients' normal, individual baselines. Measures taken within and across sessions guide the clinician in applying different bioinstruments and ancillary techniques.

A-1: SUMMARY OF CLINICAL DATA
(THERAPIST COMPLETE THIS FORM)

CARD. NO.   PT. NO.

`0` `1` ☐☐☐☐☐☐

INITIAL INTERVIEW   TERMINATION   FOL. 1 DATE   FOL. 2 DATE

☐☐☐☐☐☐   ☐☐☐☐☐☐   ☐☐☐☐☐☐   ☐☐☐☐☐☐

CHART NO.

☐☐☐☐☐☐

PATIENT NAME _____

ADDRESS _____   PHONE AREA (_____)_____

AGE ☐☐   SEX ☐   ED. ☐☐   MARITAL STAT. ☐   RACE ☐

VOCATION ☐   UNSKILLED 1. _____   SKILLED 2. _____   UNEMPLOYED 3. _____   PROFESSIONAL 4. _____

HOUSEWIFE 5. _____ STUDENT 6. _____ OTHER 7. _____

SOURCE OF REFERRAL ☐☐   OPD ____ DH ____ IN - PAT. ____ OTHER _____

THERAPIST NAME _____   THERAPIST NO. ☐☐   NO. OF SESSIONS ☐☐

DIAGNOSIS: YRS. DURA.   MEDICATIONS

MED. ☐☐☐☐ _____   ☐☐   ☐☐☐☐ _____

PSY. ☐☐☐☐ _____   ☐☐   ☐☐☐☐ _____

DISPOSITION ON TERMINATION ☐☐ _____   NO. PSYCH. HOSP. ☐☐

FOR EACH RECORD KEY PUNCH CARD CODE. PT. NO.. DATE AND GEN. TEN. LEVEL

CARD NO.   PT. NO.   DATE

`0` `2` ☐☐☐☐☐   ☐☐☐☐☐☐   GEN. TEN. LEVEL (1-9)   PT. EST. ☐   THERA. EST. ☐

PRESENTING PROBLEMS	EST. SYMP. TEN. LEVEL (1 - 9) PT.	THERA.	DATE OF ONSET MO.	YR.	PT. IMPROV. ON TERM. 1, 2, 3 (Y.N.W.)	FOLLOW-UP
1. ☐☐ _____	1. ☐	1. ☐	1. ☐☐☐	☐☐	1. ☐	1. ☐
2. ☐☐ _____	2. ☐	2. ☐	2. ☐☐☐	☐☐	2. ☐	2. ☐
3. ☐☐ _____	3. ☐	3. ☐	3. ☐☐☐	☐☐	3. ☐	3. ☐
4. ☐☐ _____	4. ☐	4. ☐	4. ☐☐☐	☐☐	4. ☐	4. ☐
5. ☐☐ _____	5. ☐	5. ☐	5. ☐☐☐	☐☐	5. ☐	5. ☐
6. ☐☐ _____	6. ☐	6. ☐	6. ☐☐☐	☐☐	6. ☐	6. ☐

DATE DATA PUNCHED: _____

Some samples of clinical records are shown in Appendices A-1 through A-5. Such records can also be designed for card-punch for computer processing, as illustrated in A-1 and A-2. Several other sources illustrate clinical data forms, particularly Brown (27, 28), Fuller (72), and Gaarder and Montgomery (74).

A-2: CLINICAL RECORD — INDIVIDUAL SESSIONS

CARD NO.   PATIENT NO.   DATE   SESSION NO.

THERAPIST

PATIENT NAME _____

MEDICATION:

PRI

SEC

PATIENT'S ESTIMATED TENSION LEVEL THIS SESSION   (1 - 9)   BEG.   END

SYMPTOMS TREATED   TENSION LEVEL (1 - 9)

THIS SESSION	BEG.	END	THER. USED	INSTRU.	SITE
1.			1.		
2.			2.		
3.			3.		
4.			4.		

DATE DATA PUNCHED: _____

METER	GAIN	FEED-BACK	RESP. TIME	SITE	EDP SCL	O_F	EEG 10-20	HZ	COMMENTS

ADDITIONAL THERAPY TECHNIQUES USED THIS SESSION: 1. HYPNOTISM: _____   2. COGNITIVE STATEMENTS: _____
3. GENERAL RELAXATION: _____   4. JACOBSON: _____   5. DESENSITIZATION: _____   6. ASSERTIVE TNG: _____
7. RECORDKEEPING: _____   8. AUTOGENIC: _____   9. VERBAL THERAPY: _____   11. IMAGERY: _____
12. AVERSIVE: _____   13. THOUGHT STOPPAGE: _____   13. OTHER: _____.
NEXT SESSION: _____

A-3: RELAXATION SESSIONS

Record in the appropriate columns your relaxation sessions. Note the date, the time of day, place, and general level of tension on scale of 1-10 (1 is deeply relaxed; 5 is moderate level of tension or stress; 10 is extreme level of tension). Add self-observations before, during and after the relaxation sessions.

Date	Time	Place	Tension Level Beg.	End	Observations

A-4: SLEEP RECORD

Record in appropriate columns information related to your sleep patterns.

Name _____ Date_____

	MON	TUES	WED	THUR	FRI	SAT	SUN
1. Time became sleepy.							
2. Time went to bed.							
3. Time (minutes) it took to fall asleep.							
4. Tension level on going to bed (1-10).							
5. Any preoccupations? (Yes, No.)							
6. Awakening (Time; feeling?)							
7. Dreams (Yes, No.).							
8. Wake up rested? (Yes, No.)							
9. Total hours slept.							
10. Naps during day? (Yes, No.)							
Comments and observations:							

A-5: RECORD OF SYMPTOM

Plot a two axis graph on one page for each day for a symptom. Note the time of the episode, duration, and intensity of each symptom, improvement in adaptive behavior, or occurrences of maladaptive behavior, such as headaches, self-assertion, phobias, etc. The reverse side of the page can be used to record self-observations, such as context of events, persons present, self-statements used, other mental content, feeling states, etc.

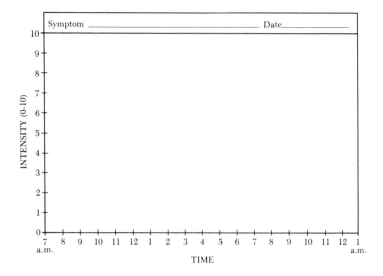

Appendix B

RATING SCALES

There are numerous personality scales and inventories that can be found in any standard text on tests and measurements. Self-rating scales have adequate reliability and validity for the clinician's use in assessing a patient's personality and any deviations from the norm. A battery of tests is ordinarily selected to fit the realities of the clinical situation and the populations being serviced. The following list has been found useful in supplementing interview data and in establishing pre- and post-treatment measurements of target symptoms and changes over time in patients treated. Their use also adds to the reliability of follow-up and evaluation studies.

The Adjective Check List
Harrison G. Gough
Consulting Psychologists Press
577 College Avenue
Palo Alto, CA 94306

Bender Gestalt Test
Lauretta Bender
Western Psychological Services
12031 Wilshire Boulevard
Los Angeles, CA 90025

California Psychological Inventory
Harrison G. Gough
Consulting Psychologists Press
577 College Avenue
Palo Alto, CA 94306

Cornell Index
Arthur Weider, Harold Wolff,
Keeve Brodman, Bela Mittelmann
and David Wechsler
The Psychological Corporation
757 Third Avenue
New York, NY 10017

Fear Schedule (Inventory)
cf: Wolpe, J. *The Practice of
Behavior Therapy.* New York:
Pergamon, 1969, Appendix 3, pp. 285–286.

Hooper Visual Organization Test
H. Elston Hooper
Western Psychological Services
12031 Wilshire Boulevard
Los Angeles, CA 90025

**Hunt-Minnesota Test
for Organic Brain Damage**
Howard F. Hunt
Western Psychological Services
12031 Wilshire Boulevard
Los Angeles, CA 90025

IPAT Anxiety Scale Questionnaire
(Self Analysis Form)
Raymond B. Cattell and I. H. Scheier
Institute for Personality and Ability Testing
1602 Coronado Drive
Champaign, IL 61820

Minnesota Multiphasic
Personality Inventory
S.R. Hathaway and J.C. McKinley
The Psychological Corporation
757 Third Avenue
New York, NY 10017

Pain Apperception Test
Donald V. Petrovich
Western Psychological Services
12031 Wilshire Boulevard
Los Angeles, CA 90025

The Personality Inventory
Robert G. Bernreuter
Consulting Psychologists Press
577 College Avenue
Palo Alto, CA 94306

Sixteen Personality Factor
(16 P-F) Questionnaire
Raymond B. Cattell
Institute for Personality and
Ability Testing
1602 Coronado Drive
Champaign, IL 61820

Stanford Hypnotic
Susceptibility Scale
A.M. Weitzenhoffer and
E.R. Hilgard
Consulting Psychologists Press
577 College Avenue
Palo Alto, CA 94306

State-Trait Anxiety Inventory
Charles D. Spielberger, Richard Gorsuch
and Robert E. Lushene
Consulting Psychologists Press
577 College Avenue
Palo Alto, CA 94306

Whitaker Index of
Schizophrenic Thinking
Leighton C. Whitaker
Western Psychological Services
12031 Wilshire Boulevard
Los Angeles, CA 90025

*Anastasi, A. *Psychological
Testing* (4th ed.). New York:
Macmillan, 1976.

*Buros, O. *Personality Tests
and Reviews*. New York: Gryphon Press, 1970.

*Cronbach, L.J. *Essentials of
Psychological Tests* (3rd ed.).
New York: Harper & Row, 1970.

INSTRUMENTATION MANUFACTURERS

American Biofeedback Corp.
Hunter Brook Road
Yorktown Heights, NY 10598

Aquarius Electronics
P.O. Box 627
Mendocino, CA 9546

Autogenic Systems Inc.
809 Allston Way
Berkeley, CA 94710

Beckman Instruments, Inc.
3900 River Road
Schiller Park, IL 60176

Betadyne Corporation
233 Broadway
New York, NY 10007

Biofeedback Instrument Co
225 West 98 Street
New York, NY 10025

Biofeedback Research Institute
6233 Wilshire Boulevard
Los Angeles, CA 90048

Biofeedback Study Center of New York
55 East Ninth Street
New York, NY 10003
(Sales representative)

Biofeedback Systems, Inc.
2736 47 Street
Boulder, CO 80301

Bio-Medical Instruments
P.O. Box 248
Warren, MI 48090

Biomonitoring Applications
270 Madison Avenue, Suite 1506
New York, NY 10016
(Tapes, publications)

Bioscan Corporation
P.O. Box 14168
Houston, TX 77021

Biotemp Products, Inc.
3266 N. Meridian, Suite 705
Indianapolis, IN 46208
(Wrist, finger thermometers)

Cyborg Corporation
342 Western Avenue
Boston, MA 02135

Edmund Scientific Co.
Edscorp Building
Barrington, NJ 08007

Electro-Labs
P.O. Box 2386
Pomona, CA 91766

Farrell Instruments, Inc.
P.O. Box 1037
Grand Island, NE 68801

Karlin Instruments, Inc.
54 East South Temple
Salt Lake City, UT 84111

Med Associates, Inc.
P.O. Box 47
East Fairfield, VT 05448

Med-Tech, Inc.
8514 N. 17 Drive
Phoenix, AR 85021

Narco Bio-Systems, Inc.
7651 Airport Boulevard
P.O. Box 12511
Houston, TX 77017

Stoelting Co.
1350 So. Kostner Avenue
Chicago, IL 60623

Systec, Inc.
500 Locust Street, Lawrence, KN 66044

Thought Technology, Ltd.
2194 Clifton Avenue
Montreal, Quebec, Canada H4A 2N5

REFERENCES

1. Abdullah, S. Biofeedback for asthmatic patients. *New England Journal of Medicine*, 1974, *291*, 1037.

2. Acosta, F.X. & Yamamoto, J. Applications of electromyographic biofeedback to the relaxation training of schizophrenic, neurotic, and tension headache patients. *Journal of Consulting and Clinical Psychology*, 1978, *46*, 383-4.

3. Adler, C.S. & Morrisey-Adler, S. Strategies in general psychiatry. In J.V. Basmajian (Ed.), *Biofeedback—Principles and Practice for Clinicians*. Baltimore: Williams & Wilkins, 1979, 180-195.

4. Alexander, A.B. & Smith, D.D. Cinical applications of EMG biofeedback. In R.J. Gatchel & K. Price (Eds.), *Clinical Applications of Biofeedback: Appraisal and Status*. New York: Pergamon, 1979, 112-133.

5. Amato, A., Hermsmeyer, C.A., & Kleinman, K.M. Use of electromyographic feedback to increase inhibitory control of spastic muscles. *Physical Therapy*, October 1973, *53*, 1063-1065.

6. Andrews, J.M. Neuromuscular re-education of the hemiplegic with the aid of the electro-myograph. *Archives of Physical Medicine Rehabilitation*, 1964, *45*, 530-532.

7. Autogenic Systems, Inc. *Handbook of Physiological Feedback*, (Vols. I, II, III). 809 Allston Way, Berkeley, California: Author, 1978.

8. Ax, Albert. The physiological differentiation between anger and fear in humans. *Psychosomatic Medicine*, 1953, *15*, 433-442.

9. Basmajian, J.V. *Muscles Alive*. Baltimore: Williams & Wilkins, 1974.

10. _____ Control and training of individual motor units. In T. Barber et al. (Eds.), *Biofeedback and Self-regulation*, Chicago: Aldine Publishing Co., 1971.

11. _____ (Ed.). *Biofeedback—Principles and Practice for Clinicians*. Baltimore: Williams & Wilkins, 1979.

12. Beatty, J. Visceral and central nervous system functions. In J. Beatty and Heiner Legewie (Eds.), *Biofeedback and Behavior*. New York: Plenum Press, 1977, 487-497.

253

13. Beatty, J. & Legewie, H. (Eds.). *Biofeedback and Behavior*. New York: Plenum Press, 1977.

14. Beech, H.R. *Changing Man's Behavior*. Baltimore: Penguin Books, 1969.

15. Bellak, L. *Ego Functions in Schizophrenics, Neurotic and Normals*. New York: John Wiley, 1973.

16. Benson, H. *The Relaxation Response*. New York: William Morrow, 1975.

17. Birk, L. *Biofeedback: Behavioral Medicine*. New York: Grune & Stratton, 1973.

18. Bleuler, E. *Demential Praecox or the Group of Schizophrenias* (J. Zinkin, trans.). New York: International Universities Press, 1950.

19. Blanchard, E.B. & Epstein, L.H. *A Biofeedback Primer*. Reading, Mass.: Addison-Wesley Publishing Co., 1978.

20. Blanchard, E.B. & Young, L.D. Clinical applications of biofeedback training: A review of the evidence. *Archives of General Psychiatry*, 1974, *30*, 530–589.

21. Bockar, J.A. *Primer for the Nonmedical Psychotherapist*. New York: Spectrum, 1976.

22. Borkovec, T.D. Physiological and cognitive processes in the regulation of anxiety. In *Consciousness and Self-Regulation*. G.E. Schwartz & D. Shapiro (Eds.), New York: Plenum, 1976, 261–312.

23. Borkovec, T.D. & Fowles, D. Controlled investigation of the effects of progressive and hypnotic relaxation on insomnia. *Journal of Abnormal Psychology*, 1973, *82*, 153–158.

24. Braud, L.W., Lupin, M.N. & Braud, W.G. The use of electromyographic biofeedback in the control of hyperactivity. *Journal of Learning Disabilities*, 1975, *8*, 21–26.

25. Brenner, C. *An Elementary Textbook of Psychoanalysis*. Garden City, New York: Doubleday, 1957.

26. Bresler, D. & Turbo, R. *Free Yourself from Pain*. New York: Simon & Schuster, 1979.

27. Brown, B. *New Mind, New Body*. New York: Harper & Row, 1974.

28. _____ *Stress and the Art of Biofeedback*. New York. Harper & Row, 1977.

29. Brudny, J., Korein, J., Grynbaum, B.B., Freidman, L.W., Weinstein, S., Sachs-Frankel, G. & Belandres, P.V. EMG feedback therapy: Review of treatment of 114 patients. *Archives of Physical Medicine and Rehabilitation*, 1976, *57*, 55–61.

30. Brudny, J., Korein, J., Levidow, L., Grynbamu, B., Liberman, A. & Freidman, L. Spasmodic Torticollis: treatment by feedback display of the EMG. *Archives of Physical Medicine Rehabilitation*, 1974, *55*, 403–408.

31. Budzynski, T.H. Biofeedback strategies in headache treatment. In J.V. Basmjian, *Biofeedback—Principles and Practice for Clinicians*. Baltimore: Williams & Wilkins, 1978, 132–152.

32. Budzynski, T.H. & Stoyva, J. An instrument for producing deep muscle relaxation by means of analogue information feedback. *Journal of applied behavior analysis*, 1969, *2*, 231–237.

33. _____ An electromyographic feedback technique for teaching voluntary relaxation of the masseter muscle. *Journal of Dental Research*, 1973, *52*, 116–119.

34. Budzynski, T.H., Stoyva, J.M., Adler, C.S. & Mullaney, D.J. EMG biofeedback and tension headaches: A controlled outcome study. *Psychosomatic Medicine*, 1973, *35*, 484–496.

35. Cameron, D.E. Observations on the pattern of anxiety. *American Journal of Psychiatry*, 1944, *101*, 36.

36. Cannon, W.B. *The Wisdom of the Body*. New York: W.W. Norton, 1939.

37. Cannon, W.B. *Bodily Change in Pain, Hunger, Fear and Rage* (2nd ed.). Boston: Charles T. Branford Co., 1953.

38. Cannistraci, A.J. *Voluntary Stress Release and Behavior Therapy in the Treatment of Clenching and Bruxism, V.1.* Cassette Tape. New York: Biomonitoring Applications, 1975–1976.

39. _____ A method of control bruxism: Biofeedback assisted relaxation. *Journal of the American Society for Preventive Dentistry*, 1976.

40. _____ Biofeedback—the treatment of stress-induced muscle activity. In H. Gelb (ed.), *Clinical Management of Head, Neck and TMJ Pain and Dysfunction*, Philadelphia: W.B. Saunders, 1978.

41. Cattell, R.B. *The Scientific Analysis of Personality*. Chicago: Aldine, 1966.

42. Chaffee, E.E. & Greisheimer, E.M. *Basic Physiology and Anatomy*. New York: J. P. Lippincott, 1974.

43. Cleeland, C.S. Behavioral tactics in the modification of spasmodic torticollis. *Neurology*, 1973, *23*, 1241–1247.

44. Cohen, M.E., Robins, E., Purtell, J.D., Altman, M.W. & Reid, D.E. Excessive surgery in hysteria. *Journal of the American Medical Association*, 1953, *151*, No. 12, 977–986.

45. Craib, A.R., & Perry, M. *EEG Handbook* (2nd ed.). Schiller Park, Ill.: Beckman Instruments, 1975.

46. Culligan, M. & Sedlacek, K. *How to Kill Stress Before it Kills You.* New York: Grune-Stratton, 1976.

47. Davis, M.H., Saunders, D.R., Creer, T.L., & Chai, H. Relaxation training facilitated by biofeedback apparatus as a supplemental treatment in bronchial asthma. *Journal of Psychosomatic Research*, 1973, *17*, 121-8.

48. Davidson, R.J. Specificity and Patterning in Biobehavioral Systems: Implications for Behavior Change. *American Psychologist*, May 1978, *33*, 430-436.

49. Davidson, R.J. & Schwartz, G.E. The psychobiology of relaxation and related states: a multi-process theory. In D.I. Mostofsky (Ed.), *Behavior Control and Modification of Physiological Activity.* Englewood Cliffs, N.J.: Prentice-Hall, 1976, 399-442.

50. Delagi, E.F., Perotto, A., Iazzetti, J. & Morrison, D. *Anatomic Guide for the Electromyographer: The Limbs.* Springfield, Ill.: Charles C. Thomas, 1975.

51. DeWitt, D.J. & Palacious, M. A treatment approach involving EMG feedback of motor disability resulting from conversion reaction. *Proceedings of the Biofeedback Society of America*, Mar. 4-8, 1977, p. 65.

52. Dhanaraj, H.V. & Singh, M. Reduction in metabolic rate during the practice of Transcendental meditation technique. In D.W. Orme-Johnson & J.T. Farrow (Eds.), *Scientific Research on the Transcendental Meditation Technique. Vol. 1, West Germany: Maharishi European Research University Press,* 1976, 137-139.

53. Diamond, S., Diamond-Falk, J. & DeVeno, T. The value of biofeedback in the treatment of chronic headache: Five year retrospective study. Read before the Ninth Annual meeting of the Biofeedback Society of America, Albuquerque, N.M., March, 1978.

54. DiCara, L.V. Learning in the autonomic nervous system. *Scientific American*, Jan. 1970, *222*, 31-39.

55. Dickinson, J. *Proprioceptive Control of Human Movement.* Princeton, N.J.: Princeton Book Co., 1974.

56. Domash, L.H. Introduction. In D. Orme-Johnson & J.T. Farrow (Eds.), *Scientific Research on the Transcendental Meditation Program, Collected Papers* (Vol. 1). Lucerne, Switzerland: Maharishi European University Press, 1976.

57. *Dorland's Illustrated Medical Dictionary, 25th ed.* J.P. Friel (Ed.). Philadelphia: W.B. Saunders, 1974, 1482.

58. Dohrenwend, B.S. & Dohrenwend,B.P. (Eds.). *Stressful Life Events.* New York: John Wiley, 1974.

59. Ellis, H.C., Bennett,T.L., Daniel, T.C. & Rickert, E.J. *Psychology of Learning and Memory.* Monterey, CA: Brooks/Cole, 1979.

60. Engel, B.T. Behavioral applications in the treatment of patients with cardiovascular disorders. In J.V. Basmajian (Ed.), *Biofeedback—Principles and Practices for Clinicians.* Baltimore: Williams & Wilkins, 1979,170–169

61. Epstein, S. Anxiety, arousal and the self-concept. In I.G. Sarason & C.D. Spielberger (Eds.), *Stress and Anxiety.* Washington, D.C.: Hemisphere Pub. Co., 1976.

62. Erickson M. & Rossi, E. *Hypnotherapy: An Exploratory Casebook.* New York: Halstead, 1979.

63. Fair, P. Biofeedback strategies in psychotherapy. In J.V. Basmajian (Ed.), *Biofeedback: Principles and Practice for Clinicians.* Baltimore: Williams & Wilkins, 1979.

64. Finley, W.W., Niman, C., Standley, J. & Ewder, P. Frontal EMG-biofeedback training of athetoid cerebral palsy patients: A report of 6 cases. *Biofeedback and Self-Regulation,* June, 1976, Vol. 1, No. 2., 169–182.

65. Freedman, R. & Papsdorf, J.D. Biofeedback and progressive relaxation treatment of sleep-onset insomnia: a controlled, all-night investigation. *Biofeedback and Self-Regulation,* 1976, *1,* 253–271.

66. Freud, A. *The Ego and the Mechanisms of Defense* (Rev. ed.). New York: International Universities Press, 1966.

67. Freud, S. *An Outline of Psychoanalysis.* (J. Strachey, Ed. and trans.). New York: Norton, 1949.

68. _____ *Collected Papers* (Vol. 1). (J. Riviere, L. Woolf & Woolf, V. and the Institute of Psychoanalysis, trans.). London: Hogarth, 1924–1925.

69. _____ *The Standard Edition of the Complete Psychological Works of Sigmund Freud.* J. Strachey, Editor. London: Hogarth, 1953.

70. _____ *The Ego and the Id.*(J. Strachey, Ed. and trans.) New York: Norton, 1960.

71. _____ *The Problem of Anxiety.* (H.A. Bunker, Ed. and trans.). New York: Norton, 1936.

72. Fuller, G.D. *Biofeedback: Methods and Procedures in Clinical Practice.* San Francisco: Biofeedback Press, 1977.

73. Gaarder, K. (Ed.). *Task Force Report on Geriatrics and Biofeedback.* Biofeedback Society of America, Aug. 1978.

74. Gaarder, K.R. & Montgomery, P.S. *Clinical Biofeedback: A Procedural Manual.* Baltimore: Williams & Wilkins, 1977.

75. Gardner, E. *Fundamentals of Neurology* (5th ed.). Philadelphia: W.B. Saunders, 1968.

76. Gatchel, R.J. & Price, K. (Eds.). *Clinical Applications of Biofeedback: Appraisal and Status.* New York: Pergamon, 1979.

77. Gazzaniga, M. & LeDoux, J. *The Integrated Mind.* New York: Plenum, 1978.

78. Gelb, H. (Ed.). *Clinical Management of Head, Neck and TMJ Pain and Dysfunction.* Philadelphia: W.B. Saunders, 1978.

79. Glueck, B.C., & Stroebel, C.F. Biofeedback and meditation in the treatment of psychiatric illnesses. *Comprehensive Psychiatry,* 1975, *16,* No. 4, 303–321.

80. Goldfried, M.R. & Davison, G.C. *Clinical Behavior Therapy.* New York: Holt, Rinehart & Winston, 1976.

81. Goldstein, G. Methodology and theoretical issues in neuropsychological assessment, *Journal of Behavioral Assessment,* 1979, *1,*23–41.

82. Goldstein-Balshan, I. The relationship of muscle tension and autonomic activity to psychiatric disorders. *Psychosomatic Medicine,* 1965, *27,* 39–52.

83. Gordon, J..E. (Ed.). *Handbook of Clinical and Experimental Hypnosis.* New York: Macmillan, 1967.

84. Grayson, H.H., & Loew, C. (Eds.). *Changing Approaches to the Psychotherapies.* New York: Spectrum Publications, 1978.

85. Green, E., & Green, A. General and specific application of thermal feedback. In J.V. Basmajian (Ed.), *Biofeedback—Principles and Practice for Clinicians,* Baltimore: Williams & Wilkins, 1979, 153–169.

86. Grings, W.M., & Dawson, M.E. *Emotions and Bodily Responses.* New York: Academic Press, 1978.

87. Hall, C.S., & Lindzey, G. *Theories of personality* (3rd ed.). New York: John Wiley, 1978.

88. Hardt, J.V. & Kamiya, J. Treating high anxiety with alpha feedback. *Proceedings of the 9th Annual Meeting of the Biofeedback Society of America.* Denver: Biofeedback Society of America, 1978, 104–107.

89. Hardyck, C.D. The elimination of sub-vocal speech activity during reading by continuous feedback. *Psychophysiology*, 1969, *5* abstract, 564.

90. Hartmann, H. *Ego Psychology and the Problem of Adaptation.* (Daniel Rapaport, Ed. and trans.). New York: International Universities Press, 1958.

91. Hassett, J. *A Primer of Psychophysiology.* San Francisco: W.H. Freeman, 1978.

92. _____. Conscious. Caution: Meditation can hurt. *Psychology Today,* Nov. 1978, 125-126.

93. Haynes, S. Electromyographic biofeedback treatment of a woman with chronic dysphagia. *Biofeedback and Self-Regulation,* 1976, Vol. 1, No. 1, March, 121-126.

94. Haynes, S.N., Moseley, D., & McGowan, W., Relaxation training and biofeedback in the reduction of frontalis muscle tension. *Psychophysiology,* 1974, Vol. 12, No. 5, 547-552.

95. Herman, S.H., & Prewett, M. An experimental analysis of feedback to increase sexual arousal in a case of homo- and heterosexual impotence: A preliminary report. *Journal of Behavior Therapy and Experimental Psychiatry,* 1974, *5,* 271-274.

96. Hess, W.R. *Diencephalon: Autonomic and Extrapyramidal Functions.* New York: Saunders, 1954.

97. Hilgard, E.R. *Hypnotic Susceptibility.* New York: Harcourt Brace & World, 1955.

98. Hinsie, L.E., & Campbell, R.J. *Psychiatric Dictionary,* (4th ed.). New York: Oxford University Press, 1970.

99. Horney, K. *Our Inner Conflicts.* New York: Norton, 1945.

100. Hume, W.I. *Biofeedback: Research and Therapy.* Montreal, Canada: Eden Press, 1976.

101. Jacobson, E. *Progressive Relaxation.* Chicago: University of Chicago Press, 1938.

102. _____. *Self-Operations Control.* New York: J.P. Lippincott, 1964.

103. _____. *Modern Treatment of Tense Patients.* Springfield, Ill.: Charles C. Thomas, 1970.

104. Jankel, W. EMG feedback in Bell's Palsy. Proceedings of the 8th annual meeting of the Biofeedback Society of America, March 4-8, 1977, p. 64.

105. Jung, C.G. *The Integration of Personality.* New York: Farrar & Rinehart, 1939.

106. Kamiya, J. Conditional discrimination of the EEG Alpha rhythm in humans. Paper presented at the Western Psychological Association, San Francisco, 1962.

107. _____. Operant control of the EEG Alpha rhythm and some of its reported effects on consciousness. In C.T. Tart (Ed.), *Altered States of Consciousness,* New York: John Wiley, 1969.

108. Kaplan, H.S. *The New Sex Therapy.* New York: Bruner/Mazel, 1974.

109. Kimmel, H.D., & Hill, F.A. Operant conditioning of the GSR. *Psychological Reports,* 1960, *7,* 555-562.

110. Kline M. (Ed.). *Psychodynamics and Hypnosis:* Springfield, Ill.: Thomas, 1967.

111. Kakulka, C.G., Brown, D.M., & Basmajian, J.V. Biofeedback training for early finger joint mobilization. *The American Journal of Occupational Therapy,* Sept. 1975, Vol. 29, No. 8, 469-470.

112. Kuhlman, W.N., & Kaplan, B. Clinical applications of EEG feedback training. In R.J. Gatchel and K.P. Price (Eds.), *Clinical Applications of Biofeedback: Appraisal and Status,* New York: Pergamon, 1979, 69-96.

113. Lacey, J.I., & Lacey, B.C. Verification and extension of the principle of autonomic response stereotypy. *American Journal of Physiology,* 1958, *71,* 50.

114. Lacey, B.C., & Lacey, J.I. Studies of heart rate and other bodily processes in sensorimotor behavior. In P.A. Obrist, A.H. Block, J. Brener, & L.V. DiCara (Eds.), *Cardiovascular Psychophysiology,* Chicago: Aldine, 1974.

115. Lader, M.H., & Mathews, A.M. A physiological model of phobic anxiety and desensitization. *Behavior Research and Therapy,* 1968, *6,* 411-421.

116. Lamott, K.C. *Escape from Stress.* New York: G.P. Putnam & Sons, 1974.

117. Lang, P.J. Acquisition of heart rate control: method, theory and clinical applications. In D.C. Fowler (Ed.), *Clinical Applications of Psychophysiology,* New York: Columbia University Press, 1975.

118. Lang, P.J., & Melamed, B.G. Case report: Avoidance conditioning therapy of an infant with chronic ruminative vomiting. *Journal of Abnormal Psychology,* 1969, *74,* 1-8.

119. Lanyon, R.I., & Lanyon, B.P. *Behavior Therapy: A Clinical Introduction*. Reading, Mass.: Addison-Wesley, 1978.

120. Lazarus, A.A. *Behavior Therapy and Beyond*. New York: McGraw-Hill, 1971.

121. Lazarus, R.S. A cognitively oriented psychologist looks at biofeedback. *American Psychologist*, May, 1975, 553-561.

122. Levine, S. Stress and Behavior. In R.F. Thompson, (Ed.), *Physiological Psychology, Readings from Scientific American*, San Francisco: W.H. Freeman, 1971, 193-198.

123. Lindsley, D.B. Electrical Activity of human motor units during voluntary contraction. *American Journal of Physiology*, 1939, *114*, 90-99.

124. Lubar, J.F., & Shouse, M.N. EEG and behavioral changes in a hyperkinetic child concurrent with training of the sensorimotor rhythm (SMR): A preliminary report. *Biofeedback and Self-Regulation*, 1976, Vol. 1, No. 3, 293-306.

125. Luthe, W., & Schultz, J.H. (Eds.). *Autogenic Therapy: Medical Applications, Vol. II*. New York: Grune & Stratton, 1969.

126. MacPherson, F.L.R. Control of involuntary movement. *Behavior Research and Therapy*, 1967, *5*, 143-145.

127. Marinacci, A.A., & Horande, M. Electromyogram in neuromuscular re-education. *Bulletin, Los Angeles Neurological Society*, 1960, *25*, 57-71.

128. Maher, B.A. (Ed.). *Contributions to the Psychopathology of Schizophrenia*. New York: Academic Press, 1977.

129. Marks, I.M., & Gelder, M.G. Different ages of onset in varieties of phobia. *American Journal of Psychiatry*, 1966, *123*, 218.

130. Martin, B. *Anxiety and Neurotic Disorders*. New York: John Wiley & Sons, 1971.

131. Martin, M.J. Tension headache, a psychiatric study. *Headache*, 1966, *6*, 47-54.

132. Masters, W.H., & Johnson, V.E. *Human Sexual Inadequacy*. Boston: Little, Brown, 1966.

133. May, J.R., & Johnson, H.J. Physiological activity to internally elicited arousal and inhibitory thoughts. *Journal of Abnormal Psychology*, 1973, *82*, 239-245.

134. McGhie, A. Attention and Perception in schizophrenia. In B.A. Maher (Ed.), *Progress in Experimental and Personality Research*, New York: Academic Press, 1971.

135. McGuigan, F.J. Interview with Edmund Jacobson. *Biofeedback and Self-Regulation,* 1978, Vol. 3, No. 3, 287-300.

136. Meichenbaum, D. Cognitive Factors in Biofeedback, *Biofeedback and Self-Regulation,* June, 1976, *1,* No. 2, 201-216.

137. Miller, N. Learning of visceral and glandular responses. *Science,* 1969, *163,* 434-445.

138. Miller, N.E., & Bunuazizi, A. Instrumental learning by curarised rat of a specified visceral response, intestinal or cardiac. *Journal of Comparative physiological Psychology,* 1968, *65,* 1-7.

139. Miller, N.E. General discussion and a review of recent results with paralyzed patients. In R.J. Gatchel & K.P. Price (Eds.), *Clinical Applications of Biofeedback: Appraisal and Status.* New York: Peragamon, 1979, 215-225.

140. Miller, N.E. & Dworkin, B.R. Effects of learning on visceral functions. *New England Journal of Medicine,* 1977, Vol. 296, No. 22, 1274-1278.

141. Mintz, B. *Marathon Groups: Reality and Symbol.* New York: Appleton-Century-Crofts, 1971.

142. Monat, A., & Lazarus, R.S. *Stress and Coping.* New York: Columbia University Press, 1977, 159-173.

143. Mowrer, O.H. *Learning Theory and Personality Dynamics.* New York: Ronald Press, 1950.

144. Mulholland, T. Objective EEG methods for studying covert shifts in visual attention. In F.J. McGuigan (Ed.), *The Psychophysiology of Thinking,* New York: Academic Press, 1973.

145. Nideffer, R.M., Deckner, W., Cromwell, R.L., & Cash, T. The relationship of alpha activity to attentional sets in schizophrenia. *Journal of Nervous and Mental Diseases,* 1971, 152, 346-352.

146. Obrist, P.A., Howard, J.L., Lawler, J.E., Galdsy, R.A., Meyers, K.A., & Gaebelein, C.J. The cardiac somatic interaction. In P.A. Obrist, A.H. Black, J. Brener, & L.U. DiCara (Eds.), *Cardiovascular Psychophysiology.* Chicago: Aldine, 1974.

147. Ohno, Y., Tanaka, Y., Takeya, T., Matsubara, H., Kuriya, N., & Komemushi, S. Biofeedback modification of frontal EMG in normal subjects. *Biofeedback and Self-Regulation,* 1978, *3,* No. 1, 61-68.

148. Orme-Johnson, D.W., & Farrow, J.T. (Eds.). *Scientific Research on the Transcendental Meditation Technique.* West Germany: Maharishi European Research University Press, 1976.

149. Ornstein, R.E. *The Psychology of Consciousness* (2nd ed.). New York: Harcourt Brace Jovanovich, 1977.

150. Pascal, G.R. The use of relaxation in short-term psychotherapy. *Journal of Abnormal and Social Psychology,* 1947, *42,* 226-242.

151. _____. The effect of relaxation upon recall. *American Journal of Psychology,* 1949, *62,* 32-47.

152. Paskewitz, D.A., & Orne, M.T. Visual effects on alpha feedback training. *Science,* 1973, 181, 360-363.

153. Patel, C.H., & North, W.R.S. Randomized controlled trial of Yoga and biofeedback in the management of hypertension. *Lancet,* 1975, II, 93-99.

154. Patel, C.H. Yoga and biofeedback in the management of hypertension. *Lancet,* 1973, *1,* 62-67.

155. Pavlov, I.P. *Conditioned Reflexes: An Investigation of the Physiological Activities of the Cerebral Cortex.* London: Oxford University Press, 1927.

156. Pelletier, R.R. *Mind as Healer, Mind as Slayer.* New York: Dell Publishing Co., 1977.

157. Perls, F.S. *Gestalt Therapy Verbatum.* Lafayette, Ca.: Real People Press, 1969.

158. Perry, J.D. Task Force Study Section on Biofeedback as an Adjunct to Sex Therapy. Biofeedback Society of America, Denver, Co., 1978.

159. Peterson, F., & Jung, C. Psychophysical investigation in normal and insane subjects. *Brain, 30,* 1907, 153-218.

160. Pickering, G.W. *High Blood Pressure, 2nd Ed.* New York: Grune & Stratton, 1968.

161. Price, K.P. Biofeedback and Migraine. In R.J. Gatchel and K.P. Price (Eds.), *Clinical Applications of Biofeedback: Appraisal and Status.* New York: Pergamon, 1979, 134-147.

162. Plotkin, W.B., & Cohen, R. Occipital alpha and the attributes of the "alpha experience." *Psychophysiology,* 1976, *13,* 16-21.

163. Rabkin, J.G., & Struening, E.L. Life events, stress, and illness. *Science,* 1976, *194,* 1013-1020.

164. Rachman, H., & Teasdale, J. *Aversion Therapy and Behavior Disorders: An Analysis.* Coral Gables, Fla.: University of Miami Press, 1969.

165. Raskin, R.H. The addition of Self-Hypnosis Training to the Standard Medical Treatment of Essential Hypertension. Ph.D. dissertation, Graduate School of Arts and Sciences, Columbia University, 1979.

166. Richards, S.A. *Temperature Regulation.* New York: Springer-Verlag, 1973.

167. Rickles, W.H. *Task Force Report on Biofeedback and Psychotherapy.* Biofeedback Society of America, Denver, Co., March, 1978.

168. Rosenthal, D. *Genetics of Psychopathology.* New York: McGraw-Hill, 1971.

169. Rugh, J.D. and Schwitzgebel, R.L. Methods and Designs: Variability in commercial electromyographic biofeedback devices. *Behavior Research Methods and Instrumentation,* 1977, *9,* No. 3, 281-285.

170. _____. Biofeedback apparatus: List of suppliers. *Behavior Therapy,* 1975, *6,* 238-240.

171. _____. Performance Variability in Commercial Biofeedback Instrumentation. *A Training Workshop for Professionals.* Sponsored by the Biofeedback Society of America. Denver: Biofeedback Society of America, 1977.

172. Russell, R.W., & Stern, R.M. Gastric motility. In P.H. Venables and I. Martin (Eds.), *A Manual of Psychophysiological Methods.* New York: Wiley, 1967.

173. Sarason, I.G., & Spielberger, C.D. (Eds.). *Stress and Anxiety, Vol. 3,* New York: Wiley, 1976.

174. Sargent, J.D., Green, E.E., & Walters, E.D. The use of autogenic feedback training in a pilot study of migraine and tension headaches. *Headache,* 1972, *12,* 120-124.

175. _____. Preliminary report on the use of autogenic feedback training in the treatment of migraine and tension headaches. *Psychosomatic Medicine,* 1973, *35,* 192-135.

176. Sargent, J.D., Walters, E.D., & Green, E.E. Psychosomatic self-regulation of migraine headaches. *Seminars in Psychiatry,* 1973, *5,* 415-428.

177. Sarris, I., Stone, R.F., & Berman, D. Biofeedback and psychotherapy in the treatment of complex psychiatric psychosomatic conditions. In *Handbook of Physiological Feedback,* Berkeley, Ca.: Autogenic Systems, Inc., 1976, *2,* 96-99.

178. Schandler, S.L. Use of muscle biofeedback relaxation in the treatment of eczema. *Proceedings of the 9th Annual Meeting of the Biofeedback Society of America.* Denver: Biofeedback Society of America, 1978.

179. Schacter, S., & Singer, J.E. Cognitive social and physiological determinants of emotional state. *Psychological Review,* 1962, *69,* 379-399.

180. Schwartz, G.E. Voluntary Control of human cardiovascular integration and differentiation through feedback and reward. In D. Shapiro et. al. (Eds.), *Biofeedback and Self-Control,* Chicago: Aldine Publishing Co., 1972.

181. Schwartz, G.E. Biofeedback and patterning of autonomic and central processes: CNS-cardiovascular interactions. In *Biofeedback: Theory and Research,* G.E. Schwartz & J. Beatty (Eds.), New York: Academic Press, 1977.

182. Schwitzgebel, R.L., & Rugh, J.D. Of Bread, circuses, and alpha machines. *American Psychologist,* March 1975, Vol. 30, No. 3.

183. Schutz, W.C. *Joy: Expanding Human Awareness.* New York: Grove Press, 1967.

184. Schultz, J.H., & Luthe, W. *Autogenic Training, Vol. 1.* New York: Grune & Stratton, 1969.

185. Sedlacek, K. Biofeedback treatment of Raynaud's. *Psychosomatics,* August 1979, *20,* 8, 25-541.

186. Selye, H. *Stress Without Distress,* New York: J.B. Lippincott Co., 1974.

187. _____. *Stress of Life.* New York: McGraw-Hill, 1976.

188. Shabain, H.S., Bahler, W.W., & Lubar, J.F. A comparison of 12-15HZ, Polandic activity (SMR) during eyes open and eyes closed conditions and its concurrence with occipital alpha. *Proceedings of the Biofeedback Society of America, 9th Annual Meeting, 1978.* Denver: Biofeedback Society of America, 165-67.

189. Shapiro, D., Barber, T.X., DiCara, L.V., Kamiya, J., Miller, N., & Stoyva, J. (Eds.). *Biofeedback and Self-Control: Aldine Annuals.* Chicago: Aldine, 1969-1980.

190. Shapiro, D. & Schwartz, G. Biofeedback and visceral learning. *Seminars in Psychiatry,* May, 1972, Vol. 4, No. 2.

191. Sheer, D. Biofeedback training of 40 Hz EEG and behavior. In N. Burch & H. Altschuler (Eds.), *Behavior and Brain Electrical Activity.* New York: Plenum, 1975.

192. Sime, W. E., & Degood, D. E. Stress testing recovery EMG for evaluation of biofeedback and progressive muscle relaxation training effects. *Proceedings of the 8th Annual Meeting of the Biofeedback Society of America,* March 4-8, 1977, p. 72.

193. Skinner, B. F. *About Behaviorism.* New York: Alfred A. Knopf, 1974.

194. Solomon, L. N., & Berzon, B., Eds. *New perspectives on Encounter Groups.* San Francisco: 1972.

195. Speilberger, C. D., Gorsuch, R. L., & Lushene, R. E. *STAI Manual for the State-Trait Anxiety Inventory.* Palo Alto, California: Consulting Psychologists Press, 1970.

196. Spiegel, H. & Spiegel, D. *Trance and Treatment: Clinical Uses of Hypnosis.* New York: Basic Books, 1978.

197. Sterman, M. B. Neurophysiologic and clinical studies of sensorimotor EEG biofeedback: Some effects on epilepsy. *Seminars in Psychiatry, 1973, 5,* 507-525.

198. Sterman, M. B., & Friar, L. Supression of seizures in an epileptic following sensorimotor EEG feedback training. *Electroencephalography of Clinical Neurophysiology,* 1972, *33,* 89-95.

199. Sternbach, R. A. *Principles of Psychophysiology: An introductory text and readings.* New York: Academic Press, 1966.

200. Stoyva, J. M. Self-Regulation and the Stress-Related Disorders: A Perspective on Biofeedback. In D. I. Mostofsky (Ed.), *Behavior Control and Modification of Physiological Activity,* Englewood Cliffs, New Jersey: Prentice-Hall, 1976, 366-398.

201. _____. Why should muscle relaxation be clinically useful? In *Biofeedback and Behavior,* J. Beatty & H. Legewie, (Eds.) New York: Plenum Press, 1976, 449-472.

202. _____. Guidelines in the training of general relaxation. In J. V. Basmajian, *Biofeedback: Principles and Practice for Clinicians.* Baltimore: Williams & Wilkins, 1979, 92-111.

203. Stroebel, C. F. The Application of biofeedback techniques in psychiatry and behavioral medicine. *Psychiatric Opinion,* June, 1979, 13-17.

204. Sullivan, H. S. *The Interpersonal Theory of Psychiatry.* (H. S. Perry and M. L. Gawel Eds.). New York: W. W. Norton, 1953.

205. Sullivan, H. S. *Concepts of Modern Psychiatry.* Washington, D.C.: The William Alanson White Psychiatric Foundation. 1940.

206. Tarler-Benlolo, L. The role of relaxation in biofeedback training. *Psychological Bulletin.* 1978, *85,* 727-55.

207. Tart, C. T. (Ed.). *Altered States of Consciousness.* New York: John Wiley, 1969.

208. Thompson, R. F. *Foundations of Physiological Psychology. New York: Harper & Row, 1967.*

209. Toomin, M.K., & Toomin, H. GSR feedback in psychotherapy: some clinical observations *Psychotherapy, Research and Practice, 12,* 1, Spring, 1975.

210. Upton, M. *Electronics for Everyone, New York: Signet Science Lebourg, 1959.*

211. Venables, P., & Martin, I. *A Manual of Psychophysiological Methods.* New York: John Wiley, 1967.

212. Waelder, R. *Basic Theory of Psychoanalysis,* New York: International Universities Press, 1960.

213. Wallace, R. K., Benson, H., & Wilson, A. F. A wakeful hypometabolic physiologic state. *American Journal of Physiology,* 1971, *221,* 795-799.

214. Watson, J. B., & Rayner, R. Conditioned emotional reactions. *Journal of Experimental Psychology,* 1920, *3,* 1-14.

215. Weiner, N. *Cybernetics.* Cambridge, Massachusetts: Massachusetts Institute of Technology Press, 1961.

216. Weiner, H. *Psychobiology and Human Disease.* New York: Elsevier Publishers, 1977.

217. Weinstock, S. A. The reestablishment of intestinal control in functional colitis. *Biofeedback and Self-Regulation,* 1976, *1,* 324 (Abstract).

218. Weiss, T., & Engel, B. T. Operant conditioning of heart rate in patients with premature ventricular contractions. *Psychosomatic Medicine, 33,* 301-321.

219. Wentworth-Rohr, I. Biofeedback applications in psychotherapy. In H. Grayson & C. Leow (Eds.), *Changing Approaches to the Psychotherapies,* New York: Spectrum Publications, 1978, 237-258.

220. _____. Symptoms, insight and behavior techniques in psychoanalytic psychotherapy. *Psychoanalytic Review,* 1970, *57,* 48-59.

221. _____. *Varieties of Psychology.* Paper presented at the meeting of the Advanced Institute for Psychoanalytic Psychotherapy, Alfred Alder Institute, New York, March, 1975.

222. _____. Clinical case studies in biofeedback therapy techniques. Unpublished, 1975.

223. _____. The reduction of anxiety in schizophrenic patients through biofeedback and behavior therapy techniques. Paper read at the Fourth Annual Meeting of the Biofeedback Society of New York, June 7, 1980.

224. Weitzenhoffer, A. M. *General Techniques of Hypnotism.* New York: Grune & Stratton, 1957.

225.   Whatmore, G. B., & Kohli, D. R. *The Physiopathology and Treatment of Functional Disorders.* New York: Grune & Stratton, 1974.

226.   _____. Dysponesis: A neurophysiologic factor in functional disorders. *Behavioral Science,* 1968, *13,* 102-124.

227.   Whitehead, W. (Ed.). Task Force Study Section on the Use of Biofeedback in the Treatment of Gastrointestinal Disorders, Biofeedback Society of America. Denver: Biofeedback Society of America, May, 1978.

228.   Wickramasekera, I. (Ed.). *Biofeedback, Behavior Therapy and Hypnosis.* Chicago: Nelson Hall, 1976.

229.   Wolpe, J. *The Practice of Behavior Therapy.* New York: Pergamon, 1973.

230.   Wolpe, J., & Lazarus, A. A. *Behavior Therapy Techniques.* New York: Pergamon, 1966.

231.   Wolff, H. G. *Stress and Disease.* (2nd Ed.). Springfield, Ill.: C. C. Thomas, 1968.

232.   Yates, Aubrey. *Biofeedback and the Modification of Behavior.* New York: Plenum Press, 1980.

233.   Yemm, R. Temporomandibular dysfunction and masseter muscle response to experimental stress. *British Dental Journal,* December 2, 1969, 508-510.

234.   Zuroff, D. C., & Schwarz, J. C. Effects of transcendental meditation and muscle relaxation on trait anxiety maladjustment, locus of control, and drug use. *Journal of Consulting and Clinical Psychology,* 1978, Vol. 46, No. 2, 264-271.

INDEX